BLOOD DISPUTES AMONG BEDOUIN AND RURAL ARABS IN ISRAEL

BLOOD DISPUTES
among
Bedouin and Rural Arabs in Israel

REVENGE, MEDIATION, OUTCASTING AND FAMILY HONOR

by

Joseph Ginat

With a foreword by
Philip Carl Salzman
of McGill University

University of Pittsburgh Press
in cooperation with
Jerusalem Institute for Israel Studies

To my children, Dina, Na'ama, and Iddo

This publication was made possible by funds granted by the Charles H. Revson Foundation of New York. The statements made and the views expressed, however, are solely the responsibility of the author.

Published by the University of Pittsburgh Press in cooperation with the
Jerusalem Institute for Israel Studies

Feffer and Simons, Inc., London
Typeset by Technosdar, Tel Aviv
Manufactured in the United States of America

Library of Congress Cataloging-in-Publication Data

Ginat, J.
Blood disputes among Bedouin and rural Arabs in Israel.

Bibliography: p. 171.
Includes index.
1. Palestinian Arabs—Israel—Social life and customs. 2. Bedouins—Israel—Social life and customs. 3. Vendetta—Israel. 4. Israel—Social life and customs. I. Title.
DS113.7.G55 1987 306'.08992705694 86-14609
ISBN 0-8229-3820-0

All photographs are by the author, except the author's Bedouin sister photo and that of a Bedouin preparing coffee, which were taken by Patricia Jarvis of Salt Lake City.

Contents

Illustrations

BLOOD DISPUTES AMONG BEDOUIN AND RURAL ARABS IN ISRAEL

Foreword

Living is a risky business. We each and all face threats from many quarters, not least from our fellow men. In consequence, much of our societal organization is oriented toward regulating relations so that the risks are restricted and reduced. The need for security in the face of potential threats from other men is a constant in human society. The arrangements for promoting security are, however, quite variable across societies and within societies through time.

One of the ways in which the organization of security varies between societies or periods is in the distribution of responsibility and capacity for the provision of security, for the acts of definition, engagement and enforcement so important in social control and in establishing to whatever imperfect degree a semblance of social order. At one (logical) extreme in the distribution of responsibility is individual self-help, each person acting on his or her own behalf. At the other extreme is the absolute sovereign, totally responsible for all aspects of internal and external security for his or her subjects.

A critical element in the distribution of responsibility and capacity for the provision of security is access to and control of the means of coercion, such as armaments and the ability to use them. The greater degree the system of social control is based upon self-help, the more the means of coercion will be widely distributed. The greater degree responsibility for social control is concentrated, the more the means of coercion will be restricted. When, for whatever reason — political, ideological, technological — there is a significant change in the distribution of access to the means of coercion, a change in the distribution of responsibility for social control and security is bound to follow.

Paralleling the distinction between security based upon self-help and security based upon a sovereign is that between stateless societies and states. Stateless societies are decentralized, decision making and enforcement resting with local populations; the means of coercion are distributed widely. States, to some degree, control security functions and maintain privileged access to the means of coercion, often claiming sole legitimate authority in the use of coercion.

We must be careful, however, to avoid reifying the notion of state society. It is more realistic to view a state apparatus as an organization with claims of legitimacy and with some capacity for enforcement. Exactly how much legitimacy it has in the eyes of its subjects or citizens and how much capacity for enforcement it actually has are matters to be established rather than assumed by the outside observer.

Stateless societies exist where there is no state capable of establishing effective control. In some areas (or periods), there is no state apparatus in the vicinity attempting to impose its authority or control, thus governance and social control rests with local populations. In other areas (or periods), one or more state organizations claim suzerainty but are ineffective or effective only to a limited degree in imposing control over local populations. It is by no means uncommon for stateless forms of governance and social control to operate in social fields claimed by state organizations.

For thousands of years of Middle Eastern history, states have waxed and waned, expanded and contracted in effective control. Stateless organization has continued to exist during these epochs, in greater or lesser operational form on the peripheries of the states, especially in the deserts and mountains, and in rudimentary form in those areas under state control. During periods of state decline, the decentralized forms of organization claim unregulated areas.

A common form of stateless organization is the tribe, a set of local groupings tied together by a symbolic idiom, often in the Middle East by patrilineal descent. Tribal organization is usually associated with control of territory and operates quite well even when constituent groups are mobile and not closely associated with particular localities. Commonly found as a part of tribal organization in the Middle East (and elsewhere) is a decentralized security system based upon self-help by groups. Small scale political action groups are formed, usually through the use of a descent criterion, which have the responsibility for the general welfare and security of members and particularly for any blood offense of injury or death involving group members. The customary understanding and usual operating policy of such groups is that each adult male member is jurally equivalent to each other member, and that all are responsible for the actions of each in the sphere of blood conflict. In this system of collective responsibility, each group member may be held responsible for the actions of each other, and an injury done to one is conventionally considered as an injury to each and all.

Security based upon small scale political action groups invested with collective responsibility works, to the extent that it does, because of two complementary forms of constraint on conflict. On the one side is the deterrence resulting from likely retribution for an injury or death stemming from conflict. An individual knows that coming into conflict with another individual means coming into conflict with that individual's group, and that a victor in individual combat becomes a target for reprisal. On the other side, each group member knows that he is responsible for the actions of each other group member, and can himself become the target of reprisal for the injuries caused by any member of his group. Thus individuals are under intense pressure from fellow group members to restrain themselves from unnecessarily inflicting injury. Should, in spite of these contraints, conflict break out and injury take place, customary equivalencies or retribution, such as similar injury to the offender or a member of the offender's group, or indemnification, as in a standard payment, remove the blood debt and return the opposed groups to debtless if not emnityless relationship.

The processes and substance, the complexities and reality of this security system based upon collective responsibility are set out and elaborated by Professor Ginat in his richly documented case material and analysis of Bedouin in Israel. He provides us with the detailed workings of the system in the actions and reactions of individuals and groups, showing the variations in development and outcome of conflicts and injuries. Integral to this system, as Professor Ginat shows in full detail, is a critical lubricating factor, mediation, which provides linkage between the action groups and elicits the healing potential in balanced opposition. Here is a crux of leadership in a decentralized polity: the mediator, encouraging, cajoling, facilitating, shaming, flattering and subtly bullying fellow tribesmen in conflict to act reasonably and responsibly and in the public interest, to fulfill their obligations as fellow tribesmen and Muslims, and to resolve their disruptive and destructive conflict by means of appropriate restitution. From successful mediation comes stature and prestige for the mediator, status and recognition otherwise unavailable in an egalitarian, stateless society.

But I have spoken so far as if the Bedouin in Israel were autonomous, functioning in a pure tribal system without other influences. This of course is by no means the case. Tribes across the world and through history have often been to a greater or lesser degree encapsulated by wider state systems. The Bedouin tribes of Israel have been encapsulated by the State of Israel, the high degree of effectiveness of the encapsulation reflecting both the strength of the Israeli state and its determination to impose control. But encapsulation, if restricting the autonomy of the tribal system, is considerably short of absorption of the tribal system through assimilation of its members to the wider society and its institutions. Thus state and tribal systems and institutions co-exist, each skewing the workings of the other and being skewed in its turn.

The mutual skewing of the state and tribal systems in Israel, and in this respect the Arab villagers of Israel can be considered as having a modified tribal system, is clearly shown in Professor Ginat's case studies and analyses: Revenge is put off or settlements made because of possible prison terms imposed by the state apparatus for acts of blood retribution. Government officials engage in mediation and guarantee settlements rather than impose judicial decisions. Mediators direct their overtly tribal activities toward covert objectives in the state system, such as timing conflict settlements to bring votes in parliamentary elections. Thus the encapsulation of Bedouin and rural Arab society by the strong Israeli state results in a mixed system, with the distinct and contradictory state and tribal structures each influencing the workings of the other.

But the challenge to the Bedouin tribal and rural Arab village systems is far greater than that posed by the Israeli state alone. For the socioeconomic system of Israel undermines the traditional basis of rural life. The decentralized, egalitarian, subsistence-oriented rural society, whether pastoral or agricultural, was based upon collectively held territory or collective land tenure, common and shared interests in the means of production, such as livestock, and a shared commitment in collective welfare, reflected in redistribution of resources and products. These common and shared interests underlay to a considerable extent the interests in and identification with the group so critical in a security system based upon collective responsibility. In many overlapping ways the individual's interest rested with the welfare of his group. But contemporary Israeli society draws many individual Bedouin and rural Arabs into its socioeconomic system, through educational and economic opportunities, through a labor and goods market system, with a resulting individuation and socioeconomic differentiation. Interests diverge, commonalities dissipate, and identity diffuses. The Bedouin with a good job in the industrial economy is less compelled by the imperatives of blood revenge. Settled Bedouin can no longer migrate away from adversaries without leaving everything behind. The commonalities and capacities of the traditional rural socioeconomic system, now to a greater or lesser degree undermined by conditions in contemporary Israel, no longer support so effectively the tribal security system.

The strains on the tribal system are reflected in the transformation of the institution of outcasting. Traditionally, outcasting was an extreme measure used to guarantee that group members acted prudently so as to avoid dragging their fellows into unnecessary blood disputes. But recently, as Professor Ginat shows, outcasting has been orchestrated by tribal leaders to sanction not deviation within the tribal system, but deviation from the tribal system on the part of individuals drawn away from traditional loyalties by the wider society. Thus outcasting serves to remind individuals of the cost of removing themselves too far from traditional patterns, while at the same time drawing together group members through participation in critical decision-making processes. The irony is in the transformation of a traditional tribal institution in order to reenforce the traditional tribal system.

As long as conditions in Israel remain much as they are today, the erosion of the Bedouin tribal and rural Arab traditional systems will likely continue. But any significant change in Israeli society, whether stemming from political, economic, territorial, or demographic developments, could lead to a shift in the evolution of the Bedouin and rural Arab systems. For example, increased contact with the wider Arab world, whether through processes of peace or war, could lead to opportunities, which would be exploited through traditional forms of organization. The contemporary mixed system reflects not only the cultural commitment of values and identity, but an appreciation of current uses of traditional forms and of their potential uses in new and different circumstances.

Professor Ginat in this volume performs the double service of enriching our understanding of the workings of the tribal and rural systems and of showing the particular developments of these systems within a strong state. The wealth of case history material in this account of Bedouin and rural Arab society in Israel provides a firm basis for the analyses presented and provides a valuable opportunity for comparison with Bedouin and rural Arabs living in other sociocultural contexts. Several cases in the ethnographic literature offer instructive contrasts.

The Al Murrah Bedouin of the Empty Quarter of Arabia, described by Donald Cole in *Nomads of the Nomads,* are encapsulated in the relatively traditional Saudi state with which they have cultural and organizational commonalities. The political system of the larger society parallels in many respects the tribal system, and actors in the tribal system are not drawn in other directions by foreign legal or electoral systems, neither of which have been instituted in Saudi Arabia. Widespread but undemanding participation in the National Guard on the part of the Al Murrah brings substantial income, which in effect subsidizes the traditional Bedouin style of rural life — emphasizing nomadic residence and pastoral production. In contrast to the effective encapsulation and sociocultural discontinuities of Bedouin in Israel, the Al Murrah in Arabia experience encapsulation and continuity.

The case of the Bedouin of the Western Desert of Egypt, described by Abdulla Bujra in *The Desert and the Sown* (Cynthia Nelson, editor), is an intermediate one, in that cultural continuity with the Egyptian state is greater than in the Israeli case but weaker than the Arabian case, and the degree of effective encapsulation is weaker than the Israeli case. Measures to "modernize" and settle the Bedouin of the Western Desert, involving the establishment of agricultural co-ops and subsidization of cultivation, not only failed to replace the traditional organization and economy, but ended up reenforcing traditional patterns. The individual co-ops were taken over by individual lineages, leadership being drawn from traditional lineage leadership, thus strengthening rather than undermining tribal social and political organization. Resources, both mechanized equipment and supplies, invested by the government in the agricultural cooperative scheme, freed the greater number of Bedouin to pursue nomadic livestock pastoralism and provided resources for investment in that other traditional Bedouin economic activity, smuggling, in this case across the Libya/Egypt border. Thus the Bedouin of the Western Desert appropriated for their tribal system the organizational forms and resources meant in the plans of state functionaries for increased encapsulation and transformation.

The Rwala Bedouin of northern Arabia, described by William and Fidelity Lancaster in *The Rwala Bedouin Today* and other works, have maintained considerable autonomy by playing off several potentially encapsulating states through shrewd movement across international boundaries (Jordan/Saudi Arabia/Syria) and astute manipulation of international rivalries within the region. Although greatly influenced by regional economic developments, such as the decline of the camel market and the intrusion of industrial technology and products, the Rwala have maintained their tribal economy by finding functional equivalents — sheep production replacing camels, smuggling replacing raiding — which allow them to continue their nomadic life in the desert and to pursue their tribal ideals of individual autonomy and social equality.

The cases of the Al Murrah, the Bedouin of the Western Desert, and the Rwala illustrate some of the ways in which Bedouin cope with and manipulate the pressures of encapsulation and cultural discontinuity where they are weaker than those for the Bedouin of Israel. The traditional tribal systems of these other Bedouin have been less compromised than that of the Bedouin of Israel because they retain access to their traditional territories, do not face such overwhelming state power and pressure, have not been engaged by a state electoral system, and have not had access to the benefits of an advanced, modern economy. Consequently, the traditional systems of residence, economy, social organization, security, and leadership of these other Bedouin have been less transformed than those of the Bedouin of Israel.

To make such comparisons, only sketched out here in rudimentary and simplistic form, we depend upon richly informative ethnographic accounts such as that provided in this volume for the Bedouin and rural Arabs of Israel by Professor Joseph Ginat. For this contribution, Professor Ginat is owed a debt of gratitude by all students of rural peoples of the Middle East.

Philip Carl Salzman

Preface

The greater part of the case history material presented in this volume was collected between 1973 and 1983. All the cases occurred in communities located among the Bedouin of the Galilee, the rural Arabs in the center of the country, and the Bedouin of the Negev, in Israel.

The nature of fieldwork in attempting to unravel the complexity of cases involving the dimensions discussed in this volume is very different from fieldwork where one studies a community *in situ*. Tracking down the circumstances of a case was sometimes in the nature of a detective's chase. Clues were never transparent and informants always tended to stress those aspects of a case that put their views or role in a favorable light. In unravelling a case history the anthropologist meets with many different persons. He hears several versions of the "facts" as well as formulating his own version of what actually occurred.

> The problem is that both the thoughts and behavior of the participants can be viewed from two different perspectives: from the perspective of the participants themselves [emics] and from the perspective of the observers [etics]. In both instances scientific, objective accounts of the mental and behavioral fields are possible. In the first instance the observers employ concepts and distinctions that are meaningful and appropriate to the participants; in the second instance they employ concepts and distinctions that are meaningful to the observers . . . The test of the adequacy of emic descriptions and analyses is their correspondence with a view of the world which the native participants accept as real, meaningful, or appropriate . . . The test of the adequacy of etic accounts, however, is simply their ability to generate scientifically productive theories about the causes of sociocultural differences and similarities. (Harris 1980, 115–16)

The interviews were carried out in the manner advocated by J. Spradley (1979, 58–59). "It is best to think of ethnographic interviews as a series of friendly conversations into which the researcher slowly introduces new elements to assist informants to respond as informants. At any time during an interview it is possible to shift back to a friendly conversation. A few minutes of easy-going talk interspersed here and there throughout the interview will pay enormous dividends in rapport."

Information gleaned tended to be piecemeal — as informants themselves learned of facts so these facts were later passed on to me. It might be thought that this temporal dimension to the fieldwork was an obstacle, and in some ways it was, for it meant that I had to make repeated visits to informants and others to verify the information I received. But the effort involved in tracking down information was not a hindrance to the final analysis; on the contrary it helped, by dint of time, to put all the facts in their proper perspective. For example, underlying political motives were usually difficult to discern clearly during an ongoing crisis. Only later did the motives for actions and stances taken become clear. I have attempted to stress this temporal dimension in relating the case histories.

I used the method of participant observation in order to gather data and to this end I met with leaders of co-liable groups when, for instance, they met to determine whether to accept a cease-fire or reject it. I also visited members of the co-liable group responsible for the homicide. I went to see the mediator or mediators they had chosen to represent them and discussed with them the chances of reaching a *ṣulḥa* (peace agreement). In interviewing the mediator and those involved in the dispute, some of these persons were often involved in earlier blood disputes already concluded. This provided additional factual knowledge and a basis for comparison. In addition to attending the formal meetings of the involved parties, I made sure always to ask regular tribal members for their opinions. In this way I could sometimes find out "political" motives behind the actions and proposals of the leaders, and, more important, ascertain how they reached their decision and whether there were any dissenting voices.

Sometimes it occurred that in talking to a Bedouin or Arab villager about a particular case, I would learn about similar cases that had occurred in the past. And this even when my acquaintanceship with the informant was not close. With informants with whom I had established bonds of mutual trust and friendship I was often told about cases, and the details regarding them, that occurred in the informant's immediate environment and even within his own family.

In some of the outcasting cases I was informed of the intention to cast out a member before a formal discussion took place; in other cases I was only informed of the events afterwards. Under both sets of circumstances the method used was to visit the co-liable group concerned, meet the outcast individual himself, and to ask dignitaries and members of neighboring tribes for their views on the issue.

In the course of investigating family honor killings I met with the actors themselves, their relatives, members of other *ḥamūla*s, and friends and rivals of the involved families. In family honor killings in particular, females were often more important sources of information than the males. Interviewing females in Bedouin and rural Arab society is problematic. In this I was greatly assisted by my wife, Dalia, who often accompanied me on visits to Bedouin camps and Arab villages. My two most important female informants are my "sister" and Sara, both of whom have provided me with much privileged information. Before relating how I initially came into contact with them, an apology is in order. Much of the ethnographic material presented here has been gathered from individuals with whom I have established close relations. This has greatly assisted in the gathering of the data, but means that in relating the case history material to my audience, my role as an anthropologist and sometime mediator comes very much to the fore. Forewarned, I hope the reader will understand the necessity of this approach.

In the winter of 1961 I accompanied the late Professor Aharoni, formerly Professor of Archaeology at the Hebrew University in Jerusalem, on an archaeological expedition in the Negev, where we were caught in a severe flash flood. Abandoning our car, which was almost covered by water, we took shelter in a worker's tent on a mound near some road constructions. Realizing that our only chance of survival was to find some warm shelter, I set out to search for help. After walking for four kilometers I reached a Bedouin's tent. The Bedouin gave me a blanket to cover myself and I explained the predicament of Professor Aharoni. The Bedouin had a problem: How could he leave his wife in the tent with a stranger? He found a novel solution. As she was preparing tea and hot bread in the other part of the tent he said to her, "Faṭma, your brother has arrived." Had he said, "My brother," that would have still presented a problem for him to leave her with me, but he said "Your brother" — a clever "message" to the two of us. The Bedouin drove off in his pick-up truck to rescue Professor Aharoni, while Faṭma served me tea and bread.

The Bedouin died in 1970, leaving Faṭma with seven children. Once a sister, always a "sister," and I visit Faṭma and her children regularly. As Faṭma's "brother" in such an extended family I am in a position to obtain much information concerning Bedouin affairs that would normally only be discussed within the family.

My contact with Sara came about as follows. In 1955, when I was nineteen years old, I worked as a herder on a kibbutz in northern Israel. A Bedouin called Muḥammad worked with me and we became good friends. Later I moved to the Negev, while Muḥammad continued to herd the cattle in the north. One day he saw a flock of sheep on the kibbutz grazing ground. He chased them away and told Sara, the young shepherdess, not to graze her flock there again. Muḥammad was attracted to her and later sought her out. An affair ensued and Sara became pregnant.

Muḥammad, a Bedouin, knew that Sara's father would consider that his daughter was of a higher status, and would therefore refuse any marriage proposal he might make. Muḥammad came to see me and explained their predicament. Could I intercede on his behalf with Sara's father? Together with some high-ranking police and military officers to whom I had explained the prevailing circumstances, I went to Sara's father's home. The father was clearly shocked (and impressed) at this unexpected delegation and said upon our arrival: "There is a purpose for your coming. Whatever you ask, I will help you." After drinking the traditional cup of coffee we spoke about the good character of the herder and told the father that Muḥammad wanted to marry Sara. The father felt duly honored by the way the request had been made, and he agreed to the marriage. At the time of the marriage ceremony Sara was some six months pregnant. Luckily, Bedouin dress for females is rather bulky, which made it easier to hide the problem for the time being, but in three months' time . . .

Muḥammad told everybody of the vow he had made that when I have a herd of my own he would come to assist me for several months. Sara's relatives were not very pleased, but she explained that her husband's vow had to be kept, especially considering that I had been so prominent in the marriage arrangements. One month after the wedding ceremony I took Muḥammad and Sara away to the Negev. I had previously arranged that they would stay with a Negev Bedouin tribe (on the pretext that Muḥammad was escaping a blood dispute), but after just one night there Sara made it clear that it was the last night. I had not considered that the customs, especially the cooking methods, of the Negev Bedouin would be so different from those in the north. I had no alternative but to rent them a flat on the outskirts of Beersheva. This presented problems because of government restrictions on the movement of Bedouin due to the security situation at the time. But these problems are another story.

Sara gave birth to Nada, a hefty baby girl who weighed over four and a half kilo. We decided that it would not be propitious to return to the north until the child was older and her true age less discernable. So they stayed an extra nine months in the Negev before returning home where the size of Nada was much remarked upon. Nevertheless, their secret remained secret. Needless to say that Muḥammad and Sara, and their daughter Nada, are informants par excellence.

Another individual with whom I established close relations was Jedū'a Abū-Ṣulb, who features in two of the case histories. In 1959 Jedū'a asked the military authorities to help him find shelter away from the Negev because he had been outcast from his tribe. I arranged that he stay with a northern Bedouin tribe where I visited him and talked to him regularly. Later on he returned to the Negev and worked there as a watchman of a forest. Jedū'a's lack of contact with his peers made him eager to talk and he used to tell me about many aspects of Bedouin life. In particular he spoke about the interaction within the co-liable group and gave me specific examples of rivalry, disagreement, and animosity. From the outside the group appeared united, but in-group political relations were far from serene. He told of his own circumstances, where the co-liable group was split in deciding whether to outcast him or not, and of the personal motivations involved in the decision.

At this time anthropology as a career was only just dawning on me. I did not recognize the usefulness of the contacts I had made until much later in my anthropological studies. My involvement was on a personal and friendship basis. When as an anthropologist I was called upon to help in various situations my willingness and enthusiasm to do so was tempered with an eye to understanding how the particular problem at hand could be understood in a cultural, anthropological context.

Acknowledgments

Professor Victor Turner read the first draft of this book and made many helpful comments. His untimely death in December 1983 was not only a great loss personally, but also to the anthropological community he served so keenly. Emanuel Marx of Tel Aviv University never tired of discussing my material with me, and made valuable comments. I am grateful to Philip Carl Salzman, of McGill University, for making many insightful remarks. I am indebted to him for the foreword he has written. I wish to thank Anthony Grahame for editing and designing the book, and compiling the index; his comments and ideas assisted greatly in the clarification of my arguments.

This book has been made possible by the support of the Research Committee of the University of Haifa. The Jerusalem Institute for Israel Studies has provided valuable assistance.

I would never have been able to write this book without the help of my wife, Dalia, who has helped me gather the case history material, especially that part relating to women's activities. Dalia also acted as hostess to Bedouin and rural Arab friends who visited our home. The late Sheikh Ḥammad Abū-Rabi'a proclaimed once that nowhere else did he feel so at home as in Dalia's kitchen! Without the complaisance of the Bedouin and villagers, no book would have been forthcoming. Their patience in answering my many queries into events that were sometimes painful for them to recall is much appreciated.

The author thanks the editors of the following volumes in which some of the material collected here has previously appeared in shorter versions. Those chapters previously published are substantially different from their earlier versions in both their theoretical framework and their much enlarged ethnographic material. Chapter 2 appeared in a shorter version in *The Changing Nomads,* ed. Emanuel Marx and Avshalom Shmueli (Tel Aviv: Shiloah Center for Asian and African Studies; New Brunswick, N.J.: Transaction, 1983); Chapter 4 appeared in *Nomadic Peoples,* vol. 12, February 1983, ed. Philip Carl Salzman; some of the case histories in Chapter 5 previously appeared in *Israel Studies in Criminology* 5, ed. Giora Shoham and Anthony Grahame (Tel Aviv: Turtledove Press, 1979).

CHAPTER ONE

Introduction

The central theme of this book concerns blood homicide in Bedouin and rural Arab society in Israel. Each chapter focuses on a particular topic, but there are many interrelations between the four main topics of revenge, mediation, outcasting, and family honor. These interrelations are described and analyzed fully in case histories. My purpose here is to gain a perspective of the conflict that the populations under study are undergoing in terms of how they reject and adapt their moral code relating to blood homicide in the face of their rapidly changing social and economic environment, and how they have adopted western methods of settling such conflicts.

In Israel the Bedouin and rural Arab societies are encapsulated physically, politically, and economically within the wider Israeli society. Physically, they are surrounded by Jewish settlements. Politically, they have to obey the legal system of the Jewish state. And economically, they work for wages in the Jewish sector. The whole spectrum of interactions with the wider society, especially in terms of the sedentarization process that Bedouin are undergoing, is causing profound changes to their values and behavioral norms.

In the Galilee, Arab villages and Bedouin settlements are surrounded by Jewish towns and agricultural settlements; only in the late 1960s, when more Jewish settlements were built near the villages, were roads built as throughways to the area. The Arabs of the central part of the country live in the Triangle.[1] Only in the mid-1950s did this group begin to develop contacts with the wider Israeli society, although Jewish settlements were always situated close to the Arab villages and these settlements were always an important source of employment for the Arabs. In the 1970s additional settlements were built between some of the villages.

In 1960 the city of Arad was established in the eastern Negev. The new highway to Arad crossed the Bedouin tribal lands and they soon found themselves surrounded by Jewish towns and agricultural settlements. In the mid-1960s their sedentarization began with the building of the first Bedouin settlement of Tel-Sheva. Later, a second Bedouin settlement was built in the western Negev at Rahat, close to several kibbutzim. Many Bedouin moved northwards and settled in two mixed Jewish–Arab cities, Lod and Ramle. Other Bedouin settled in Arab villages, and in orchards belonging to Jewish families, in the Triangle area.[2] The 1979 Israeli–Egyptian peace treaty caused a big change in the Negev Bedouin sedentarization process. Israel's evacuation of Sinai resulted in the building of a military airfield in the heart of Bedouin tribal lands. Part of the compensation agreement was that the authorities assist the Bedouin in building two new settlements in the eastern Negev.

The process of sedentarization of the Negev Bedouin, as well as for the Bedouin of the Galilee, is similar to that of nomads all over the Middle East. The sedentarization process brings with it dramatic changes in their ways of economic livelihood. Emanuel Marx (1984, 7) quotes Donald Cole on a Bedouin tribe of Saudi Arabia: "Many tribespeople have settled in shanty town complexes . . . all of them have settled because of their activities in industrial occupations." Marx notes that only a few Israeli Bedouin still engage in farming. These economic changes affect their social structure: "Some nomads achieve a large measure of economic security in town and break away from the tribe, they neglect the kinsmen they left behind, their herds and gardens and even their tribal friends in town" (ibid., 2).

Collective Responsibility

In Bedouin society the basic unit of the tribe is the *khams.* Marx (1967) coined the term "co-liable group" to describe this unit, which is a group formed by all descendants of one ancestor to the fifth generation. A basic ideology of the co-liable group is collective responsibility — any act or omission by one individual reflects on the group as a whole in the sense that the group is responsible for and must accept the consequences of that act or omission. Collective responsibility manifests itself in two major ways: blood revenge and mutual aid. In blood disputes, mutual responsibility "constitutes the ultimate obligation of members of a co-liable group" (Marx 1973, 24). Ernest Gellner (1981, 37–38) says that kinsmen are co-responsible

> for the conduct of any one of their members, sharing in the risk of becoming object of retaliation, or of contributing to blood-money as an alternative to feud if any one in the group commits an act of aggression against a member of another group, and similarly, being morally bound to avenge aggression against any fellow member, and standing to benefit from compensation.

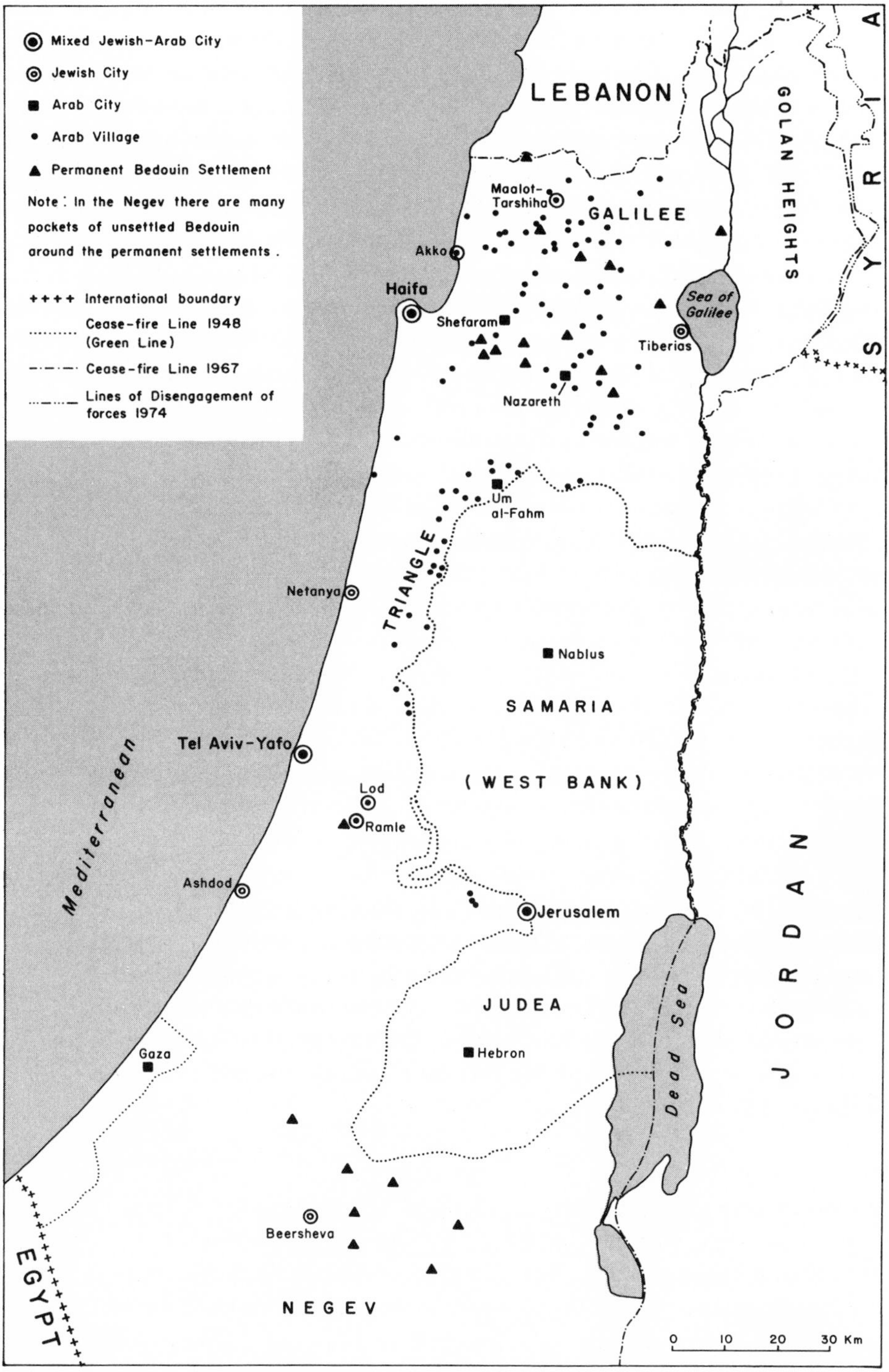

Mixed Jewish-Arab City
Jewish City
Arab City
Arab Village
Permanent Bedouin Settlement
Note : In the Negev there are many pockets of unsettled Bedouin around the permanent settlements .
++++ International boundary
Cease-fire Line 1948 (Green Line)
Cease-fire Line 1967
Lines of Disengagement of forces 1974
LEBANON
GOLAN HEIGHTS
SYRIA
Maalot-Tarshiha
GALILEE
Akko
Haifa
Shefaram
Sea of Galilee
Tiberias
Nazareth
Um al-Fahm
TRIANGLE
Netanya
Nablus
SAMARIA
Tel Aviv-Yafo
Mediterranean
Lod
Ramle
(WEST BANK)
Ashdod
Jerusalem
JUDEA
Hebron
Dead Sea
JORDAN
Gaza
Beersheva
EGYPT
NEGEV
0 10 20 30 Km

Map of Israel showing areas of Bedouin and rural Arab settlement

The second dimension of collective responsibility, mutual aid, provides a perspective on inter-Bedouin relations as a whole. Strong ties with kinsmen are necessary in an environment that at the best of times provides only a meager living. Marx (1984, 9) cites a Sinai Bedouin construction worker who spoke explicitly about the two kinds of insecurity to which every Bedouin was exposed: "Any Jewish workman can throw you out of work, even if we have been three years on the job . . . What happens if there should be another war. When the October (1973) war broke out we were left stranded . . ." Marx continues: "The mutual help given among kinsmen is practically unlimited. It may be given grudgingly but it is not usually withheld . . ."

Mutual aid in Bedouin society is reflected in a number of different attitudes and customs. For example, if a father of children dies, the co-liable group will look after the children's upbringing. The sense of collective responsibility is also seen in the way visitors are entertained. When a member of another tribe comes to visit a member of the co-liable group he does not come to the personal tent of that member. Instead, he comes to the *shiq* (guest tent) of the group.[3] Guests are served the traditional bitter coffee and are always offered a meal. If the offer is accepted the host has to kill a goat or a sheep, for it is customary always to serve meat. However, it is not the group member that is being visited who provides the animal for slaughter. Each member of the co-liable group acts as a "host" to *shiq* guests in a rotation system. The collective responsibility system is also practised in marriage and circumcision ceremonies; group members take turns to erect the tents and serve food to the guests.

The collective responsibility unit for the Arab rural villagers is the *ḥamūla*; the ideology of collective responsibility is the same as for the co-liable group. The term *ḥamūla* has been used as an equivalent for lineage (Cohen 1965, 2–3), and for the clan (Antoun 1972, 44–45). Neither term adequately translates the Arabic *ḥamūla*, which is the patronymic group made up of persons having the same surname. In addition to the members of a descent group, that is the offspring of one ancestor, the *ḥamūla* includes individuals who have joined the core of the descent group. Together, all these persons constitute the patronymic group called the *ḥamūla*. The term lineage is used here to mean a segment of the descent group consisting of up to five generations. Thus the rural collective responsibility unit only comprises members of the descent group; in a blood dispute, *ḥamūla* members who are not members of the descent group are not collectively liable as far as revenge is concerned. In cases where blood money is paid, however, many of the *ḥamūla* members contribute toward the blood payment in order to demonstrate their affiliation with the descent group. As regards the mutual aid aspect of collective responsibility, there is no difference in the actions between the descent group and the wider *ḥamūla* unit.

Bedouin of the Galilee have adopted the term *ḥamūla* from the rural villagers, but in reference to blood disputes they use the Bedouin term and its collective liability meaning. The adaptation of *ḥamūla* was the result of their pitching tents in unsettled areas among the Arab villages. They were encapsulated by the surrounding peasant society and the tribes adopted the peasants' term.

Bedouin and Rural Arabs in Transition

The Bedouin of the Negev are in an advanced stage of sedentarization.

> By the 1970s, Bedouin derived only about 10% of their cash incomes from cultivation. Flocks of sheep and goats, which had formerly been the second major source of income in most households, had declined in importance and sheep raising was now practiced by a small number of Bedouin who owned relatively large flocks of several hundred head. Most Bedouin men had become wage earners, in factories, farms and offices, and some had done well in business, mainly as building contractors. (Marx 1981, 120)

In many cases jobs are secured. Most of the employed Bedouin are members of the Federation of Trade Unions (the Histadrut) and cannot be dismissed without notice.[4]

The sedentarization of the Bedouin took on a new dimension after the 1979 peace agreement between Egypt and Israel. As a result of the Israeli withdrawal from Sinai, the area of the Negev became a much more strategic area for Israeli economic and military development than was previously the case. In particular, a large air base has been built in the Negev; it is located in the eastern Beersheva plain, in the heart of Bedouin tribal homelands:

> The outcome [of these plans for the airfield] was a draft law to expropriate an area six times that needed for the air base, and the proposal did not allow the occupants of the expropriated land recourse to the courts. Compensation for the land was to be nominal: however, each Bedouin household, whether it had owned land or not, would be entitled to a fully developed building site in one of the seven Bedouin towns to be established in the Negev. (Marx 1981, 121)

These changes in the socioeconomic organization of the Bedouin, resulting in a situation where incomes are now derived mainly from wages rather than from flocks and herds, have brought about a corresponding change in their sociocultural structure. This change has manifested itself in a loosening of the collective responsibility structure. The coliable unit is not deemed by the Bedouin themselves to be as important as it was in the past; the younger generation, especially, consider it a burden and question the validity of its rules in the light of their new social situation. As one Bedouin physician put it: "How can I explain to the hospital that because of a blood dispute I cannot come to work? Everybody knows where I work; the avenging group will look for me first."

In discussing the nomads of Baluchistan, Philip Salzman (1980, 106) says that:

> One noteworthy change is the decline of lineage corporateness and solidarity. This is manifested in a decline among lineage mates of coresidence, of mutual economic and political support, of identification with the lineage and of feelings of solidarity. Lineage mates live together less frequently and with members of other lineages more frequently. They are less prepared to provide economic assistance (to bail someone out of jail, for example) and even customary redistribution (as in ritual gift occasions, such as weddings, births, etc.). Political support is forthcoming only in more and more restricted contexts. Tribesmen no longer see their welfare as being so closely congruent in the way that it was felt in traditional times.

Additional to the sedentarization process, Salzman (ibid., 107) says that there are other factors that tend to undermine lineage corporateness and solidarity: "One is the decline of self-help as a means of social control. National government presence in the forms of rural police and courts circumscribes and limits the extent to which the tribesmen depend upon their lineage mates for protection and redress. A second is the economic inequality that results from differential participation in nontraditional economic sectors, such as the labor market and agriculture."

Much of what has been said about change to the Bedouin is also valid as regards the Israeli rural Arabs. Most rural Arab villagers derive their main source of income from wage labor outside the village. Some return to the village after their day's work; for others their working place is so distant that they only return at weekends. For these latter workers their village becomes a mere dormitory town; most of their time is spent within the wider Jewish society. The attitude of the Arabs who spend most of their time away from the village is such that they are reluctant to allow themselves to be drawn into collective responsibility commitments. This is reflected in the ways they have created to settle disputes and the paucity of blood dispute cases that end in a revenge being taken.

Reference was made before to the decline of lineage corporateness and solidarity among nomads. The effect of economic change is also having an effect on the political structure of rural Arab communities. The organizational basis of the *ḥamūla* has already been explained. A political faction within a village is not based on kinships ties, but on a relationship between a leader and his followers. In many instances first cousins, or even brothers, belong to opposing factions. The main difference between the *ḥamūla* and the faction is in terms of the political struggle. Struggles for resources *outside* the village are between factions; struggles for resources *within* the village are between *ḥamūla*s. In case of a dispute between two descent groups, an individual must stand with his descent group against his political friend who belongs to the rival *ḥamūla*. Up to the present time it was not easy to make a "true friend" of someone who belonged to a different descent group. The preference of loyalties was always to the descent group. But nowadays, members of different descent groups are often partners in business. Loyalty to the group is still strong, but where it comes into conflict with the individual's economic livelihood, such loyalty is put to a severe test.

Bedouin and rural Arabs, distinct societies encapsulated within the wider framework of Jewish society, face rapid changes in their economic, political, and social structures. These changes put severe strain on their traditional normative framework. The case history material shows that the settlement of blood disputes does not follow any particular pattern: Some disputes are dealt with traditionally, others can be seen to incorporate more modern attitudes, and in yet others tradition will be over-emphasized as a means to strengthen the cohesiveness and the unity of the group.

Before presenting the ethnographic material in the form of case histories, the rest of this introductory chapter will be devoted to examining blood disputes and the law, and political assassination as it relates to blood disputes. Lastly, the role of the anthropologist who also acts as a mediator will be explained and elaborated.

Blood Disputes and the Law

Blood revenge as a reaction to homicide was well known in ancient times. In the Bible there is a clear distinction between premeditated murder and killing. An example of the former is "when a man goeth into the forest with his neighbor to hew wood, and his hand swingeth with the axe to cut down the tree, and the hand slippeth from the helve and lighteth upon his neighbor, that he die . . ." (Deut. 19:5). In cases of killing without intent the Bible contains specific instructions on how to prevent blood revenge. "He shall flee unto one of those cities, and live, lest the avenger of the blood pursue the slayer, while his heart is hot, and overtake him, because the way is long, and slay him; whereas he was not worthy of death, inasmuch as he hated him not in times past" (Deut. 19:5–6). The Bible expressly emphasizes "that innocent blood be not shed in this land . . ."

In cases of premeditated murder the Bible states that the murderer should be killed in revenge. "But if any man hate his neighbor, and lie in wait for him, and rise up against him, and smite him mortally that he die, and fleeth into one of these cities, then the elders of his city shall send and fetch him from there and deliver him into the hand of the avenger of blood, that he may die. Thine eye shall not pity him . . ." (Deut. 19:11–13). In contrast to biblical law, premeditated murder in Bedouin and rural Arab societies does not necessarily lead to blood revenge, but may be settled through payment of *diyya* (blood money).

In rural Arab and Bedouin societies, blood disputes are not handled by the judiciary but instead are resolved through a quasi-legal procedure based not on law but on custom. In addition, in Bedouin society there is no distinction between premeditated murder and unintentional killing. Revenge may take place in either case. In the past, Bedouin society was basically a military society: If a man was killed by accident or by murder, the result was the same in that the group had one soldier less than before the homicide. Revenge is essentially a settling of scores, in biblical terms an "Eye for eye, tooth for tooth: as he hath caused a blemish in a man, so shall it be done to him" (Lev. 24:20). The Bedouin slogan is that "There should be one grave opposite the other grave."

The law in Israel neither reflects nor mentions Arab norms relating to blood disputes. The situation is different, however, in neighboring Middle East states. In Jordan, for example, murder is punishable by life imprisonment, but in cases of blood revenge the court is empowered to set a sentence of not less than eight years in prison (article 99). William Lancaster (1981, 79) discusses the norms relating to blood disputes in Saudi Arabia:

> In the past the killer could seek protection where he thought best and anyone with sufficient reputation could act as mediator. Nowadays only the courts can act as mediators and only Ibn Saud can give protection. In practice this means that the killer is imprisoned until the case is sorted out and compensation paid. During this time, and it is usually months, the killer's family are at risk and he has no opportunity of raising the money for the compensation. This interference by the state in what is regarded as a family matter is much resented.

In some Arab countries there are legal rates for *diyya*. The legality of such payment is indicative of the legal sanction pertaining in that country to killing for blood dispute reasons. In Oman, a person who unintentionally causes a death has to pay $14,500 to the injured family. In cases where a woman is killed the *diyya* is fifty percent of this amount. There is also a distinction between Muslims and non-Muslims.[5]

Defense of family honor in homicide is recognized in the legal systems of Arab countries. Jordanian law (No. 16, 1960, article 340[2]) states that in cases where a husband or a brother surprises their wife or sister having illicit sexual relations, and injures one or both partiees to the illicit act, the judge may prescribe a penalty between six months to two years in prison. But according to a different article (340[1]), the judge may absolve the attacker from his crime, even from murder. Jordanian law thus clearly recognizes the concept of family honor in homicides. Lebanon differs from other mid-east countries in that there is a strong Christian community there. There is a Christian dominance in many areas of Lebanese life, including the legal system. According to Lebanese law (article 562) a person who surprises his wife, sister, mother or daughter in committing illicit sexual relations will be convicted but will not be punished if he kills her. That is he will be judged to be guilty of the crime, but will not be sent to prison. In deciding the punishment of the avenger, the court will also take into consideration whether the normbreaker was caught in the act or whether the killing was carried out on suspicion only.

Lawyers from Lebanon,[6] the West Bank, and the Gaza Strip state that in cases where murderers were convicted for family honor killings, they are many times released, on appeal to the court, after serving only a short prison sentence. While in prison, inmates of family honor crimes who have been convicted under Arab legal jurisdiction are treated differently than the rest of the prisoners. The prison authorities do not classify them as criminals, and they are respected by other prisoners. Sudan has recently adopted Islamic law. The authorities there claim that Islamic law proclaims that if a man or a woman is caught committing illicit sexual relations they will be sentenced to death. In other Arab countries the law refers to the punishment of a person who killed a guilty woman. In Sudan, the law actually implements the societal value norms concerning illicit sexual relations.

In Israel, if premeditated murder is proved, the judge has no other option but to sentence the murderer to life imprisonment.[7] The Supreme Court in Israel has made it clear that blood revenge or a killing for reasons of family honor are not mitigating circumstances. In other words, the motive for such a killing is immaterial as far as criminal responsibility is concerned. A Supreme Court judge has said that *if* blood revenge was recognized as a justification for a homicide, then "the land would be filled with blood revenge."[8] In a case where an uncle murdered his niece because she had illicit sexual relations, the District Court decided that the murder was for reasons of family honor. In the appeal judgment of the Supreme Court it was pointed out that proof of motive does not reduce the criminal responsibility of the offender.[9]

Although the Israeli legal system makes no distinction between homicide for different reasons, the Israeli administration does. A murderer of a woman who engaged in illicit sexual relations, or a person who took revenge in a blood dispute, can be released by presidential pardon after no longer than 8–12 years in prison. Such release is not automatic and must be applied for, but it is the usual pattern in most cases. Under Arab legal jurisdiction, as practised on the West Bank and Gaza Strip, it is the courts that are empowered to reduce sentences on appeal, but in Israel it is only the administration that can do this in cases of blood revenge and family honor killings.

Although Israeli law holds no legal provisions for Arab mores relating to honor crimes and blood disputes, the courts are flexible in their attitude in that they will recognize customary ways of handling such disputes (provided that there has been no homicide), in so far as it promotes a satisfactory legal solution. In some cases of blood dispute it is customary to establish a committee whose function it is to secure *ṣulḥa*. (peace agreement). The *ṣulḥa* committee, as it is known, negotiates a settlement between the disputants, in this way preventing further bloodshed. There is always at least one official representative of the police or of the political administration on the committee. Gideon Kressel (1981, 188, 130) states that in one case he studied the police made it clear that if the disputants did not agree to the *ṣulḥa* as proposed by the committee, then the case would be referred to the court.

It sometimes happens that the prosecution will agree to a lesser charge against the accused when a *ṣulḥa* has been negotiated between the disputing parties. For example, a charge of murder might be reduced to the lesser charge of manslaughter. Judicial authorities state that the public interest is served because the peace agreement reduces tension between the parties, and thus reduces the chance of further antagonism.[10] In July 1978, in a Triangle village, different sections of a *ḥamūla* fought against each other. Several people were seriously injured. At the subsequent court case the prosecution and defense attorneys explained to the judge that a peace agreement had been reached between the disputing parties. The agreement stipulated that, providing the judge agreed to the provisions, the attackers would not be sent to prison but would have to pay a fine only. The judge agreed to this suggestion.[11]

A blood dispute between a Druze village, and a mixed village of Christians, Druze, and Muslims, but predominantly Christians, reached a higher level of conflict than just between two descent groups and could have led to fierce interethnic strife in the region (see case history XV). A peace agreement was reached after much effort by mediators from all three ethnic groups, and representatives from the police and government. An unprecedented feature of the agreement was that the government participated in the *diyya* payment. The government rationalized this payment as being for the damage caused in the fighting (some 60 homes of Christians were damaged by the Druze). However, all the money went to the families of the deceased — not to the families who suffered material damage. The fact that the director general of the prime minister's office handed over the checks brought about comment that the money was actually blood money. According to some commentators the authorities' legitimization of blood payment could be viewed as condoning blood revenge. Although there have been cases where high officials (deputy prime minister or chairman of the Knesset [Israel's parliament] for instance) have participated in the signing of a peace agreement — the purpose being to add weight of authority — this is the first time that the government has paid the blood money.

In instances where the blood revenge "failed" and the revenger did not succeed to kill his victim, although attempted to do so, the courts can exercise discretion in determining sanction. An Arab from the Galilee stabbed his sister-in-law with whom he had engaged in illicit sexual relations.[12] While the trial was in progress the *ṣulḥa* committee, which was composed of a Greek Orthodox minister, three Arab dignitaries, a Jewish social worker, and a representative of the police, decided that the woman should return to her husband, and the husband's brother who had sexual relations with his sister-in-law should pay all the expenses involved. In convicting the attacker to eighteen months in prison the judge stated that a peace agreement had been submitted to him, and that it indicated that the husband had forgiven his wife. It is difficult to know whether the agreement influenced the judge's sentencing decision, but the very fact that details of the agreement were mentioned in the judge's summing up is evidence that the judge took this aspect of the case into consideration.

A Bedouin was accused of killing another Bedouin from a neighboring co-liable group.[13] The killing was a result of a quarrel over land boundaries between the two groups. Before the judge passed sentence several Bedouin were called to act as character witnesses. Apart from testifying to the previous good character of the defendant, one of them explained the Bedouin tradition of waiting one year before *ṣulḥa* negotiations could begin. The judge commented that as ten months had passed since the murder, *ṣulḥa* negotiations would soon take place. The Bedouin concurred, emphasizing that he believed that a peace agreement would be reached and that he hoped that the judge would take this into consideration when passing sentence.

Israeli Arabs are, of course, subject to Israeli law. If they take revenge in a blood dispute or if they kill for the sake of family honor, they must bear the full burden of the law without the extenuations that exist under Arab legal jurisdiction. Nevertheless, there are cases where the threat of life imprisonment does not discourage an individual from taking revenge or from satisfying family honor. In discussing killings of women for reasons of family honor, Kressel (1981, 147) states that "[Israeli Arab] attackers [fled] to Jordan, where murderers under circumstances of restoration of honour are not dealt with harshly." In Arab countries it is usually customary to announce publicly that revenge will be taken. (This is especially so in cases of political assassination, and among high status families.) Israeli Arabs, on the other hand, because of the more stringent legalities, will keep their revenge plans on a low profile. In several cases representatives of injured families stated that "time heals" and that: "We don't think that killing by revenge is a good solution." Such statements are made only for the authorities. As some of the case histories in later chapters show, revenge was taken anyway.

Blood disputes are a critical and enduring element in Middle Eastern society; such disputes bring a traditional society into conflict with the perceptions, norms and laws of the modern state. In pluralistic societies, blood disputes bring to the fore questions regarding the limits of the communities' autonomy vis-à-vis the sovereignty of the state. In Israel, the state institutions refuse to legitimize acts of violence in the course of blood disputes, yet officers of the state (high government and local officials, military and police officers, and public personalities), acting as official mediators, find themselves involved in an effort to contain or resolve blood disputes. These people actually invest the authority of the state in a serious effort, on the border of legality, to reduce the damage incurred in blood disputes. In some cases, in order to end the dispute, the official mediators intercede with the legal authorities on behalf of the perpetrators. This is not a violation of the law nor a relaxation of its enforcement. Officials simply tend, in these situations, to use their judgment to the limit of their legal authority.

The Israeli legal system makes no distinction between homicide performed in blood disputes and homicide taking place under different motives. The Israeli administration, however, does. It may be easier to commute a sentence or obtain an early release from prison in cases of crime for blood revenge or for reasons of family honor. The partial recognition by the state of traditional customs may indeed contribute to their continuity. But more probably the responsiveness shown limits the alienation of the traditional communities within the modern state. Further, informal involvement with members of the governing and social elite enhances the process of socialization of the more traditional members of Israeli society.

Although many Bedouin and rural Arabs remain loyal to traditional customs, the demands of these customs have ceased to be the single overriding factor in determining their social behavior. Considerations of punishment and less official consequences within the wider society play a larger role. This increases the chance for a peaceful resolution of the dispute, helps to limit the degree of violence used, and may lengthen the time given to the process of mediation. The process of Bedouin sedentarization, which is proceeding rapidly in Israel, increases the degree to which they interact with the wider society, in this way bringing about the above mentioned changes, and in particular increasing the pressure to modify the traditional patterns in blood disputes.

Political Assassination

Comparison between political assassinations in Arab societies and western societies reveals some fundamental differences. A political assassination in an Arab society brings about a change in the balance of political power and the threat of revenge against those who are collectively responsible. This can be compared to two well-known political assassinations that occurred in the west. When John Kennedy was assassinated, the Kennedy family as a clan did not organize themselves to take revenge by killing the killer's family. Moreover, when Robert Kennedy was assassinated by an Arab, there was no threat to the killer's family. In the John Kennedy case there was no immediate change in the balance of political power. On the whole, political assassinations in the west are not "politically" motivated in the sense that the object is to remove one person from power and replace him by another. In the west, assassinations are usually against the individual as a symbol of authority. In Arab societies, however, especially where political parties represent different ethnic groups, political assassination creates a tension the ramifications of which are usually severe. The following two topical case histories of political assassination add a further perspective. The first concerns political assassination and revenge in Lebanon; the second the assassination of an Israeli Bedouin parliamentarian.

Suliman Franjiyya was the president of Lebanon in the 1960s, and now leads a Maronite faction in northern Lebanon. In 1978 fighting took place between rival factions and in the affair Franjiyya's son, Tony, his wife and their three-year-old daughter were assassinated. Franjiyya accused Bashir Jamaiel as being responsible for the murders. Franjiyya not only deponed that he would take revenge, but built a special chapel to house the coffins, proclaiming that he would bury his kin only after he had taken revenge.

In 1982 Bashir Jamaiel was elected president of Lebanon, but was killed one week before his inauguration. In an interview,[14] Franjiyya stated that he was happy that Bashir was dead, but that his joy was not complete as he himself was not responsible for the killing, and that he was still determined to take revenge by killing other members of the Jamaiel family. Because of their high status the two families cannot allow themselves to settle their dispute through a *ṣulḥa* and payment of *diyya.* If they take money it will affect their long-term status — people will use it against them in other disputes and will be wary of entering alliances with them. For their honor to be effected, revenge is the only solution.

Fredrik Barth (1968, 85), referring to Swat Pathans, says that monetary compensation is unacceptable to an individual with any political ambition.

> A gift of money would do nothing to repair the damage to the personality; on the contrary it would further emphasize the superiority of the murderers. Clients and tenants accept blood money; chiefs are forced, because of the importance of honour to their political career, to pursue revenge. In revenge, complete submission is sought from the opponent where possible. If that is not feasible, equality in retaliation is attempted, not as a principle of justice, but because such equality expresses the existing stalemate in power; it brings the feud to a halt by implying no loss of honour to either party.

The question of status is important, as indicated by the following episode. In 1957, Franjiyya and his followers assassinated members of a rival family during a prayer ceremony in church.[15] Franjiyya took shelter in Syria until a *ṣulḥa* was successfuly negotiated and *diyya* paid, at which time he returned to Lebanon without fear that revenge would be taken against him. In this case the injured family was of a lower status, thus blood revenge could be avoided.

The assassination of an Israeli Bedouin parliamentarian took place in January 1981. Sheikh Ḥammad Abū-Rabi'a, head of a Bedouin tribe in the Negev, was assassinated outside his hotel in Jerusalem, after attending to business arising from his position as a member of the Knesset. Abū-Rabi'a was first elected in 1973, the first time in the history of Israel that a Bedouin was elected to the Knesset. His election came about as a result of a decision between sheikhs of the Negev and of the Galilee to unite under one political umbrella to further the political aims of Bedouin as a whole. In the past these two Bedouin groups had only minimal contact with each other, but they hoped that their combined group would win at least two seats in the Knesset. The election campaign was full of tension because this new party struggled to obtain votes against a rival and long established Arab party headed by Saif al-Dīn Zu'abi, from Nazareth, and a Druze leader, Sheikh Gaber Mu'adi. The newly formed Bedouin party took away from the Arab party votes that in previous elections had been theirs. The result of the elections was that the Bedouin party won one seat, taken up by Abū-Rabi'a; the other established Arab party elected two members.

In the 1977 elections the prediction of the leaders of the Labor party, to whom the Bedouin and Arab parties were affiliated, was that if the two were not joined no seats would be forthcoming for either party. It was therefore recommended that the order of any seats won by the combined parties would be as follows: Saif al-Dīn, one of the leaders of the established Arab party; Abū-Rabi'a, of the Negev Bedouin; Gaber Mu'adi, of the Druze. On the promise that Saif al-Dīn would resign immediately after the elections, Abū-Rabi'a agreed. Only one seat was won although two had been hoped for, and under the circumstances Saif al-Dīn refused to resign because he did not want Abū-Rabi'a to have the only seat. Two years later a written agreement was signed to the effect that Saif al-Dīn would resign immediately, and that Abū-Rabi'a of the Negev Bedouin would hold the seat for one year and would then resign in favor of Gaber Mu'adi of the Druze.

After the year passed, Abū-Rabi'a refused to resign. His reason for refusing was because Saif al-Dīn had not kept his original oral agreement and because he considered himself the only person capable of negotiating on behalf of the Negev Bedouin regarding the expropriation of Bedouin land, which was to be used for the military airfield to be erected in the Negev as a result of Israel's withdrawal from Sinai. Abū-Rabi'a felt most strongly about this because the area of the proposed airfield was where his tribe came from.

After his declaration of not resigning, and concerned about threats to his life, Abū-Rabi'a traveled with Bedouin bodyguards. Then, suddenly, he chose to do without them. In answer to his friends' protestations regarding his safety he answered, "My life is in the hands of God." His friends and acquaintances did not understand this answer, but after his murder members of his family related that he had told them that he had reached an agreement to pay Gaber Mu'adi U.S. $10,000, ostensibly for the expenses incurred by the Druze sheikh in taking the matter to court. In return for this payment, Gaber Mu'adi would allow Abū-Rabi'a to continue to hold his seat in the Knesset without interference. Gaber Mu'adi, however, denies that any such arrangement was made. At present the Bedouin analyze this as a trick to fool Abū-Rabi'a into thinking that by paying money the threat to his life would be absolved.

During the police investigation after the murder, Gaber Mu'adi's three sons were arrested and one of them confessed to the crime. In normal circumstances the names of those arrested would be made public. In this case, however, the police felt that if it was publicly known that the sons of the Druze leader had been arrested in connection with the assassination, it might have brought about an immediate retaliation by the Bedouin. Although the police withheld the names of those arrested for eleven days, it was common knowledge among Bedouin, the information having been broadcast over Jordanian radio and also leaked to the Bedouin by rivals of Gaber Mu'adi living in his own Druze village. At the trial, all three sons of Sheikh Gaber Mu'adi were found to have participated in the murder of Abū-Rabi'a and were sentenced to life imprisonment.

Immediately after the assassination, Sheikh Gaber Mu'adi began to travel everywhere with bodyguards, and his home in the Galilee was given 24-hour armed protection by group members. Gaber Mu'adi knew that the finger of accusation was upon him, and that revenge could be taken at any time. A particular irony of the situation was that Gaber Mu'adi automatically became a member of the Knesset on the death of Abū-Rabi'a.

This unprecedented blood dispute (Abū-Rabi'a was the first member of the Knesset ever to be assassinated) is unlikely to be settled by payment of blood money. Such a payment, however large, would be beneath the dignity of the Bedouin against the life of such an important personage. At this juncture there are just two possible ways of settlement with honor. Because the family of the accused murderer is Druze and not Bedouin, the revenge could be ignored, and the minimal interaction that now takes place between the two communities could be completely foregone. The second solution would be for the Bedouin to act according to custom by taking blood revenge. Several mediators have been sent by Gaber Mu'adi's family to the new sheikh of the Bedouin tribe in the hope that a peaceful settlement will be achieved, but the Bedouin have so far given no indication that they are prepared for a peaceful settlement. Bedouin who are not related to Abū-Rabi'a state that revenge, if taken, would be directed only against Gaber Mu'adi personally. Their thinking is that irrespective of whoever did the deed, the idea came from the Druze leader. It is perhaps indicative that during the period of condolences, when the family were asked about what steps would be taken to effect honor, the family of Abū-Rabi'a remained silent. Such silence from Bedouin is a sign of determination.

In the majority of blood disputes a certain pragmatism can usually be discerned — changes in the structure of political factions and alliances are often a potent reason for settling blood disputes. But an act such as building a chapel to house the caskets of a murdered family precludes any settlement other than revenge; in the Israeli Bedouin parliamentarian case, there has so far been no indication that revenge will be taken. A story related amongst Bedouin probably puts this state of affairs in its proper perspective. A man walked into a guest tent and told the other guests that he had just killed the son of a man who had killed his (the man relating the facts) father — forty years after the first killing. There was silence in the tent as the Bedouin did not know quite how to react. At last one old man said, "What was the hurry young fellow?" and the tension broke.

The Anthropologist/Mediator

In order to be successful a mediator must be trusted by both parties to the dispute. This is equally true for instances where the mediator mediates between members of the public, and where he mediates between the authorities and the public. In the latter case it is not necessarily a Bedouin or Arab who mediates, but can be someone with previous government experience, or an anthropologist or field worker who is in some way involved in their society. For example, Marx mediated between the Negev Bedouin and the authorities over the relocation of Bedouin resulting from the 1979 peace treaty between Egypt and Israel. As a result of the treaty, the Negev, the southern part of Israel, became a strategic area for Israeli economic and military development. This area was occupied by some 40,000 Bedouin. Marx acted as an anthropologist/mediator, as part of the Negev Planning Team, in the Bedouin resettlement negotiations.

Mediating anthropologists work with all the parties involved in any

> particular matter and seek to achieve a workable solution acceptable to all. They assume that the parties concerned possess power and more or less clearly defined aims. I use the term mediator for persons who have an "interjacent commitment" to the negotiating parties (Gulliver 1969, 62). Gulliver rightly notes that these are usually also people of influence with resources of their own, who often take the lead in negotiations. (Marx 1981, 119)
>
> The planner-anthropologist thus becomes a mediator in the sociological sense, who must be seen by all parties concerned to be impartial and not a tool of employees and who must facilitate communications all around and, thus, create conditions for agreement and exchange. In the process, he or she will acquire power, which must be used constructively in the support of new ideas, compromise, and persuasion. In this role the planner-anthropologist comes to manipulate and change the field of power, by introducing new participants, neutralizing others, and redefining issues. Finally, he or she must pave the way for gradual withdrawal, in a manner that will permit the parties to continue unaided. (Ibid., 124)

Marx (ibid., 126) states that the "central object of the mediator [is] the balancing and manipulation of power." In the Negev Bedouin case the government authorities knew that the Bedouin trust Marx, while the Bedouin knew that Marx had the power to influence government decisions regarding the Bedouin sedentarization. The difference between my experience and that of Marx is that in most instances in which I acted as a mediator, only one side needed me. Nevertheless, the criteria related by Marx is basically valid for my mediating experience. The following three case histories are indicative of the sort of mediation requests that have been made to me. In determining how to react to each individual case I bore in mind that what often looks like a minor case to an anthropologist/mediator is sometimes of the greatest concern to the individual requesting mediating services. Mediation is part of rural Arab and Bedouin way of life, and a request to act as a mediator must always be viewed in this light.

Sometimes the anthropologist/mediator just happens to be on the spot, and so it was with me in the case of a family honor killing that took place in August 1973 in a small hamlet situated in the Triangle. The case history is fully analyzed in chapter five, but the sequence of events that led me to play the role of anthropologist/mediator are related here.

A girl had intercourse with a young man of her lineage. When the murder occurred the mother of the girl screamed that her husband had just killed their daughter. Her son, Sa'id, who had been sitting in a local cafe, heard his mother's screams and rushed home to find the dead body. Sa'id then determined to spare his father the imprisonment and claimed

A collection for the blood money payment is made among descent group members.

Two Bedouin started fighting with a sword and a stick. A neighbor quickly ran to bring a goat, and invited the combatants to settle their differences over a meal with him.

Druze and Christian leaders conclude a peace agreement by shaking hands.

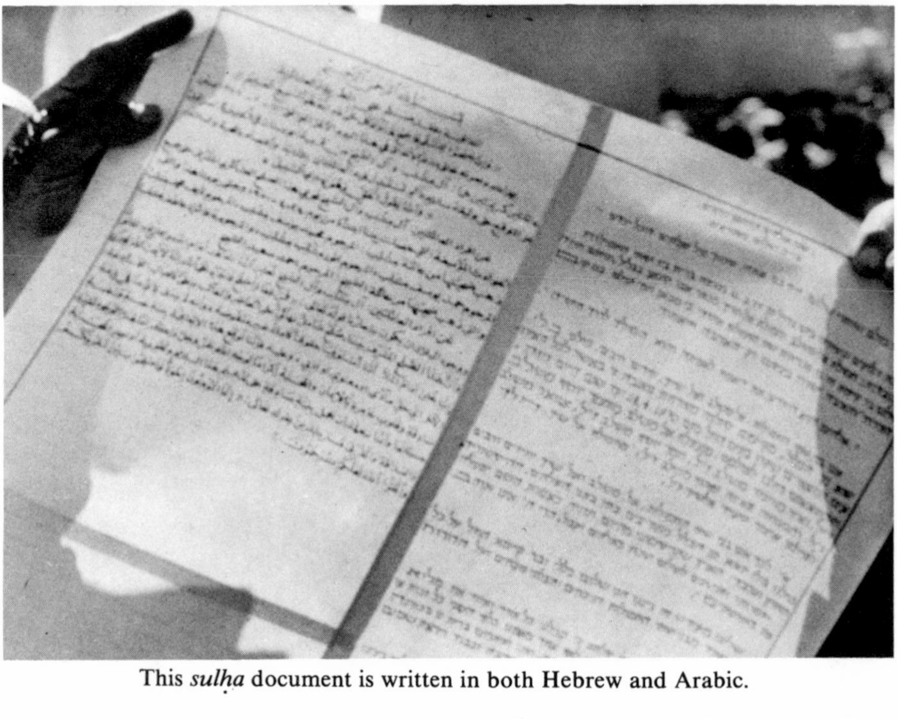

This *sulḥa* document is written in both Hebrew and Arabic.

that he was the one who had killed his sister. However, Sa'id did not know that his father had already made a statement to the police confessing that he had killed the girl without accomplices. Although Sa'id later retracted his confession, both father and son were found guilty and sentenced to life imprisonment. In 1975 the head of the *ḥamūla*, who is also the head of the hamlet, asked me to help them in soliciting a presidential pardon for the father and son. The family was concerned for both their members, but especially for the father. A *ḥamūla* elder expressed the sentiment, shared by the rest of the family, that, "It would be a *shame* for us if the old man dies in prison." Like the villagers, I was convinced that the father had killed his daughter without an accomplice.

Beginning in 1975 I wrote several letters to the president, and to the minister of justice. The purpose of this correspondence was to put before them full details of why I believed the son was innocent, and a detailed explanation of Arab society norms concerning family honor, which in this case had two different dimensions: under what circumstances an individual is pushed to kill his sister or daughter, and why a son would take upon himself a murder committed by his father. In the course of this appeal I met President Itzhak Navon four times, and met several more times with officials from the ministry of justice. In 1978 the president agreed to change the category of sentence,[16] first for the father and then later for the son, from life imprisonment to a period of 27 years. This change of category was an important step for it meant that they were now eligible to limited parole from the prison on religious holidays and at certain other times such as family bereavements and family festivals. After a prolonged illness in prison the father was released in 1983 on humanitarian grounds. He had served nine years.

Due to reduction of sentence by presidential decree and remission of sentence due to good behavior, by 1983 the innocent son had just five more years to serve. Because Itzhak Navon's term as president was at the end I felt that an all-out effort should be made to release the son before Navon was succeeded, as he was well acquainted with all the facts of the case. I further felt that a ground swell of public opinion might be all that would be needed for the president to pardon the innocent young man. To this end I suggested to the family and *ḥamūla* heads that I organize a television program where the villagers, both young and old, present their views concerning illicit sexual relations and family honor. The villagers agreed to this suggestion and it was further proposed that the father who murdered his daughter should also speak, as well as his son in prison who would explain why he confessed to a crime he did not commit.

The night before the T.V. crew was to come to the village I received a telephone call from the head of the *ḥamūla* saying that they had decided to cancel the filming in the village. After some inquiries I found out that a younger brother of Sa'id was the cause behind the sudden change. The younger brother was planning to marry a girl from a neighboring village. The girl was from a higher status family than his own and he thought that the television program might jeopardize his marriage prospects. He was not ashamed that his father had killed his sister, but was afraid that the bride's family might object to giving their daughter to someone whose sister was a "prostitute." The younger brother feared that his future in-laws would be influenced by the television program and cancel the marriage. And it was he who put pressure on the *ḥamūla* heads to cancel the filming. I went to see Sa'id in prison and explained the situation to him. After visiting Sa'id in prison the younger brother acquiesced in this matter and another date for filming was agreed upon. The documentary was shown on Israel television in May 1983. The morning after the program I received a telephone call from the presidential office to say that the president had signed papers that allowed the releasing committee of the prison to free Sa'id.

The above events involved me in mediation between the authorities and members of the public; my second example concerns inter-Arab mediation. In June 1983 I was approached by Khair, an Arab peasant whose mother and wife were of Bedouin origin. He requested that I put forward a proposal for a *badal* marriage between his siblings and the siblings of an Arab whom I have known personally for many years. (A *badal* marriage is an exchange marriage where one man's son marries another man's daughter and the first man's daughter marries the second man's son. The two unions are linked — if one union breaks up, the other union automatically breaks up too.) Khair chose me as a mediator because he knew of my close friendship with the family with whom he wishes to become related with. Khair explained that he had recently requested a relative of the other party to propose this *badal* arrangement, but that the proposal had been rejected outright. Nevertheless, the Arab did not take "no" for an answer and in requesting me to be his mediator he suggested that I take along my wife, Dalia; the idea being that Dalia would mention the good qualities of his daughter, whom Dalia knew, while I "sold" the son. When I presented the *badal* proposal to my friend he explained that Khair had made a terrible mistake by first sending a relative who was of a lower status than his own. "You have to honor me and to send an important person as a mediator," he said. He then told me that because he had previously rejected the proposed *badal* he would like to wait for several months before he would refer again to the matter.

The third example of my mediating activities concerns Muḥammad and Sara (see the Preface). Recently, Sara suspected Muḥammad of having sexual relations with a woman from a neighboring village. After the woman in question admitted her part in the liaison Sara refused to speak to her husband, who approached me to act as mediator. This kind of mediation is very unusual; in such cases a wife will return to her natal family and stay there until the problem is solved. There are then direct negotiations between the woman's father and brothers, and her husband. Under these circumstances the woman is described as *ḥardana* ("offended and angry"); such affairs usually end in the husband coming to take his wife back by bringing her an expensive gift. In this case, however, Sara did not go back to her natal family; furthermore, she was against any reconciliation. When I explained that it was important for their children that they reestablish normal relations, she relented and agreed to begin speaking again with her husband.

The three descriptions of my role as mediator show a type of fieldwork that can be distinguished from the participant observation type of fieldwork related in the Preface. Usually, there is not too much personal involvement with the society under study.[17] The three mediation cases described above are also fieldwork, but with the difference that I assisted in some way. This assistance toward them resulted in their assisting me in the form of providing me with inside information on other issues.

Mediation cannot be over estimated in Bedouin and rural Arab societies. Bedouin and rural Arabs are highly politicized. The conduct of their daily life and the main topic of their daily conversation is related to political activity and intrigues within their society. A man's political standing is akin to his honor — to be safeguarded and if possible increased. Marx (1973) tells how circumcision ceremonies are used to promote the political standing of the father. Mediation is one channel by which political relations between individuals are conducted. It is their way of doing things. For example, it would be considered impolite for a politician to ask the leader of a faction to vote for him. Instead, the politician will ask his friend to do the asking. The friend will act as an intermediary — he will promote the qualities of the politician. This indirectness is a hallstone in political relations in Bedouin and rural Arab societies. And it is mediation that is the bridge for this indirectness.

There are various connecting links between the elements of blood revenge, the role and status of the mediator, outcasting, and family honor. These links are power, exchange, and honor. In blood disputes, in cases where the injured group decides to take revenge, the head of the group accumulates power through the cohesiveness built up as a result of a formal decision to act. In cases where the group agrees to *ṣulḥa* and accepts *diyya,* the exchange relations are on the basis of the relative strength of the two groups. For example, if the group whose member caused the homicide is stronger than the injured group, it is in the interests of the injured group to establish a situation whereby they can in the future rely on the support of the more powerful group; they try to establish a situation of permanent indebtedness.

The mediator, by negotiating between disputing groups, and in this way making the groups dependent on him, accumulates power. The mediator's power derives not from implementing the prescribed and customary rules of mediation, but rather from his manipulation of the power he has to bring about a settlement. In other words, his power comes from manipulating intergroup relationships.

In cases where an individual is cast out from his group, it is the proposer of this action who attempts to alter intragroup power relations. Although ostensibly the act of casting out an individual from the group is done in order to achieve cohesiveness within the group, such an act affects the balance of power, from which personal benefits may accrue.

The killing of a woman because she brought shame on the family is an established Arab norm. Yet behind the carrying out of this norm lie power, control, and exchange relations. Illicit sexual relations imply free mate choice, whereby the father loses control over his daughter and thus the chance of making a politically advantageous match. This not only applies to daughters, but to his sons also. The norm may be even more strictly applied because nowadays sons do not have to rely on their father's inheritance. Thus control over the sons is viewed very much in terms of a continuing close control over the marital choice of the daughters. Free mate choice also means that the customary role of the mediator in matchmaking would become redundant. The mediators, who gain prestige from their matchmaking undertakings, are thus strong proponents of strictly maintaining the sexual norm.

An example of power in Arab society is where a leader has more persons under his control than a rival leader. In cases of conflict such a difference will award him more manpower, but even in normal times the leader of the larger group operates from a position of strength, which manifests itself in being economically stronger, or being able to grant favors to a wider circle of people. Power considerations also relate to promoting the cohesiveness of the group, to the status of individuals, and to other aspects, which are elaborated in the case histories. Even in cases where power and exchange relations cannot be discerned, there is almost always some honor element. The very act of taking a position, let alone accusing another of some misdeed, means that honor is at stake. The accuser cannot back down without losing face and the accused has to protect himself against the accusation. The honor standing of both parties is thus at stake. If it is not resolved through mediation, it has to be satisfied through perhaps more violent means. The aggravating factor is that the honor standing of an individual is related to that of his co-liable group, and this aspect intensifies the honor conflict.

CHAPTER TWO

Blood Revenge

This chapter is concerned with blood revenge in Bedouin society. Blood disputes in rural Arab communities are usually settled through mediation rather than through revenge, and are dealt with fully in chapter three.

Instances of murder among the Bedouin who live within the borders of Israel, and in other Arab countries, are frequently reported in the news media and in professional literature.[1] The Bedouin themselves often explain after such incidents that the killer did not have homicidal intentions but was carried away by the heat of an argument: The consequences were not intended and neither was the act premeditated. One example of a cause for squabbling is over who should go first when shepherds meet at a well to water their flocks. Even so small a controversy may lead to a homicide. Although the first killing may occur on the spur of the moment and without prior planning, this is not the case when a murder takes place for revenge. The very idea of retribution — in this case killing someone who has killed another — is intentional and premeditated.

The Bedouin themselves explain blood revenge by arguing that if a man has been slain, there must be one grave opposite the other grave. Despite this apparently simple explanation, its realization is hardly satisfactory. A Bedouin may sometimes shrug off the importance of one human life, but if such an attitude were deeply anchored in the thought and feeling of the community, no blood revenge would follow. Revenge is in essence a rebellion against the shedding of blood; it is a reaction that expresses outrage. Sometimes the word "feud" is incorrectly used in place of blood revenge.[2] When there is a feud there is a chain of reciprocal murders, one following the other, between the rival groups. Revenge for the first killing, which terminates the dispute, cannot be defined as feud. Blood revenge refers to a single killing to avenge a murder that has taken place.

Collective responsibility means that each member of a co-liable group knows that if he murders someone, or even if he kills him unintentionally without any premeditation, he creates a conflict with the injured co-liable group that might lead to blood revenge, the exile of his co-liable group, or, at the very least, payment of *diyya* (blood money).[3] The blood dispute is not ended until there is a *ṣulḥa* (peace agreement) or revenge is taken. Sometimes the dispute can last for many years. It is not always the individual who caused the murder upon whom revenge is taken. It can be any member of the murderer's co-liable group — somebody who is completely innocent and apart from the original argument is murdered in revenge because of collective responsibility. Although any member of the group can be killed as a revenge, members of the injured group will usually try to kill a close relative of the murderer.

There may be additional members in the group of the murderer who are not of the co-liable group, but such persons are not forced into exile after a murder, they do not participate in the payment of blood money, nor do they receive a share of any blood money paid to the group they have joined. It is customary, however, for every male member of the group who is not of the co-liable group to give the family of the murdered man a camel or its value in money. This payment is called *be'ir al-nom* ("camel of sleep") and once it is accepted the giver can sleep in his tent without fear. The payment is really an "insurance policy," a wise precaution that prevents a possible hasty act. 'Āref al-'Āref (1933, 78–79) points out that members of the sixth and seventh generations, as well as those who have joined the group, pay for the *be'ir al-nom*.[4]

An important distinction in blood revenge in Bedouin society is whether the killer and his victim are members of different co-liable groups, or whether they both belong to the same co-liable group. Different norms and procedures apply according to whether there is any kinship relation between the killer and his victim.

Killer and Victim from Different Co-liable Groups

As a reaction to the killing of a member of a certain corporate group, a single retaliation will follow by killing a member of the murderer's co-liable group. The blood dispute can also be ended through the payment of *diyya* following negotiations through a mediator. Blood revenge or blood money payment usually stops the cycle of hostility between the two groups. But until revenge has been taken or until *'aṭwa* (a cease-fire, in the sense of a cessation of hostile action) has been concluded, every member of the murderer's co-liable group lives in constant fear of death. The time period during which *'aṭwa* is effective is not clearly defined, though it is usually valid for at least one month. There is, however, no obligation to prolong the agreement.

The custom regarding *'aṭwa* among the Bedouin in the Negev differs from that in the Galilee. *Ṣulḥa* negotiations in the Negev are not opened before one year after the murder, and sometimes *'aṭwa* will be agreed upon for several years until a *ṣulḥa* is concluded. No money changes hands during the *'aṭwa*, which is termed *'aṭwat sharaf* — an agreement of honor. The Bedouin claim that it is easier to violate an agreement based on payment of money than one that concerns a man's honor.

In the Negev the group whose member has inflicted injury hopes that *'aṭwa* will be followed in due course by a *ṣulḥa*, but there is no binding obligation on the part of the injured group to agree. If the group is prepared to accept blood money an interim agreement is reached covering the period between the time that *'aṭwa* is agreed upon and the *ṣulḥa*. This contract is called *jira* (based on payment of money or the handing over of a bill). At the *jira* ceremony an amount of money is paid by those who are collectively responsible for the murder (al-Āref 1933, 90). After the money is paid, revenge cannot be taken. The money is entrusted to the mediators until the time of the *ṣulḥa* ceremony when the *jira* payment is deducted from the total blood money payment. Even if *'aṭwa* has been agreed upon, if the conditions of the cease-fire have not been strictly adhered to by the group of the killer,[5] then revenge can still be taken up to the point when the *jira* payment is made. In the Negev the interim payment of *jira* is made near to the time of the *ṣulḥa*. This extension in time before there is recognition by the injured group that they can no longer take revenge presents an additional danger to the killer's group. Among the Bedouin of the Galilee this interim payment usually takes place on the occasion of the *'aṭwa* agreement. (There are instances in which the injured party among the Bedouin of the Galilee refuse to accept money during the *'aṭwa* ceremony, for the same reason that the Bedouin of the Negev prefer *'aṭwat sharaf*. It is possible that the custom of giving money became a norm among Bedouin of the Galilee under the influence of Arab villagers.) The important difference between Bedouin custom in the north and south is that in the south *'aṭwa* may not be renewed; because the interim *jira* payment has not yet been made, the injured group can still take revenge. In the north the interim payment is made at the time of the *'aṭwa* agreement; after the interim payment is made, no revenge can take place. In both the north and the south, the party responsible for the murder is not required to pay any sum to the mediators, but unofficially some token payment, and sometimes more than just a token payment, is made.

The ethnographic data presented in the following case histories refer to killing for blood revenge and also to the payment of blood money for manslaughter. The particulars throw light on the conditions under which an injured group will oppose a cease-fire and insist on murder as the only possible form of revenge, as well as conditions under which an injured group will conclude a peace agreement after payment of blood money. An attempt will be made to find a general explanation for the reaction of the injured group.

It is important to recognize the significance of the effects of violent death on those emotionally close to the victim. It is true that a man's feelings are often akin to those in his group, whose members are linked to him through bonds of blood relationship. But there may also be especial relations of friendship or good comradeship. Collective responsibility does not mean that everyone relates to everyone else within the group in the same way, or that sympathies and antipathies cannot develop on an individual basis. Although an individual will formally react the same way as other members of his group concerning the death of a member of the co-liable group, the deceased may or may not have been his close friend. Although the individual acts according to prescribed norms, he may urge normative action more passionately and more convincingly when his feelings are aroused. A man whose feelings are hurt may refuse blood money and insist on physical revenge. When he is indifferent he may wait for others to advocate revenge.

Students of society must bear in mind that human beings are not only part of economic, social and political structures, but are also individuals who react to the same challenges in unique ways — even if they live in an identical or nearly identical manner. Their duties and privileges may be the same, and their patterns of behavior dictated by custom, but even within this system there is still room for a variety of emotions and reactions. Sometimes a person's strong emotional reaction may result in an outburst that presents a dramatization of the incident, arousing feelings of empathy and compliance. An individual who feels personally injured may not acquiesce when blood money is accepted for a murdered relative to whom he has been close. He may even resort to action without the consent of the group.

Not only factors of personal hurt and honor must be taken into consideration. The outraged individual of the injured group may well refrain from taking revenge if prolonged imprisonment would result. Emanuel Marx refers to a case where the potential avenger would have had to go to prison for a long time if he had acted out his revenge (1967, 193–94). After *'aṭwa*, when the heat of the moment for revenge may have subsided somewhat, economic and political considerations often guide the decision of how the injured group reacts. For example, imprisonment might not only take away the breadwinner of the family but also weaken the group if this individual has a high political standing. Consequently, it often happens that revenge is abandoned, especially in cases where the murderer lives at a distant location,[6] or where the group of the murdered man has no economic, political or other relations with the group that inflicted injury on it.

Killer and Victim From Same Co-liable Group

Where the corporate group functions well a way is usually found to appease and compensate the injured family without recourse to blood revenge or blood money. Emrys Peters (1967, 264–65) says that revenge is not taken within the group. If it is taken, the loss to the group will be twice as great. A killing within the group is resolved through the killer's exile for a period of several years. If the immediate family demands revenge or blood money, this indicates that the group is not functioning well. In such a case the same conditions apply as when the killer and victim are members of different co-liable groups. When the killer and his victim are members of the same co-liable group it is the Bedouin norm that the group resolve the crisis with the least disruption to the group's activities. This is achieved (providing of course that the injured party is not bent on revenge) by (1), as stated, the murderer going into exile, and (2) the murderer giving his closest unmarried female relative to the closest male kin of the victim.

It is the norm that the killer exiles himself to a place outside of the area where the co-liable group lives. If the killer does not initiate his own exile, he will be forcibly exiled. The elders of the co-liable group determine the length of exile only after the man has left the encampment; their decision will depend on the circumstances that led to the homicide. Clearly, a premeditated murder will be viewed differently than an accidental death. The exiled person will then enlist the services of a mediator to help reduce the period of exile. There are instances where the closest relatives of the victim initiate the return of the exiled individual back to the fold of the group as well as instances where the exiled individual feels that he has been unfairly treated by his group and builds a new life attached to a different group.

In cases where the murderer goes into exile he gives his closest unmarried female relative to the closest kin of the person who was killed (i.e., his daughter or sister to the deceased's father, brother, or son). The girl who lives in such a relationship is called a *ghura*. The *ghura* lives with the closest male kin of the victim until she gives birth to a male offspring.

This is done in order to compensate the family for their loss. After giving birth the woman may return to her family. If the relationship was satisfactory, however, a marriage is arranged, and this is the norm in most cases. Because the woman is no longer a virgin, even though it was the "husband" who deflowered her, the bride price is usually about half of the regular price. When the marriage takes place the exile of the murderer is terminated. There is a paradox in this Bedouin norm for both the family to which the murderer belongs, and the injured family, may be brought closer through a marriage union.

Factors Affecting Revenge or Settlement

A group whose economy is based on wage labor will be anxious to resolve a blood quarrel quickly because their daily and regular trips to their places of work will make them vulnerable to the revenging group. If the economy of the group is based on the raising of herds the movements of group members are not regular. Consequently, in contrast to the wage labor situation, a revenge is less likely to be perpetrated. When groups lived in tents it did not present a problem to repitch the tents of one group at some distance from another group in case of a dispute. But now that many Bedouin live in houses, daily interaction between the groups is unavoidable and thus the chance of a continuation of the conflict is higher. The rapid pace of sedentarization of the Bedouin in Israel has also been accompanied by a change in their manner and method of growing food. Nowadays many of the Bedouin who are not already engaged in wage labor practise intensive cultivation techniques, not just for their own use but for sale on the market. Intensive cultivation requires regular daily looking after. This regularity and the danger inherent in it makes it important to negotiate a quick settlement.

More and more Bedouin are now entering the wage labor market on a permanent basis. In undertaking such work a Bedouin accepts a certain responsibility to attend work regularly. If for reasons of a blood dispute he decides one morning that it is unsafe for him to attend, it is highly likely that his job will not be waiting for him when he decides that it is safe to attend. The wish to keep one's job and the benefits of a regular income are strong reasons to make sure that blood disputes are settled quickly.

The major factor affecting revenge or settlement is the political "condition" of the avenging group. A leader who is anxious to promote cohesiveness within the group will encourage revenge. Mutual (collective) responsibility "constitutes the ultimate obligation of members of a co-liable group" (Marx 1973, 241). By deliberately increasing tension a leader can make his group aware of their collective responsibility, in this way promoting group cohesiveness. Even if the leader does not advocate a revenge he can achieve cohesion by not permitting a cease-fire agreement. There are also political circumstances where it is in the interests of the injured group to agree to a settlement.

Case History I

Some Bedouin groups, whose members are of peasant origin originally from the area in which the fortress (*qal'a*) of Khan Yunis is located, live among the Bedouin of the Negev and are called Qla'iyya (Marx 1967, 197). Until 1968 they did not constitute a tribe of their own but were subject to the authority of three tribes in the Ẓullām subfederation and the Qderāt al-San'a tribe. The Qla'iyya and other peasant groups had previously owned no land where they originally resided. They migrated to regions inhabited by Bedouin, particularly the lowland of Beersheva–Arad. The dispersion of the Qla'iyya among the Bedouin tribes is indicated in figure 1. The situation of the Qla'iyya is described by Marx (1967, 77):

> The peasants acquired land wherever and whenever they were able to obtain it, and then remained under the protection of the tribe from which the land had been bought. Thus one now finds that the members of many peasant groups are formally divided up among three or four tribes though other groups will be concentrated in one tribe.

Despite formal membership with several tribes, the Qla'iyya pitched their tents together and in this way succeeded in creating their own political framework. As early as the 1950s the heads of the Qla'iyya asked the authorities to grant them independent status, a resolution that was reflected in the 1959 Knesset election campaign. In 1968, the head of the largest co-liable group among the Qla'iyya was finally nominated head of the tribe and awarded the coveted sheikh's seal. After recognition by the authorities, a split occurred in the tribe (figure 2). In 1970 a group within the newly formed Qla'iyya tribe seceded from the tribe (stage I). This group, group A, convinced the authorities that its members had nothing in common with the other Qla'iyya members, except their peasant origin. The head of the seceding group A was appointed head of his tribe (thus group A became tribe A) and was permitted to use the sheikh's seal as a symbol of his position, as well as to carry a pistol. In the fall of 1971 another group seceded from the Qla'iyya tribe. This group, group B, also tried to be recognized as an independent tribe (stage II), although this request was not granted until nearly a decade later.

FIGURE 1

Dispersion of the Qla'iyya among the Bedouin tribes

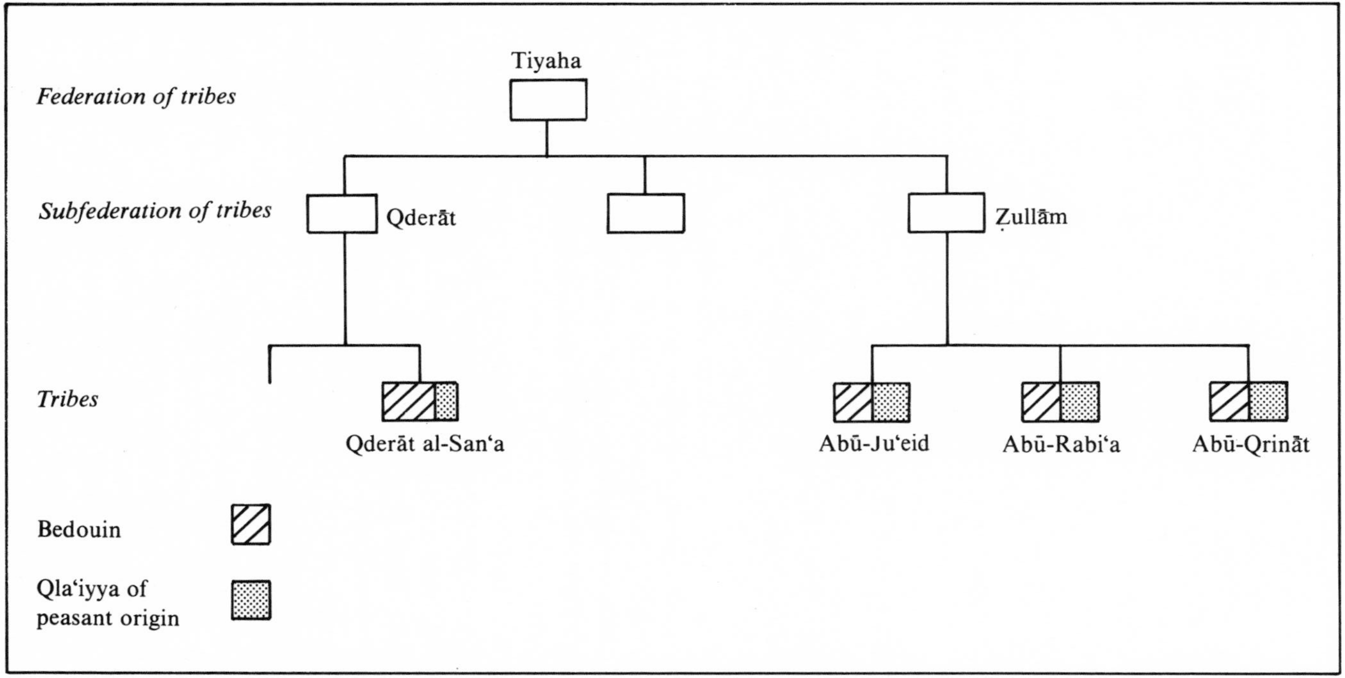

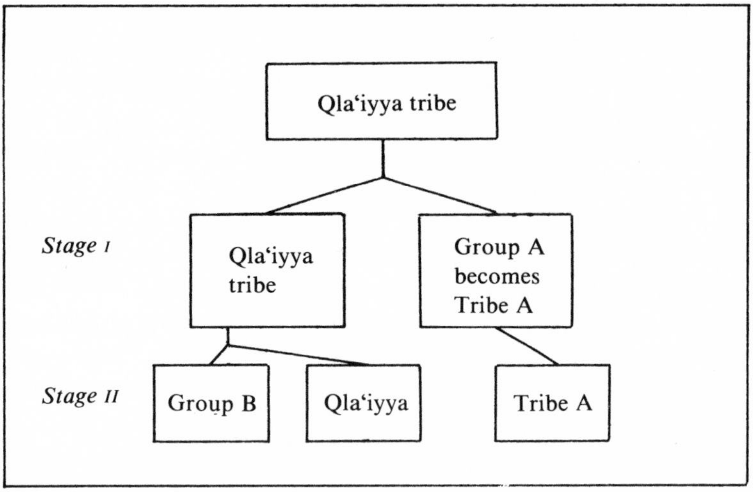

FIGURE 2
The split in the Qla'iyya after recognition by the authorities as a tribe

The head of tribe A did his best to persuade members of group B to join his tribe. Verbal clashes between tribe A and group B created tension, which focused on pasture and the right to draw water from certain wells. (Prior to the political maneuvering of the involved parties in attempting to gain recognition as independent tribes there had been no conflict over the shared use of these scarce resources.) Finally, a murder took place. In May 1972, members of tribe A ambushed members of group B close to Beersheva; in the fight a member of tribe A was killed.

Those from group B belonged to the same co-liable group, whereas the tribe A ambushers came from three different co-liable groups. (There are altogether four co-liable groups in tribe A.) Police investigation did not establish the identity of the murderer and the incident was defined as a mass quarrel. Immediately after the murder took place, several Bedouin notables declared *'aṭwa mafrūda* (an enforced cease-fire).[7] The head of the injured group turned a deaf ear to every suggestion of peace and only submitted *nolens volens* to *'aṭwa*, which lasts three and a third days as custom prescribes. An enforced cease-fire enables the co-liable group, one of whose members killed a man, to find shelter in the encampment of another tribe.[8] Such a cease-fire takes place irrespective of the wishes of the injured group. If they do not submit willingly to the cease-fire then they must accept it unwillingly, but accept it they must.

The head of group B and other group B members argued that the head of tribe A was preventing the head of the injured co-liable group of his tribe from concluding a peace agreement. The head of tribe A, however, maintained that it was not for him to decide but depended on the members of the injured group, who were not prepared to accept blood money. After several meetings in the sheikh's tent, one of the elders said that there was no hope of reaching an agreement and that the members of the injured co-liable group were determined to murder a member of the attacker's co-liable group. Other Bedouin notables supported this view, and it was therefore suggested that a *ṣulḥa* committee be set up. This is not the custom in the Negev, although it is common in the north of Israel. *Ṣulḥa* committee members are chosen from the ranks of Bedouin leaders and representatives of the administration. In this instance the governor of the district, a representative of the prime minister's office, and a representative of the police, in addition to the sheikhs, served on the committee — but their efforts proved futile. Pressure was exerted by the authorities on the leader of tribe A by confiscating his revolver and suspending him from office. Talks were held with the leader of the injured co-liable group and he received certain assurances in the event that he would accept blood money. These actions were to no avail and at the end of May 1973, one year after the murder, the injured co-liable group of tribe A avenged the death of their member by murdering the brother of the head of group B. Three of the members of the avenging group were found guilty of murder and sentenced to life imprisonment in January 1974.

In the early 1970s the Qla'iyya numbered about 1,800; at that time there were about 7,000 Bedouin of the Ẓullām tribes.[9] Marx (1967, 78) points out that:

> Even though the peasant group [the Qla'iyya] own some land, it would still be true if one called them "landless", for the land is never sufficient for their requirements, and they still have to obtain the larger part in share-cropping arrangements, wherever available. There is, of course, some connection between the source of a man's land and his political allegiance, so that the peasants are in many ways politically tied to their Bedouin landowners. But this economic and political dependence on the Bedouin does not in any way detract from the peasants' allegiance to their own co-liable groups.

In recent years the economic and political dependence of the peasants on the Bedouin has decreased. Although the Qla'iyya also lease land from the ministry of agriculture, it is not enough for their subsistence. Many young men have become wage earners and commute long distances to work.

Well before the antagonism amongst the various Qla'iyya members erupted, one of the leaders of the four co-liable groups of tribe A moved close to Lod where he bought a stone dwelling house; in 1967 he became a member of the committee of Trustees of the Muslim *Waqf*[10] in Lod. Some families from two of the co-liable groups, one from that of the injured group that took revenge and others from the sheikh's group, pitched their tents close to one of the Arab villages in the Triangle and lived there all year round. They were employed in Jewish agricultural settlements, or leased land from Arab villagers on which they grew vegetables, utilizing modern systems of cultivation including irrigation and plastic covers during the winter season. The fourth group had for several years grazed flocks in the Beit Shemesh–Ramle area, where they stayed with their flocks during the lambing and milking season, from October to April. In sum, a considerable number of tribe A members stayed away from the tribal encampment for most of the year. Although there is agricultural land near the encampment, its cultivation requires no more than a few weeks' work a year. This situation of a much dispersed tribal community meant that the tribe was lacking somewhat in cohesiveness.

After the murder the leader of tribe A saw a chance to unite his tribe, and he assembled all the males of the co-liable groups for consultations. Had the leader of tribe A agreed to *'aṭwa*, tension would have abated. Not only would the members of the other co-liable groups have returned to their occupations in the north of the Negev, but also the members of the injured co-liable group would have left the Negev to return to the place that they have inhabited for the last decade — the Triangle and the Ramle–Lod area. The leader of tribe A set up a large guest tent, which was crowded all hours of the day. The sheikh even asked the ministry of education to add further classes to the school attached to the tribe in order to accomodate the children of the assembled families. The sheikh fully understood that his suspension from office was temporary, a ruse in order to exert pressure and make him agree to *'aṭwa*. In his eyes the consolidation of the tribe was of the greatest importance. The blood dispute offered an opportunity for exercising formal power and in this way strengthening his position. The appearance of sheikhs and other notables in his tent for consultations clearly added to his status. Usually unity is achieved by decreasing tension in the group, but in this case unity was achieved by increasing tension.[11] It was possible to do this because only the injured party is in a position to agree to *'aṭwa*.

The sheikh of tribe A understood that a cease-fire agreement, even if it was not subsequently renewed, is an indication of a lessening of tension and would have an adverse effect on his aim of consolidating his tribe. The political unity factor was decisive when the leader of tribe A incited the injured co-liable group to revenge. The murder of the brother of the leader of group B, who had been ambitious for official recognition as sheikh, is also politically significant. The revenge could have been implemented through the killing of any member of the co-liable group, but the intention was to injure the leader.

Case History II

Emanuel Marx (1967, 239) describes the case of Jedū'a Abū-Ṣulb, who was expelled from his co-liable group by his agnates. Marx states that "Gadū' Abu Ṣulb was haunted by bad luck, as one man put it. Time and again he became involved in bloodshed." The first occasion was in 1951, when Jedū'a broke a man's hand in a quarrel. The second occasion took place in 1953, when Jedū'a went hunting and accidentally shot and wounded a shepherdess. The dispute following this incident was prolonged because the wounded shepherdess subsequently died from gangrene. Jedū'a's group ended this dispute, but he was proclaimed a *meshamas* (an outcast). No one could now hold the group responsible for his actions. (The case of Jedū'a is analyzed from the outcasting point of view in case history XXIV.)

Some time after his *tashmīs* (expulsion) Jedū'a crossed the border between Israel and Egypt into the Sinai Desert, and again got into trouble. When the Egyptians discovered his illegal presence he tried to escape, injuring a Bedouin in the shooting that occurred during his flight. He returned to Israel and was employed as a watchman by an agricultural company whose fields bordered on those of the al-Huzayel tribe. Several young men of the Ṭawāra group (whose origin is from southern Sinai) conspired against him, claiming that they had priority in employment in this region because they were of local origin. Jedū'a was attacked and in the ensuing fight a man was killed. In the subsequent trial, Jedū'a pleaded self-defense. The Ṭawāra knew that he was expelled from his co-liable group and decided to kill him at once, so before the trial opened several young Ṭawāra men staged a fight close to the prison. One of them insulted a policeman and made several derogatory remarks about the State of Israel. He was arrested and found to be in possession of a knife that he had hidden in his shoe, and which was clearly intended to be used in order to kill Jedū'a. The court sentenced Jedū'a to three years' imprisonment but he was released after two years.

Jedū'a asked the military authorities to help him in finding shelter away from the Negev and in the winter of 1960 he went to live with a

Bedouin tribe close to the Israeli–Lebanese border, where I visited him on several occasions. His hosts refused to accept payment from him, although he himself received wages for his labors during his stay with them. Despite the kindness he received from the Bedouin in the Galilee he could not forsake the Negev and in the summer he returned to work as a watchman in the United Jewish Fund forests close to Dimona. At night he slept in different creeks, never remaining in one place all night. In 1962 he married and had a son, but in the spring of 1964 fate caught up with him and he was killed in a fight by two men (not from the Ṭawāra co-liable group) with whom he was in dispute.

Members of the Ṭawāra still claim that the blood dispute between Jedū'a and themselves is not yet at an end and that they will murder his son when he grows up. They believe that even after he was expelled from his co-liable group, agnates kept in contact with him and that the expulsion from his group, made known to all tribes prior to the last quarrel, was a fake (Marx 1967, 24–42). For many years the issue lay dormant, but since 1984 members of the Ṭawāra co-liable group have proclaimed in public that now Jedū'a's son is a man, they will take revenge by killing him. The young man, who works in the construction industry, fears that an attempt will be made on his life. However, he too claims that he will avenge his father's death. Many of the Ṭawara work for wages. Some have moved from the Negev and settled in Triangle villages, others work in the area of Ramle and Lod. That the co-liable group is very much dispersed is of great concern to that part of the group which remained in the Negev. In order to counter the dispersal of the group, some of the Negev members have made the blood revenge threat, hoping in this way to re-unite the group through an issue that demands a group decision.

Case History III

In Spring 1975 a thirty-year-old Bedouin, a building contractor of the Abū-Karīr tribe, was killed by his father's brother's son. Both the father of the killer and the father of the victim used to be herders. At the time of the killing the father of the victim, though financially supported by his sons, possessed herds for which he leased a certain pasture. Several years prior to the killing, members of his brother's nuclear family had invaded the pasture after which there were verbal insults[12] that led to physical violence in which a son of the man who had leased the pasture was stabbed in his arm. The event led to tension between the two families. The man who had previously been stabbed in the arm (son of the man who had leased the pasture), was attacked and killed by a paternal cousin. The court sentenced the killer to four years' imprisonment. His father and brothers went into exile as the accused man would have done had he not been incarcerated (Hardy 1963, 92). The exiled father and brother decided to live with the al-Ḥubeshi tribe at a distance of about twenty kilometers west of their own residence. Although they had formerly lived in shacks they now pitched tents, which they attached to one of the co-liable groups of the host tribe.[13]

The victim's brother maintained that revenge would be taken and several Negev Bedouin, anticipating revenge, did their best to bring about *'aṭwa* But they were unsuccessful in their attempts. The head of the co-liable group in whose vicinity the victim's relatives now resided explained that the reason for the unsuccessful attempts at promoting *'aṭwa* was due to the fact that the sons supported their respective families by a non-agricultural livelihood. As a result there was little interaction between the two families and a corresponding loss of mutual cooperation, which is necessary where close families are engaged together in full-time agriculture or herding.

Coincidentally, the wealthiest among the sons of both families was the victim. When sons derive their livelihood from sources other than the land or herds there is a separation of interests, and envy and rivalry are often the consequence. The men in this case were no longer dependent only on their ascribed status, which was identical because of their close blood relationship, but on their achieved status. That the victim had succeeded most among the descendants of the two families clearly created a difference between the achieved status of the individuals. This distinction must have been a source of tension between them. Where one's livelihood is largely dependent on the cooperation of other family members, such as in tilling the land or minding flocks, disputes do not usually develop.

Neighbors of the victim's nuclear family were convinced that there had been a premeditated deliberate killing and not a spontaneous flare-up of passion during which a man had hit out blindly and had accidentally caused death, as often happens according to Bedouin evidence. They explained that in the first fight the stabbing had been carefully planned and was only the first phase of the murder plan. The decision of the father and brother of the murderer to live outside the camp, but still to remain in the region, was unsatisfactory to the family of the victim. The need for revenge might have been obviated if the family of the murderer had moved elsewhere instead of remaining on the periphery. The fact that it was necessary to ask for *'aṭwa*, even though the killing was within the group, is indicative of the dysfunctioning of the group. It would be expected that a powerful individual within the group could have directed events so that *'aṭwa* was not necessitated, but formal power within the group was lacking. This case history illustrates that cleavage within the co-liable group may result when there is no economic cooperation between close relatives, and eventually this may impede the group's effectiveness.

Case History IV

In October 1983 a quarrel took place between two neighboring co-liable groups in the Abū-Karīr tribe. Members of group A claimed that a small dam, which had been built to collect water for cultivation, was situated on their land. Members of group B insisted that it was within the boundaries of their land. Several males from each group participated in a verbal dispute that led to a fight, which resulted in the death of a member of group A. The police arrested all seven men of group B, claiming that all of them had taken part in the killing.

After 14 days of police investigation, five out of the seven arrested were released until the trial took place. The two who remained in prison were the head of the group and Aḥmad, one of his sons. The five who were released presented alibis to the police that they were not present at the dispute. Aḥmad, however, being a religious Muslim, told the truth and said that he was present at the time the dispute took place but emphasized that he did not participate in the fight nor in the killing. Aḥmad's wife, Laila, is from the al-Aṭram tribe, which is encamped close to the area inhabited by groups A and B. Laila's mother belongs to Aḥmad's group (group B), and two of Laila's brothers are married to female relatives of their mother. Thus there are close relations between some group B members and the al-Aṭram tribe. Because no cease-fire was agreed between the two groups the males of group B did not dare to return to their homes for fear that group A would take a revenge. Group B did not, however, take their families to shelter in a neutral tribe, as custom prescribes. The male members of group B came at night to their in-laws in the al-Aṭram tribe and met there with their wives. Having affines close to their own homes they could leave the women and children in their own encampment to graze their small flocks and continue their daily life more or less normally. The women were in no danger, for revenge, if taken, would be directed toward a male member of the group. This case illustrates that prescribed norms can be disregarded if a way round the norms can be found (as well as illustrating an advantage afforded by out-group marriage).[14] The norm of seeking shelter in a neutral encampment was disregarded because of the possibility of meeting the wives regularly, close to their homes, with the help of al-Aṭram relatives. These secret meetings could only take place, of course, with the acquiescence and help of the male members of the al-Aṭram, for they were the ones who had to make sure that the meetings were not discovered by members of group A.

The boundary quarrel that began the blood dispute must be viewed in terms of a more general disagreement — both groups want to separate from the Abū-Karīr tribe and to establish themselves as separate tribes. The split was not approved and group B accused group A of not presenting the case to the authorities in an appropriate way. In particular, the elders of group A were blamed for not using an influential mediator. After the killing took place the head of group B sent a mediator to explain to group A members that if they take revenge they will weaken their chances of being accorded a separate tribal status. If the achievement of tribal status is viewed as achieving power, acceptance of blood money and a negotiated *ṣulḥa* are the means to achieving this power. The exchange of killing by receiving blood money, rather than the exchange of blood for blood, would contribute to both groups' political aspirations in their quest for separate tribal status.

Case History V

Bedouin who are employed as teachers or clerks often express their fear of verbal clashes between members of their group and another group, knowing that such clashes may eventually involve them in a blood dispute. One Bedouin, referred to here as Ḥassan, wished to leave his group in order to avoid being involved in any blood dispute that might arise. Ḥassan, who held an important public position, feared that he might be cut off from his extra-tribal source of income as a result of tribal affairs in which he no longer had an interest, and he anxiously watched for potential disputes with other groups. To him, group membership had become a burden for he was not in need of economic cooperation or group protection. Ḥassan knew that revenge usually focused on the person himself and his close relatives when injury was inflicted, but this was not always the case: All members of a co-liable group are not really safe until *'aṭwa* is granted, a situation which he, for obvious reasons, feared and resented.

Ḥassan spoke to several elders of different tribes, all of whom told him that an individual cannot renounce his belonging to a co-liable group, for no Bedouin would recognize such a renunciation. This "belonging" can only be terminated by being declared a *meshamas* (outcast), an action he could not initiate because of the stigma it involved; because no Bedouin will interact with a *meshamas,* he would lose the honor and power now accorded him through holding a public position. He therefore took other measures to safeguard his security and those close to him. He persuaded the heads of several nuclear families in his group to expel a cousin whose conduct was likely to involve the group in disputes, and the cousin was duly pronounced a *meshamas* (see case history XXVIII).

In 1977, however, Ḥassan's fears were justified. A fight occurred between a number of teenagers belonging to Ḥassan's group, and others from a different group and another tribe. There were casualties on both sides. The notables of the respective tribes attempted to solve the dispute internally by telling the police that the culprits could not be found. But the reconciliation attempt was unsuccessful and the culptrits were eventually handed over to the authorities. Tension mounted sharply after the incident, both groups making mutual accusations and each group disclaiming responsibility. As Ḥassan knew that he could not detach himself from his co-liable group, he argued in favor of a modification of the norms of collective responsibility. He felt that these norms should not now be strictly adhered to when the Bedouin were living in a world so dramatically changed from when the norms were first promulgated. This is certainly possible, as representatives of Bedouin of the Negev discovered in Jordan (on a visit of condolence to King Hussein after his wife's death). The Bedouin of Jordan now restrict blood revenge to just three generations within the co-liable group instead of five.[15] This change in custom is due to changing socioeconomic conditions. Once the conditions surrounding the customs no longer prevail, they are likely to be relinquished.

Case History VI

In 1974 bloodshed occurred among the Bani-Ḥajar tribe, which is settled in the Galilee. The owner of a combine harvester started to harvest the field of a member of another co-liable group of his tribe. The owner's son appeared and demanded that the man leave the field immediately, whereupon the owner of the combine harvester went home carrying a sack of grains he had already harvested. The son of the owner of the field came afterwards to demand the grain but the combine owner said he wanted his payment first. The dispute escalated from words to blows, and the combine owner knocked his opponent out by hitting him on the head with a rock. The man died and the combine owner was arrested.

The head of the tribe, who usually acts as a judge and mediator in blood disputes among the Bedouin and the villagers of Galilee, immediately secured a cease-fire. Fifteen days later a *ṣulḥa* took place, even before the trial opened. Police charged the man with manslaughter in self-defense and agreed to release him on bail prior to the opening of the trial, in which he was later pronounced innocent.[16] The negotiated *ṣulḥa* settlement was such that he had to pay compensation of $1,700 to the family of the dead man and to exile himself to the Negev for seven years. Even though the members of the tribe knew that he had acted in self-defense it was still necessary for *'aṭwa* to be renewed several times before a *ṣulḥa* was agreed upon. Even if a killing is accidental and recognized as such by those involved, it is still necessary to secure a peace agreement. There have been cases where revenge has been taken even though the first death was accidental.

The incident described above occurred in a permanent settlement of the tribe where field cultivation is a minor livelihood and most of the tribe are permanently employed in wage labor outside the settlement. These circumstances, and the fact that the shepherds of the tribe do not have close grazing for their flocks (and would thus be in greater danger from the injured group because of the distance from the camp), were compelling reasons to negotiate a quick peace agreement. The head of the tribe, the mediator, wanted to make sure the dispute did not threaten their economic livelihood. His suggestion that the murderer be exiled for seven years, despite the recognition that he had acted in self-defense, made the quick arrangement of the *ṣulḥa* possible. Since the beginning of 1977 the exiled man has pleaded with the head of the tribe, through various people, for permission to return. The reasons for his request are given in case history XIII, where the role of the head of the tribe (the mediator) is analyzed more fully.

Case History VII

In 1966 a wedding ceremony took place among settled Bedouin who lived approximately fifty kilometers north of Beersheva. At weddings and other happy events it is customary to fire revolver shots in the air as a manifestation of joy.[17] During this particular festivity, however, a Bedouin was killed and the sheikh of one of the tribes arrested and accused of murder. Although the fatal shot was proved to have come from his revolver, the sheikh was pronounced innocent for lack of evidence. The man killed was a member of a co-liable group of a tribe living in the vicinity of the sheikh's tribe. There were ambiguous facts regarding the circumstances of the shooting. Several Bedouin mentioned an exchange of insults between the sheikh and the murdered Bedouin, several minutes after both had left the *shiq*. A shot was heard and the

Bedouin was found dead lying in a pool of blood. Others testified that the killing had been unintentional. In the course of the police investigation *'aṭwa* was agreed upon by the two co-liable groups involved. Discreet negotiations were held to prolong the period of *'aṭwa* until the end of the trial because it was feared that the true state of affairs might come to light.

About one year after the incident the members of the injured co-liable group accepted a proposal of *jira*. In the discussions regarding the blood price they defined the killing as murder. The negotiations resulted in an immediate arrangement of a *ṣulḥa*. The injured co-liable group was relatively small, being a section of the tribe that was not strongly organized. The sheikh who paid the blood money (thus indirectly confessing to the manslaughter) was the head of his tribe. He was popular with representatives of the government, who frequently consulted him, and he enjoyed high status in the region. The members of the injured group were of low socioeconomic status and a peace agreement with the co-liable group of the sheikh was considered most desirable, promising many economic and political advantages.

Case History VIII

Another case involving groups of dissimilar strength occurred in the al-Ḥubshi tribe. In 1966 a member of the sheikh's co-liable group unintentionally killed a member of the same tribe of a different co-liable group. A stray bullet escaped from his rifle while he was cleaning it. Not only was *'aṭwa* granted immediately, but representatives of the injured group argued that there was no need to pay *diyya*. A member of the sheikh's co-liable group repeatedly offered to make payment, but was met with a firm refusal. The family of the murdered man did not enjoy high status in the group, partly the result of the family having separated several years previously, some of its members having moved to the Ramle region.

In general, when a certain group renounces payment of blood money, they do not divulge this intention beforehead. After the sum stipulated as blood money has been handed over, and at the end of the *ṣulḥa* ceremony, the head of the group declares that the peace concluded is a true one, but payment of money is renounced. In the presence of the guests he returns the money to the representative of the killer's family. The money is returned in the same transparent plastic bag in which it is given in order to let those invited see as well as hear that it has been returned.

The reason for the refusal of blood money is to be found in the different status of the involved parties. The sheikh enjoyed much higher status than the group whose relative was accidentally killed. The weaker group sought to create a relationship in which the stronger group was indebted to it by refusing to let the latter pay their debt. Had the injured group accepted blood money the matter would have been closed and the status quo preserved; by not accepting indemnity, the imbalance between the two groups was reduced. The stronger group would now be obliged to the weaker one. This obligation would most probably be effected through some form of economic help, and under certain circumstances it would mean having to support the weaker group. The just claim (with respect to receiving blood payment) of the weaker group was thus put to their material and political advantage. These shifts were perhaps never spelled out in so many words, but members of both groups were conscious of the state of affairs. The stronger group, aware of the implications that the request implied, repeatedly tried to pay its debt.

A distinction was made in this chapter between where the killer and victim belong to different co-liable groups, and where they belong to the same co-liable group. In the former case, in order to ensure greater cohesion within the group, a leader may try to use the murder of a member as a basis for unification. Through the exercise of formal power, tension is artificially intensified to make members feel they have to stand together, the leader hoping that the solidarity formed within the group will outlast the blood dispute. A refusal of *'aṭwa* may lead to the murder of the killer or any co-liable member of the group to which the killer belongs. If a man expelled from his group, or even someone who joined a certain co-liable group, becomes a murderer, there will not as a rule be a peace agreement. The members of the injured group will attempt to murder him if he remains in the area.

Socioeconomic and political variables are usually the main determinants in the reaction to blood disputes. The political factor should be examined on two different levels: the political relationship of the two groups involved in the blood dispute and the political structure of the injured group itself. Solutions are structured by the situation in which they occur. One should not assume that because different co-liable groups have the same physical environment and the same economic basis that they will react in the same manner to the murder of one of their members, particularly when the internal political organization of the two groups are different.

CHAPTER THREE

Role of the Mediator

A mediator in Arab society is known by the term *wāsiṭa* (or *wāsṭa* in colloquial Arabic). Sami Farsoun (1970, 269–70) states that the term *wāsiṭa* means "a go-between, or the process of employing an intermediary go-between . . . One needs a wastah in order not to be cheated in the market place, in locating and acquiring a job, in resolving conflict . . . and in establishing and maintaining political influence, bureaucratic procedures . . . and in finding a bride . . ." The term go-between is also used by Elizabeth Colson (1962, 176) who, in discussing the social organization of the Gwembe Tonga, says that

> many matters are privately settled through the services of a go-between acceptable to both parties. Elopement damages, marriage negotiations, marital disputes, quarrels betweeen kinsmen, arguments over damages to crop or livestock or persons, are usually first a matter of private negotiations, if either party is dissatisfied with the result, he can press for a higher hearing . . .

Aharon Layish and Avshalom Shmueli (1979, 30) refer to the role of arbitrator: "Each tribe has its arbitrators . . . persons not holding political office. Some arbitrators have won fame even outside their tribe and are resorted to also by members of other tribes . . . Arbitration generally passes by inheritance within certain families. The economic position of the arbitrator is sound (he is paid for his judicial work)." The role of arbitrator, however, is quite different from that of mediator, the function of the former relating to Bedouin judicial matters.

The role of the mediator has been studied by several scholars.[1] In this chapter mediation among Bedouin of the Negev and the Galilee, Arab villages of the Galilee, and villages from the Triangle will be discussed. The focus here is on the roles and status of the mediator as they relate to the way disputes are dealt with.

Mediators are usually persons who have some authority, such as being heads of a tribe or of a co-liable group, but this is not always the case. An important quality of a successful mediator is his reputation. William Lancaster (1981, 43) writes that "Reputation is based on how closely a person demonstrates virtues — honour, bravery, generosity, political acumen and mediation abilities." The "power" of influence and persuasion from a position of authority and respect enables the mediator in the majority of cases to settle the blood dispute through payment of *diyya* (blood money) and arranging *ṣulḥa* (peace agreement), rather than through the taking of revenge.

Because of the dangerous possibility of revenge it is in the interest of all members of the co-liable group, one of whose members killed a member of another group, to solve the conflict by peaceful means. And it is to this end that the group would use the services of mediators (occasionally only one mediator is used) to negotiate with the injured party. It is always the accused group that seeks out the services of mediators. The mediators recommend a certain course of action but the actual decision whether to take revenge or accept *diyya* is always made by the group collectively responsible for the individual who was killed. Negotiations to obtain the agreement of the injured family to accept *diyya* are often long and difficult. Nevertheless, in many cases the mediators' recommendations are heeded, and circumstances that at first precluded any other action except revenge have been "mediated" so that a non-violent end to the dispute has been arranged. The mediating services may be used not only to obtain a formal settlement of a dispute but also afterwards. For example, a mediator might be asked to negotiate a reduction in the stipulated period of exile of a group member.

In most cases the mediators are outsiders. Each individual mediator is thus a "stranger" to the groups involved in the dispute. Georg Simmel's analysis of the "stranger" stresses that he is objective and that both sides trust him. He is both close and distant at the same time, and therefore helps to reduce tension. Simmel (1971, 146) states that "the objective man is not bound by ties which could prejudice his perception, his understanding and his assessment" of the dispute. According to Simmel the "stranger's" position within a group "is fundamentally affected by the fact that he does not belong in it initially and that he brings qualities into it that are not, and cannot be, indigenous to it" (ibid., 143). The mediator is usually a member of the wider circle of the two co-liable groups in the case of Bedouin society, or descent groups in rural Arab society, that are involved in the blood dispute. He might, for instance, be a member of the same tribe or subfederation[2] of tribes that one or both groups in question belong to, or he might just live in the village where one or both of the descent groups dwell. The mediator is usually in some way on the periphery of the lives of the two groups involved in the dispute. From this position he can be both near and distant at the same time.

The plan of the chapter is to first examine the position and functions of the mediator in four other societies. The different facets of the role of the mediator in each of the four societies will assist, by comparison, in revealing important characteristics of the mediator in Bedouin and rural Arab societies in Israel. I have chosen to examine (1) the Saints among the Sanusi in Cyrenaica; (2) the Saints of the Atlas mountains in Morocco; (3) the Saints among the Swat Pathans; and (4) the leopard-skin chief of the Nuer. Comparison will also be made between the role of mediators in these societies with the above analysis of the "stranger."

1. In discussing the Bedouin of Cyrenaica, Edward Evans-Pritchard (1949, 65) says that they are "inveterate devotees of saints, the *Marabtin* (sing. *Marabat*) or Marabouts."

> The Grand Sanusi derived his sancity, and thereby his power, from the fact that he was a Marabout . . . To [the Bedouin] the Grand Sanusi was . . . a man with *baraka,* an ample measure of God's grace which flowed through him to ordinary folk.

Evans-Prichard (ibid., 66) states that "the word *Marabat* . . . derives from the root RBT, to bind . . ."

> The marabouts in their lifetimes were regarded as standing outside the tribal system . . . Their chief political role was to act as mediators between tribes and between one tribal section and another. (Ibid., 67–68)
>
> So, long centuries before the Grand Sanusi began his mission in Cyrenaica, the Bedouin were used to the sign of the 'alim, a learned man . . . such a man was also a *muhakham,* one who arbitrated in their disputes . . . He could arbitrate among them because he was not of them. (Ibid., 68)

2. In *Saints of the Atlas,* Ernest Gellner compares the religious status of the saints in urban versus tribal life. He emphasizes that where in urban life there is absence of mediation, in tribal life the tribesman needs the religious man "not only to mediate with God, but also to help with inter- and intra-tribal political mediation." Gellner says that:

> The "saints" of the Atlas are . . . charismatic leaders: they are identified and legitimated by possession of *baraka* . . . which is about as close to the sociologists' notion of "charisma" as one could hope to find. (Ibid., 12)

The Berbers recognize that the election of a chief, whom they elect annually, should be a unanimous decision, otherwise his authority would not be complete and the tribe would suffer as a result.

> In those [election] negotiations, mediation, persuasion and pressure by the saints play an essential role (as it does in the settling of inter-group disputes and in legal cases). This part is so great that when the saints describe the

> procedures of elections in lay tribes, they frequently claim that they, the saints, appoint the tribesmen's chieftains for them. (Ibid., 85)

Gellner states that "effective igurramen [hereditary saints] . . . claimed not to feud or litigate at all. A mediator who was himself involved in a network of hostilities and alliances would not be much use for mediation and sanctuary" (ibid., 126). The saints also provide sanctuary, which

> serves in at least two ways: for one thing, it is useful to have a secure place in which rival tribes or groups in conflict can meet to negotiate without danger. Secondly, the lodges are useful for murderers fleeing vengeance, and for their kin during the early period following a murder, before blood-money is agreed and accepted. The murderers may spend prolonged periods of time in the lodges, before being either "forgiven" and allowed to return home, or resettled by the igurramen . . . (Ibid., 136–37)

3. In *Political Leadership among Swat Pathans,* Fredrik Barth (1968, 96–97) states that "the status of Saints makes them particularly suited to the role of mediator or arbitrator. Though any respected person may play this role, Saints are generally preferred . . . And their functions in mediating in disputes have been conventionalized to such an extent that they are indispensable for certain standard procedures." In cases of blood dispute, when one party determines to beg the pardon of the other party, the concerned man will seek the assistance of a saint who guarantees the safety of the suppliant and who serves as the concerned man's spokesman. "The chances of success depend on the persuasiveness of the saint in pointing out the reasonableness of the settlement . . ." Where a saint is chosen as arbitrator in a conflict

> the party or parties who appoint the Saint . . . surrender control of the conduct of their own affairs . . . Furthermore, he [the Saint] has very considerable freedom in reaching his decision . . . he is frequently able, on the basis of the same facts, by choosing different ways of arriving at a settlement, to reach widely different conclusions. (Ibid., 97)
>
> The dilemma of the Saint is that he is in a position more or less to propose settlements in favour of either of the conflicting parties; but if his proposed settlement is not accepted, though this in no way reduces his religious merit and repute, it does immediately reduce his political influence. His political influence depends on the extent to which he can modify the actual course of any conflict or dispute, as judged by his past performance. (Ibid., 24)
>
> The political authority of Saints derives also from the reputation for holiness and piety which they may gain by appropriate actions.

4. The last society example is the role of the leopard-skin chief as mediator among the Nuer. Evans-Pritchard (1940, 172), who studied the

Nuer tribe in the Sudan, states that "Feuds are settled through the leopard-skin chief and he plays a minor role in settlements other than homicide." The power of the leopard-skin chief is limited. Although the leopard-skin chief has both power and authority, it is the power of persuasiveness and the authority of a highly regarded individual. This power and authority does not derive from a surfeit of material possessions, such as possessing a large number of cattle and the economic benefits that arise from this, although it is no doubt influenced by such circumstances. As a mediator the chief gives "his final decision as an opinion couched in persuasive language and not as a judgement delivered with authority" (ibid., 163–64). His authority is not so extensive as to allow him to make definitive and binding judgments.

The major distinction between Simmel's "stranger" and the saint as a mediator lies in the fact that the saints in the first three society examples are outsiders in the sense that they live physically outside the community (although in close proximity). In Simmel's analysis the "stranger" lives within, and is involved in, the daily life of the community, but is recognized as being somehow apart or different. Mediators in Bedouin and Nuer societies are part of the same ethnic group of the community in which they live; mediators in both societies have qualities that fit the "stranger" analysis. In the case of rural Arab society the mediator is also an outsider in the sense that he is often not born locally but somehow attached himself to the kinship group, through marriage for example. This apartness or difference of the "stranger" results from certain qualities attributed to him, such as being a respected person with the ability of good judgment, in other words possession of the saints' *baraka.* In the first three society examples an individual needs power, in the form of being a saint, in order to be a mediator. It is not enough that he is a respected person. Barth (1968, 96) states that "though any respected person may play this role, Saints are generally preferred . . ." This is in marked contrast to the situation in Bedouin and rural Arab societies where it is *because* a particular individual is a respected person that he may be called upon to mediate. In many cases it is the heads of tribes and co-liable groups that serve as mediators. Obviously the head of a group has more power than a regular member of a tribe, and this power accords him a certain respect and status.[3]

The different facets of the role of the mediator in each of the four societies exampled will help us, by comparison, to understand the strengths and weaknesses of the mediator in Bedouin and rural Arab societies in Israel. Before highlighting the similarities and differences, I present the ethnographic data. The comparisons will be more meaning-

At a judicial hearing at the home of a Bedouin judge a man bringing an accusation sits with his *kafīl* (guarantor), and his *kabīr* (spokesman).

In this *ṣulḥa* ceremony the payment by the government of "official" blood money to the injured party was a precedent.

The mediator successfully negotiated a settlement between the disputants after a boy was injured in a quarrel with neighbors.

Druze dignitaries attending the home of their religious leader wait for the director general of the prime minister's office to append his signature to a *ṣulḥa* agreement.

fully judged after presenting the case histories, and discussing the social exchange relations between mediator/judges and their clients.

Case History IX

Mediation is highly regarded and an important aspect of rural Arab daily life. The importance attached to the role of the mediator is well illustrated in the following circumstances, which took place in 1975. A 19-year-old girl was stabbed in an attack, the blade only just missing her heart. The girl identified the stabber as the brother of the mayor of the local council. Both the mayor and the father of the injured girl belonged to the same political faction, and prior to the council elections these two men had signed a voluntary agreement according to which the mayor would resign after two years (half of the term in office). The mayor broke the agreement by not resigning after the stipulated time and this caused a split in the faction. Prior to the stabbing, the father of the injured girl had recruited various members of the faction against the mayor and had also met with the head of the opposition party to arrange a vote against the incumbent mayor.

In regard to the murder attempt on the young girl, the analysis of the local villagers was that the mayor sent his brother to murder the young girl close to her home so that the police would have arrested her father and brother as suspects. The justification for this process of thinking made by the villagers (and to all accounts on behalf of the mayor and his brother) is as follows. Ginat (1979, 181) writes that "the media frequently announce the murder of a young Arab girl . . . It is usually seen as an act intended to remove the stain of shame from the name of a family due to illicit sexual relations." The scenario as presented by local gossip was that if the young girl had been killed, the mayor would have immediately acted as a mediator to assist in the release of the girl's father and her brothers from prison. Under these circumstances the father of the girl would have been grateful for the efforts of the mayor and would have been indebted to him to the extent of not pursuing any course of action that would oust the incumbent mayor. It is important to note that the explanation by the villagers focused on the mayor's role as mediator. That an individual is prepared to go to the extent of asking his brother to murder for him so that he can act as a mediator is an indication of the importance that the role of the mediator is accorded. The purpose of the incumbent mayor was to relegate the political nature of the dispute, a situation where both protagonists were on equal footing, and in its stead promote a personal need, a situation where the two men would be on unequal terms — one the mediator and the other his client.

Bedouin of the Negev

A mediator in the Negev can serve in several different capacities. He can be the one to initiate *'aṭwa*; he can be a "professional" mediator in the sense that he has performed this function before and people know this; he can act in the capacity of a judge, and he can be a spokesman for his group. In the capacity of mediator or judge, the role of the individual fits Georg Simmel's analysis of the stranger. An individual who represents his group as a spokesman, however, is an "insider." (This is in marked contrast to the role of saints, who cannot be "insiders.") If a weaker group is in conflict with a stronger one, the weaker group will often ask an individual from their own tribe, who is known as having judged or mediated on previous occasions, to act as spokesman for them. They feel that the authority of the spokesman, expressed by the Bedouin as *kabīr* (big, important) will influence the power balance between the two groups. Such a role contributes significantly to an individual's status. Being asked to perform as a spokesman provides an individual with an opportunity to gain power within his group.

In blood disputes there are no judges or judgment. In non-homicide disputes among Negev Bedouin it is usual for the two parties to the quarrel to agree to go to the tent of a judge or mediator. The meeting that takes place is known as *malām*.[4] In Arabic this word is known as "getting together" — a meeting or a gathering; in Bedouin terminology, however, it is known not as a regular meeting but as a specific meeting about a dispute between two parties in the home of a person from whom they might accept advice, or who might become a judge to their dispute if they do not agree to his advice.

Before the dispute has reached the stage of the meeting in the tent of the *malām* there must have taken place the accusation about which the dispute is concerned. When a man comes and accuses another man he often brings a representative of his family, and a neutral man, someone who is not a member of his co-liable group. This neutral man is also a sort of mediator in the sense that he listens to the arguments of both sides. If the parties in dispute do not come to an agreement at this first initial meeting, the neutral man will be asked to be a witness to this meeting. Whatever he says was said at the meeting is accepted by the *malām* and by any subsequent judges. Both sides thus have no recourse to denying any statement this man makes about what went on in the meeting. This neutral man is called *mardawi* (from the word *radi*, which means to be pleased with). Both sides have to be pleased with his statements.

If the problem is not solved during the accusation stage the parties then decide who to approach as a *malām*. On this same occasion the accused is entitled to choose two other judges in case the hearing at the tent of the *malām* has no satisfactory solution. At this stage the *malām* is a passive mediator. If there is no solution the passive mediator becomes the first judge to the dispute by asking for his fee. There is no rule about who should choose the *malām*, either party is entitled to suggest someone and either party is entitled to reject a suggestion. Neither the *malām* nor the subsequent judges have any legal qualifications. They are chosen solely on the criterion that each party to the dispute feels that "this man is fair." This reputation of fairness may have been achieved by the judge having been known to act in previous disputes, either in the same capacity as judge or in the capacity of mediator; or just because the man is considered a fair man. Clearly, the two disputing groups will choose someone who they think will view their side of the case more favorably. But it is usually not difficult to achieve agreement over the choice of the first judge. The choosing of the two subsequent judges, however, may involve some dispute for they are chosen by the accused party, yet the choice must be agreed upon by the injured party.

If both the accused and the accuser belong to the same tribe or to the same subfederation of tribes, then the accused must choose the other two judges from the subfederation of tribes (which, of course, includes his tribe). If both parties belong to tribes that belong to a different subfederation of tribes, but within the same federation of tribes, then the judges must be chosen within the boundaries of the federation.[5] If the accused is from a different federation of tribes, then two out of the three judges can be chosen from the federation of the accused; the third has to be chosen from the federation of the accuser.[6]

As stated above, the transition from *malām* to judge is made by the asking of a fee from both sides to the dispute. Whatever amount the judge states that his fee is, he receives this sum from each of the disputants. The total fee can be from several hundred to one thousand dollars and must cover the cost of hospitality to all those who come to listen to the arguments presented. Those who come include not only the immediate families of the parties involved but also others who are interested in watching the outcome of the dispute. The procedure of arranging visits to the judges for all those involved takes a long time and much organization. It is also expensive; sometimes guest tents have to be erected to accomodate those supporting the two parties to the dispute. The losing party is responsible for the costs relating to the hospitality offered at the various judgments.

Each side brings with him a *kafīl* (guarantor), who is responsible for paying the judgment fines. If both sides agree to the decision of the judge there the matter ends, but if one side feels "hard done by" he will ask the judge to transfer the case to a second judge. Even though the accused was the one to choose the two judges, it is the accuser who now has the option of choosing which judge to go to next. The second judge will not, however, be told about the first judge's decision. Again the facts will be related, the representations made, and the judge will decide. If the second judge finds the party in favor that the first judge found, then there the matter ends. If it is a case of one judgment for each side, then the parties, at the request of either side, may go on to seek the decision of the third judge, whose decision will decide the affair. The idea of having three judges is so that each side has a chance to appeal once. If the fine levied by the second or third judge is more than that of a preceding judge, it is the fine upheld in the last judgment that has to be paid. The loser of the case cannot, after hearing a second judgment against him, choose which judgment in respect of the fine he has to pay he will accept.

If there is some chance of quickly solving the dispute the parties will go first to a *malām*. If the two sides cannot agree to the advice of the *malām*, the *malām* makes the transition (at the behest of the two parties) from being a passive mediator to being a judge. Where the nature of the dispute is more serious the parties will often dispense with the *malām* stage and ask the individual they have chosen to act immediately as first judge. The following case history is unusual in that a situation arose where the judge declared himself a mediator.

Case History X

Two tribes, A and B, both in the same subfederation of tribes, were in dispute. The head of tribe A accused the head of tribe B of selling land belonging to the first tribe in order that the authorities would decide to impose permanent settlement in an area near to where the second tribe was settled.[7] For Sheikh B this was a very serious matter. In Bedouin society, land and honor (*arḍ* and *'arḍ*) are the two most frequent reasons for serious dispute. They chose as a first judge the head of a tribe that was within the same subfederation of tribes. Because it was a serious accusation the accused sheikh wanted to keep the case within the subfederation.

The judge to whom they went was the sheikh of his tribe, a young man who not many years ago succeeded his father, a very famous judge and mediator. This sheikh suggested that instead of judging them he would be an "active" mediator between the two. The accused refused to accept this, demanding that a judgment be made because of the seriousness of the matter. The sheikh retorted that if he was not accepted as a mediator he could only suggest that the parties go to a new judge, whom he would recommend, and who would be considered the first judge. The sheikh stated that his offer of mediation meant that he could not now act as a judge in the dispute. The recommendation of going to a new "first judge," who was a member of a tribe that belonged to the same federation of tribes as the two men involved in the case but not from the same subfederation of tribes, was accepted. This last statement is important because the idea of going to the original first judge was to keep the issue within the boundary of the subfederation only, in order not to disclose the dispute to the wider society. The outcome, however, was that the choice of the new judge meant that the dispute became more generally known. In the subsequent judgment the accused was found innocent.

Instances of a judge declaring himself a mediator are rare. In this case the mediator was younger in age than the two disputing sheikhs. The young mediating sheikh recognized that any judgment he made on such an important matter would mean that he would be on bad terms with at least one of the sheikhs. By making the suggestion he did he was able to remain on good terms with the two disputants; what is more, by recommending a particular individual to act as judge, especially between such important personages, he laid up a debt to that person.

Case History XI

Among Bedouin of the Negev the harvesting is usually done by the males; they uproot the wheat complete with roots, while the women of the same co-liable group load the sheaves of wheat onto trucks. On one occasion the women worked alone. Some young boys who worked in the construction industry in Beersheva came along on bicycles and demonstrated the supposed inferiority of these women by tilting their *'aqāl* (a black cord that holds the headdress in position) to the side of their head.[8] It is customary for men to wear the *'aqāl* in the middle of the head. By tilting the *'aqāl* to the side they showed contempt for the girls. The girls told their male relatives about the event, and the next day these same relatives ambushed the boys and broke two of their bicycles. They were careful, however, not to harm the boys physically. Fearful that even stronger revenge would be taken by the relatives of the girls, the families of the young boys consulted a mediator. The case became so complicated that it took over six months to solve the matter satisfactorily. When a case takes a long period of time to solve the mediator not only gains in prestige for his continuing task but also accumulates power through the continuing dependence on him of the parties to the dispute.

Case History XII

In this case a mediator used other peoples' problems for his own interests. A man killed a member of a different co-liable group. He was sentenced to nine years in prison but because of good behavior was released after six years. Shortly after his release, he died. His family immediately referred to a mediator in order to arrange a *ṣulḥa* with the injured co-liable group. It was thought that the death of this man would allow the injured co-liable group to negotiate a *ṣulḥa*, which had previously been rejected during the man's life. The mediator did not succeed in his mission and, furthermore, he was accused by those who used his services of hardening the attitudes of the injured co-liable group. The family of the murderer maintained that since the mediation attempt the injured co-liable group supported the mediator politically. The family members were most concerned about this development: The unsuccessful mediation attempt was viewed to be a reminder to the injured party of the previous events, and it made the threat of blood revenge much greater than before the mediation. Cases where the family loses trust in the mediator are always a point of discussion in the *shiq* of the group, and become a focus for gossip by the wider community. In this instance the status of the mediator was much reduced.

Bedouin of the Galilee

As a result of various wars in the desert over grazing areas and water sources, the Bedouin from the Syrian desert and Transjordan who settled in the Galilee came not as whole tribes but only as parts of tribes. Their interaction with the peasants proceeded at a faster pace than that of the Bedouin of the Negev; this interaction changed the mores and traditions of their society to the extent that there are fewer Bedouin notables in the Galilee capable of acting as judges "in true Bedouin fashion" than among tribes from the Negev or Sinai.

Because of the small choice of such notables it has become increasingly necessary to use the services of judges and mediators from rural villages. This also works the other way — villages involved in disputes ask Bedouin notables to officiate in their disputes. Bedouin notables used in disputes between villagers greatly enhance their reputation. As a way of emphasizing their Bedouin heritage, the form of judgment for the Galilean Bedouin is the same as for the Negev Bedouin.

The important difference is, as stated, that outside notables are asked to serve as judges.

Case History XIII

The circumstances related here have been analyzed from the blood revenge point of view in case history VI. In 1974 bloodshed occurred in the Bani-Ḥajar tribe, which is settled in the north of Israel. The owner of a combine harvester started to harvest the field of a member of another co-liable group of his tribe. The son of the owner of the field appeared and demanded that the man leave the field immediately, whereupon the owner of the combine went home carrying a sack of grains he had already harvested. The son of the owner of the field came afterwards to demand the grain but the combine owner said he wanted his payment first. The dispute escalated from words to blows, and the combine owner knocked his opponent out by hitting him on the head with a rock. The man died and the combine owner was arrested.

The head of the tribe, a well-known judge and mediator among the Bedouin and villagers of the Galilee, immediately secured *'aṭwa.* Fifteen days later a *ṣulḥa* took place *before* the man's trial on a charge of manslaughter in self-defense. Although the man was later pronounced innocent, the mediator had already suggested that he be exiled for seven years and this stipulation formed part of the peace agreement. Since the beginning of 1977 the exiled man has pleaded, through various people, with the head of the tribe for permission to return. He argues that the conditions of the *ṣulḥa* were agreed in his absence, while he was still under arrest and before the court found he had acted in self-defense. The head of the tribe, the mediator, thought the request premature.

There are two ways of looking at the outcome of this mediation. It can be argued that the mediator's suggestion that the murderer be exiled for seven years, despite the generally held opinion that he had acted in self-defense (later confirmed by the trial verdict), made the arrangement of the *ṣulḥa* possible. The most important thing was to secure a peace agreement before a revenge could be taken. A second way of looking at it is that the mediator acted too hastily. But why? Well, there was indeed a political motive for organizing a quick *ṣulḥa.* In 1973, a Bedouin political party was established for the first time in the history of the state. As first on the list, Sheikh Abū-Rabi'a became a member of the Knesset (see the Political Assassination section in chapter one); the mediator who organized the quick *ṣulḥa* was second on the list, although first in line to represent the Galilee area. The mediator was in a unique political situation for he was not only the head of a tribe but also a political leader of a party that unified Bedouin from different tribes all over the country. By arranging the *ṣulḥa* quickly he showed his political adversaries that he had a strong influence over his own tribe. The quick *ṣulḥa* was not necessary for he could quite easily have avoided blood revenge by arranging a long-term *'aṭwa*, with the *ṣulḥa* to be arranged at a later date. His motive was completely political. Other mediators state that they have never known such a quick *ṣulḥa*.

ARAB VILLAGES IN THE GALILEE

During the last two decades there has been a standing *ṣulḥa* committee for disputes in the Arab villages of the Galilee. The committee is composed of 7–8 members, all of whom participate in each case. There is no option for a villager in dispute to have a particular mediator. In cases of blood dispute those members immediately available are called quickly to begin the mediating process between the parties. In the villages there is an immediate 24-hour "disengagement of forces," similar to the *'aṭwa mafrūda* (enforced cease-fire) in the Negev.[9] If the dispute involves people from the same village the members of the *ṣulḥa* committee stay in the village to make sure that the disengagement is carried out. Before this 24-hour time period is over the committee negotiates with the deceased man's family (the injured party) to arrange *'aṭwa*. In the last decade there has not been one case where the injured family refused to accept a cease-fire. Thus, in Bedouin society it is customary (but not always the case) to accept such a cease-fire, but in the rural area of the Galilee this has become the pattern. During the *'aṭwa* ceremony the committee takes an interim amount of money from the accused party. This money is known as *frash al-'aṭwa* (at the beginning of 1980 this sum was between $1,000–$2,000.) As soon as the *'aṭwa* is agreed, the *frash al-'aṭwa* is paid over to the mediators; this signals that revenge cannot now be taken.

The difference in procedure between the Bedouin encampment and the rural village is the result of two major causes. First, sedentarization brings with it a greater tendency to accept blood payment rather than to take revenge, and secondly, it is clearly impractical to exile the entire descent group of a family in a village during the negotiation period. Instead, the *ṣulḥa* committee arranges matters so that no physical confrontation will arise between the parties to the dispute by dividing the village into various areas where the parties may or may not go. Arrangements are also sometimes made in respect of services. In some cases it has happened that the school teacher or teachers have been members of the accused group. In such a case other teachers from other tribes will be brought in during the negotiation period so that no difficulties arise between children of the injured group and their teacher. Where there is a clinic facility in the village, for instance, attendance by the involved groups will be arranged for different days. Full settlement of blood disputes are clearly more necessary in rural settlements. Village life, with its high level of interaction, could not function if there was open tension.

The arrangements described above, where, in the case of blood dispute, each member of the *ṣulḥa* committee is a mediator, are regarded by the community as quite routine — a formal procedure that brings life back to normal as soon as possible. Even the designation of the committee, the *ṣulḥa* committee, implies that at some stage in the proceedings a peace will be initiated. Thus, whereas in the Negev the accused party looks to help from the mediator to avoid blood revenge; in the Galilee (and in the Triangle) it is more a question of negotiating conditions — it is (almost) taken for granted that revenge will not be taken.

In minor cases the mediator conducts the negotiations by himself, and the committee does not stand (also the case in the Triangle). Even a minor dispute, such as a teacher who reprimands a pupil by spanking him, might involve much mediation. The mediator might have to arrange matters between the police, the school authorities, the teacher, and the parents of the child. Although Arab society recognizes the authority of the teacher over his pupils, the law of the land expressly forbids that a child be manhandled under the jurisdiction of a teacher. The mediator's job is to prevent such an event being taken to the process of law. Furthermore, such an event would provoke bad feelings between the family of the pupil and the family of the teacher. A mediator must always be careful not to allow a minor case to develop into something serious like a blood dispute.

Case History XIV

A mediator is not always neutral, especially where his own interests are at stake. In one of the Arab villages of the Galilee there was a blood dispute that was not resolved for several years. The main mediator was a member of the Knesset, and when the time of the elections came round he made special efforts to arrange a *ṣulḥa*. Several informants told me that about two years prior to the *ṣulḥa* there had been a good chance of arranging matters satisfactorily then. But before a solution to the dispute was found, tension between the families involved increased. My informant stated that the mediator was to be blamed for this — the insinuation being that the more politically advantageous time for arranging the *ṣulḥa* was nearer to the elections and not at the time of two years prior.

It is customary to have several mediators when the official committee does not stand. In this particular case the Knesset member brought in two Bedouin mediators to help him. Ostensibly their help was required because of their experience in settling blood disputes. But the real reason was that the mediator cum Knesset member wanted Bedouin support in the forthcoming elections and he felt that this was a good way of securing such support. For the Bedouin mediators the invitation was prestigious and enhanced their standing in their own society.

Case History XV

In Spring 1981, in the course of a football game between a team from a Druze village and a team from a mixed village of Christians, Druze, and Muslims, but predominantly Christians, a quarrel on the field led to fighting among the spectators. A young man from the Druze village was killed in the affray and in retaliation, the next day, members of the Druze village attacked their opponents killing two and injuring several others. The revenge was an over-reaction that left many buildings damaged and two boys dead. One of those killed was a Druze, and the other a Christian, whose home became a pilgrimage for many Christians of the surrounding villages. The two boys killed from the Christian village had not been involved in the original affray.

The first priority of the *ṣulḥa* committee of the Galilee was to arrange *'aṭwa* in order to stop the hostilities. I was present when the committee, traveling as a group in cars, went to the Christian family from the mixed village to determine their demands for *'aṭwa*, and I observed the differences of opinion amongst the committee members. At the home of the Christian family one of the committee members, a prominent Druze from a neighboring village, who was concerned for his status as a leader among the local Druze community, opposed their cease-fire demands and stated that *'aṭwa* would be more easily attained if the conditions were softened. This was a difficult moment that nearly led to the ending of the visit, which would have meant failure of reaching a cease-fire agreement and a continuation of hostilities. In reply to this stipulation, a Muslim member of the committee, a well-known and respected mediator, suggested that the conditions laid down by the Christian family nevertheless be brought to the Druze notables. (Note that the Muslim was ethnically neutral in this situation.) No one objected to his suggestion and the committee left for the Druze village.

On the way to the village the Druze leader who had opposed the cease-fire demands of the Christian family called a halt to the convoy of cars. He suggested to the other mediators that they wait for an hour among the olive trees instead of entering the village, and then return to the Christian family and say that Druze notables had agreed to *'aṭwa*. He reasoned that any conditions imposed by the Christian family would be humiliating to the Druze notables. He felt that it would not be difficult to persuade the Druze villagers to agree to *'aṭwa* and begin negotiations for *ṣulḥa*, but he did not want a surfeit of conditions imposed by the Christian family to be a stumbling block to the negotiations. The Druze leader was concerned for his status. He wanted to avoid facing the Druze notables, to whom he was ethnically related, with all the Christian family's conditions.

The Muslim member of the committee felt that it was important to take the demands of the injured Christian family for approval to the Druze notables. His reasoning was that by transmitting the conditions to the Druze notables the Christian family would feel honored, and that this would most certainly lead to a reduction in tension. And this was the prevailing view of the majority of the mediators. It was obvious in the subsequent negotiations that the status of the Muslim mediator was much increased for having forcefully replied to the proposal of the other committee member. In the event consent was obtained from the Druze notables and *'aṭwa* arranged, one of the conditions being that no Druze enter the Christian village until the *ṣulḥa* had taken place.

Arab Villages in the Triangle

The pattern of mediation for blood disputes is the same as in the Galilee except that there is no official committee. In addition to mediators who comprise each *ad hoc* committee, there is usually also an individual who is not generally known as a mediator. Such a person is always someone who is involved in political issues around the time of the case.

Case History XVI

Prior to the elections to the Knesset in 1977 there was a case in one of the Triangle villages of a blood dispute between two families. One of the disputing families was from the *Maṣārwa* wave;[10] the other family to the dispute had been established in the area for a long time.

Two men, both with previous mediating experience, wished to be nominated as candidates for the Knesset by the Labor party and were in competition with each other for the candidacy. The political aspirations of the candidates would be enhanced by their acting as mediators in the dispute, especially as the ascribed status of each of the two mediators reflected the difference in origin of the two disputing families. Both men recognized the potential gain to be made by acting as a mediator in support of the family to which his ascribed status was closest.

An event such as a blood dispute is a focus of discussion and the persons involved in the mediating process will be in the public eye. This is a fact of much importance to the opinion-conscious politicians. In this case the advantages of playing the role of mediator were on two levels. Blood disputes are socially important events to the older generation. Such disputes involve the whole range of Arab–Muslim mores, about which the older generation is much concerned. On the second level, each mediator was in a good position to gain the support of the younger generation, who would be duly impressed by the fact the mediator (in this case both mediators were in their early 40's) has progressive ideas. By acting as mediator an individual places himself in a good position to gain political support.

Case History XVII

In 1977 a blood dispute occurred in the southern part of the Triangle. A quarrel between two lorry drivers concerning the transportation of a group of workers escalated from curses, to rock-throwing, and then to knives. The young man killed was from the same village as his antagonist, but not from the same descent group. The mediators on the *ṣulḥa* committee were: a leader of a third descent group in the village; the two young politicians mentioned in case history XVI; two other dignitaries who had previously participated in other cases; and a person from a small village in the region whose experience as a mediator was limited. It was in the interests of the two politicians to reach a *ṣulḥa* as quickly as possible (for the same reasons as cited in the previous case history). All the other members of the *ṣulḥa* committee agreed with the two politicians that an early end to the dispute was best. However, the individual with limited mediating experience did not work toward nor wish for an early end to the dispute. It was in his interest to prolong the negotiations in order that his role on the committee be seen to be important. He suggested that a clause in the peace agreement stipulate that after the killer's release (he was sentenced to three years), the injured party (the father of the victim) would determine when the killer of his son would be allowed to return to the village. On the release of the killer the mediator invited the released person to stay in his home. He then attempted to persuade the father of the victim to forego the stipulated clause.

Normally such a case would be ended with the *ṣulḥa*. By inserting the clause about permission to enter the village the mediator very cleverly made sure that his services would be used at some future date, thus focusing attention upon himself for the ulterior motive of being recognized as an important mediator, rather than as just another member of the *ṣulḥa* committee. An additional aspect is that in the years prior to the mediator being used as such, this individual had carefully nurtured relationships with the authorities. His being called to serve in the *ṣulḥa* committee was the result of recognition of his interactions with representatives of different government offices. A mediator accumulates power not only from the dependence on him by the parties to the dispute or from political support, which acting as a mediator between disputants gives him, but also through his contacts with the authorities, a topic that is discussed in terms of social exchange.

Social Exchange

Peter Blau (1964) defines "social exchange" as "the voluntary actions of individuals that are motivated by the returns they are expected to bring and typically do in fact bring from others." The relationship between mediators and judges, remembering that more often than not both act in both capacities, and the relationship between this set of individuals and the public at large, is well suited for examination in terms of social exchange.

Peter Ekeh (1974, 205), in discussing Levi Strauss' distinction between mutual reciprocity and univocal reciprocity, says:

> By univocal reciprocation Levi-Strauss meant that system of social interaction in which, say, A does not expect a direct rewarding activity from B to whom A does benefit, but rather from another individual, say, C or Z . . . Univocal reciprocity means first and foremost that an actor does benefit to another actor from which he does not expect immediate or direct reciprocation.

Univocal reciprocity is seen in the relationship between mediators and judges because of the fact that recommendations made at one time cannot obviously be reciprocated immediately due to the irregularity of instances that arise which require the services such individuals offer.

In the relationship between the set of mediators and judges (mediator/judge)[11] together, and the public at large, the judge or mediator in question will have accrued a debt from the family that sought advice, or the family or individual who obtained a winning judgment. This debt is repaid by supporting the mediator/judge politically, not only by voting for him if elections are at hand, but also in the sense of "speaking up for him" and thus contributing to his status. When an individual requires the services of a judge or mediator he will remember those who have been spoken well off. As judges are paid for their services[12] this results in a clear financial benefit. (Remember that an individual who at one time is a mediator will often serve in his next case as a judge.) The expected benefit provides the motivation for acting as a mediator; the voluntary act of mediating is done on the basis that it will lead in the future to acting in the capacity of a judge, with its consequent financial gain — a clear case of social exchange, which fits Blau's definition quoted earlier.

Once the public at large know that the authorities use the services of a particular mediator they will use him to intercede for them in their dealings with the authorities. This type of mediator would most likely be an influential person who has close contacts with the authorities. For example, a family, one of whose members is about to finish teacher training college, would use the services of a mediator to make sure that the teacher placement authorities will place the individual in a teaching post near the village where the family is located. This type of mediator would also be used by a farmer to influence the representative from the ministry of agriculture in order to obtain a water quota (Huxley, 1978, 17). Another example of this type of mediation is where a potential sheikh uses a mediator to influence the authorities to give him the seal indicating that he is the representative of the tribe. This occurs when a sheikh dies, for it is not always automatic that the title of seal holder pass to the eldest son. Such a situation of asking a mediator to negotiate the recognition of seal holder with the authorities might also occur when a group detaches itself from a tribe and wishes to be recognized as an independent tribe.[13]

The authorities are quick to recognize the achieved status of a mediator and will use him in cases where they need to persuade members of the public to adhere to certain government directives. For example, in the Galilee and Negev the authorities use influential people to persuade the Bedouin to settle at permanent sites. In the Negev, when the government began the first settlement projects in 1964, the man hired by the ministry of housing to explain the sedentarization project to the Bedouin was a well-known mediator. When the Bedouin use a mediator again and again they do it simply because of his qualities — they see that the mediator is a fair man and choose him over other mediators for this reason. If the authorities use the same man to mediate between themselves and the public, this gives the mediator power. He is seen to have successful contacts with the authorities, and the Bedouin and Arab public now look toward him to act on their behalf in their dealings with the authorities. A situation thus develops, a sort of self-perpetuating network of relations, where, because the mediator is successful in inter-Arab disputes, the authorities will use him to mediate between themselves and the Arab public. Knowing that the mediator has good relations with the authorities, the public will use him in obtaining government-appointed jobs (Farsoun 1970, 269–70), and in obtaining the release of an individual from prison (Huxley 1978, 10, quoting Ayoub).

Cooperation between mediators/judges and the authorities is highlighted in the settling of some blood disputes. For example, in one of the Druze villages in the Galilee not only did members of the Israeli cabinet and Knesset participate in the *ṣulḥa* ceremony, they also appended their signature to the written agreement. In this instance the foreign minister, the minister of police, the chairman of the Knesset and the director general of the Prime Minister's office attended.[14] The reason why high government and senior officers of the police sometimes attend the *ṣulḥa* ceremony is that the avoidance of blood revenge is more effectively guaranteed if the parties to the dispute recognize the standing of an agreement signed by such important signatories. This has an important psychological effect on them "to keep their part of the bargain." Nevertheless, as the following case history shows, there is never any "guaranteed effective" avoidance of blood revenge.

Case History XVIII

This case occurred in the early 1970s in a village on the southern slopes of the Hebron mountains. It is a tradition that in the *ṣulḥa* ceremony the injured group line up and members of the group deemed responsible for the killing come and shake hands, in turn, with all the members of the injured group. In this instance a younger brother of the murdered man, while standing in the line, pulled out a *shibriyya* (a sickle-shaped dagger) and killed the brother of the murderer. This most unusual occurrence is not regarded as blood revenge, but is considered a new event. Such an action puts the mediators in acute embarassment for clearly their mediation has not only been unsuccessful, but a new revenge situation has developed that did not exist previously. Such an event has obvious repercussions on the political standing of the involved mediators.

Case History XIX

The relationship between mediators and judges themselves, and between them and their clients, does not always reflect the highest moral standards. Sometimes a party in dispute will send a "secret mediator" to influence the judge. Informants state that not all the judges will turn down such a delegate. An informant who served as a judge told me that cases of secret mediation bribing had occurred: He explained that not only from the ethical point of view a judge should not agree to any secret mediation in the form of accepting a bribe to find a favorable decision, but also from a practical point of view such an arrangement can be a double-edged sword. There is no guarantee that the secret mediator or the party to the dispute who engaged his services will not, at some later time, disclose this arrangement. If this occurs people will no longer use the services of the judge who accepted the bribe.

The political circumstances surrounding the events described here are related fully in the Political Assassination section of chapter one. An agreement was signed between a Bedouin, Sheikh Ḥammad Abū-Rabi'a, and a Druze, Sheikh Gaber Mu'adi. According to the agreement the Bedouin had to resign his seat in the Knesset at mid-term in favor of the Druze. This agreement had resulted from them both being on the same voting list in the 1977 elections. The Bedouin, however, abrogated his part of the agreement by declining to resign at the appointed time. Mediators were then sent by the Druze to persuade the Bedouin to change his mind, but to no avail. According to the Bedouin, more than a few of the mediators who came on behalf of the Druze did not try to persuade him to fulfill his part of the agreement, by resigning, but on the contrary, encouraged him to remain in office.

Generally speaking, if a mediator feels that there are no proper grounds for his mission, he should decline to undertake the mission. In this case some of the mediators actually did the opposite of what they were asked to do. It is probable that those mediators who did not try to persuade Abū-Rabi'a to resign were motivated to behave as they did for fear of antagonizing both sides. On the one hand they did not wish to refuse the mission, and on the other hand they did not want to carry it out. The path they chose meant that they remained on good terms with both sides, and both sides were indebted to the mediator. One can also speculate that some of the mediators had political motives for not wanting the Druze leader to take his place in the Knesset. The outcome of this unkept arrangement was that the Bedouin was shot and killed one night in Jerusalem, close to the entrance to his hotel, after attending a Knesset session. Subsequently the three sons of the Druze were arrested and later sentenced to life imprisonment (one son was released in 1984). Recently, Sheikh Gaber Mu'adi asked a close friend to visit the Abū-Rabi'a *shiq*. The purpose of the visit would be to find out if there was any chance of resolving the dispute.

The status of judges and mediators is determined by the particular situation they happen to find themselves facing in relation to the conflict at hand. Each different set of circumstances and their resolution determine the way judges or mediators are regarded by the participants to the conflict and by the wider circle of interested persons. The following three case histories each show different aspects of this role of the mediator.

Case History XX

After many years of unsuccessful mediation in a blood dispute a senior distant relative of the murderer entered the tent of the family of the murdered man whose paterfamilias had just returned from the pilgrimage to Mecca. Bedouin tradition is such that even if your enemy comes to your tent you must give him hospitality. In this case the senior relative humiliated himself by crawling into the tent. Prostrating himself he refused to be served the traditional cup of coffee until the family of the murdered man agreed to a settlement of the dispute. In order to preserve his honor regarding the Bedouin tradition of offering hospitality even to enemies, the paterfamilias relented and agreed to an end to the blood dispute. This unprecedented behavior was frowned upon by mediators because it indicated that blood disputes could be settled without their services, albeit by strange behavior. An additional facet to the story is that agreement was probably also easier to come by because of the important need for unification amongst the tribes with regard to the expropriation of Bedouin land by the authorities.[15]

Case History XXI

One can anticipate a number of changes concerning the use of mediators and judges as the Bedouin become more and more sedentarized. A man accused his nephew of stealing some steel reinforcing rods. Both men were building contractors. The accuser did not approach his nephew, nor did he go to the father of his nephew (who was, of course, his own brother). Instead, he went and filed a complaint with the police. As the Bedouin become more sedentarized they will use the legal system of the state more and their internal judgment process less. It is most probable, however, that the Bedouin will continue to prefer their own unique way of settling blood disputes through a mediator. Some customs are disappearing due to sedentarization, but other customs are being revived as a result of the free movement of peoples between Egypt and Israel, as the following case history illustrates.

Case History XXII

Two men had been in bad relations with each other since 1967. One man accused the other of lying about certain facts. In order to determine the truth both men recently traveled to Egypt to consult an Egyptian Bedouin judge and mediator. The two men had heard that this mediator conducted the *bish'a* ceremony from which it is possible to determine whether an individual speaks the truth.

The Bedouin have several methods that purport to determine whether a man tells the truth or not. For minor matters they would ask the person to swear that he did not do the thing he was accused of doing. Because a Bedouin will not swear a false oath, his refusal to swear is an indication of where the truth lies. A second degree would be to ask the suspect to join the accuser in a trip to a tomb of a Holy man and to take an oath of innocence. Again, a refusal to comply with such a request is indicative. The most important test of truth, however, is the *bish'a* ceremony. Several men witness the accused person wash his mouth with water three times in front of the accuser. Then the man who conducts the ceremony, the *mebash'a*, pulls a metal plate out of the fire and the accused person licks the plate *(bish'a)* three times. If the accused person's tongue burns he is deemed guilty; if his tongue remains without blisters the accused is declared innocent. The idea behind the *bish'a* test is that the saliva of a guilty man will dry up thus causing blisters on the tongue, whereas the saliva of an innocent man who has nothing to fear will remain and prevent the hot plate from causing a burn. Clearly, the temperature at which this plate is licked is of paramount importance and the skill involved in presenting the metal plate accords the *mebash'a* a certain status. In this case the man was deemed to be innocent.

At the present time there is no Israeli Bedouin *mebash'a*. Neither is one to be found on the West Bank. The last *mebash'a* serving Israeli Bedouin was from northern Sinai, but he died in the 1950s without passing on the skills of his profession. Since the peace agreement with Egypt there have been three missions of Israeli Bedouin to the Egyptian *mebash'a*. If the *bish'a* ceremony is reinstated as a Bedouin custom, it may well reduce the status of judges and mediators, for their services will then be in competition with such a test. Yet even though the need for mediating/judging services may be reduced, the mediator's presence in terms of authority and prestige involved still remains an important factor. Recently (September 1985), some Bedouin traveled to Egypt to attend a *bish'a* about an issue not connected with the case history related above. It is customary at the *bish'a* ceremony for each side to the dispute to bring along a witness. In this instance the Bedouin asked a famous mediator to perform this function. It is probable that they did this in order to promote the prestige of their group.

Interactive Comparison

I present here an interactive comparison between the role of mediator in the four society examples presented earlier, and the role of the mediator in Bedouin and rural Arab society.

1. Kinship is not a prerequisite in Bedouin society as it is among the Sanusi. Nevertheless, it is often the case that offspring of mediators and judges have themselves taken up their father's profession. When this does occur, especially where there is a tradition of mediators in the family, there is an added prestige to the mediator.
2. The Marabouts can arbitrate among the Sanusi because they are not of them, in the sense that they do not belong to their society. The same applies to the Saints of the Atlas. In Bedouin society the mediators are society members, but are "outsiders" to the community (co-liable groups) in which they live and practise their mediation.
3. The Saints of the Atlas are reputed to have a certain charisma concerning their person. Similarly, mediators in Bedouin society are endowed with Simmel's "qualities."
4. In the annual elections of the Saints of the Atlas the "chief must be . . . one who is accepted unanimously" (Gellner 1969, 85). The saints serve as mediators in all kinds of dispute, including blood disputes, and in all cases there has to be a consensus of decision amongst the group whom the mediator represents. (In the case of the elections a consensus of the whole tribe is required.) Only one saint at a time serves as the mediator. Where no satisfactory outcome can be agreed between the disputing parties they will refer to a different saint/mediator.[16] In Bedouin and rural Arab societies there are cases where only one mediator is used but it is more usual, and always in blood disputes, for there to be more than one mediator. (And in the Galilee there is even a committee.) In cases where there is just one mediator and his mediation does not result in an end to the dispute, the outcome is the same as for the saints — a different mediator will be asked to perform. In cases where more than one mediator is involved and there is disagreement among the mediators as to the correct course of action, the recommendations put forward will reflect the majority.

   The same consensus requirement, whereby members of the co-liable group must unanimously accept the recommendations put forward by the mediator *before* he carries them out, also applies to Bedouin and rural Arab societies. Disagreement in the group as to the correct course of action will delay the settling of the dispute. Kressel (1982, 130) has noted a case where the younger generation opposed the traditional way of dealing with the matter, and this caused a delay of the *ṣulḥa*. If the mediator sees that his persuasive arguments do not lead to a settling of the dispute he may well resign in the hope that other mediators, with different mediation tactics, may be more successful. He may even resign in anger, hurt that his advice has not been taken.

5. Among Saints of the Atlas a "mediator who was himself involved in a network of hostilities and alliances would not be much use for mediation . . ." (Gellner 1969, 26). This is in contrast to the mediator in Bedouin and rural Arab societies, who is automatically involved in a dispute if his group is involved. But such involvement in no way affects his status as a mediator.
6. In cases of blood dispute a murderer may apply to the Saints of the Atlas for sanctuary, the saint being the only authority that can grant such a request. In Bedouin society, however, a murderer may go to any Bedouin and enjoy his protection.[17] It is not necessarily the mediator who is asked to protect the murderer in cases of blood disputes.
7. Swat Pathans who appoint saints to represent them in disputes "surrender control of the conduct of their own affairs. Their relation to the saint becomes temporarily one of complete dependence" (Barth 1968, 97). This is in marked contrast to the authority of the mediator in Bedouin and rural Arab societies where the mediator must always gain the consent of the group that he represents before he puts forward proposals to the other party for settling the dispute. He will, of course, initiate ideas and persuade the group he represents to follow a certain line of action, but he will never act without their agreement.
8. Among Saints of the Swat Pathans, if a "proposed settlement is not accepted, though this in no way reduces his religious merit and repute, it does immediately reduce his political influence" (Barth, 1968, 98). Unsuccessful mediation by a Bedouin or rural Arab mediator is also detrimental to his political standing and his reputation as a mediator. The religious aspect does not apply because a mediator is not looked upon as a religious authority. Even in the capacity as "judge" a mediator has no legal authority. Among Swat Pathans and Saints of the Atlas, mediators are religious authorities. In Bedouin and rural Arab societies a religious authority *can* act as a mediator, but

generally speaking these two functions are separate.

9. Although the leopard-skin chief of the Nuer does have some power and property, his status is more of a ritual nature. Among the Bedouin, power is an important attribute for mediators, but there are instances of mediators without power and property who are respected, not on the ritual level, but solely as a result of their mediating qualities.
10. Among Saints of the Atlas, "ideally, a saint should not work at all. But this ideal can seldom be attained" (Gellner 1969, 156). Many of the Negev Bedouin mediators are heads of tribes or of co-liable groups. Their daily duties focus around the needs and administration of the tribe. It is most often the case, but not always, that mediators are persons of means. This is especially so among rural Arabs. One can predict, however, that in the future this pattern will change. As wage labor increasingly becomes the norm it will be those individuals with contacts resulting from their work who will be best placed to act as mediators, rather than those individuals with traditional authority.

The detailed description of the saints' function in the three societies, and of the leopard-skin chief in the fourth, together with the analysis of Simmel's "stranger," has helped gain an understanding of the role of mediator among Bedouin and rural Arabs. In discussing the role of the mediator in Bedouin and rural Arab societies in Israel I have used as a basis for my arguments an interactive comparison between four other societies each with their own particular environment and economy. It is usually difficult to compare societies living under widely different economic and environmental conditions, but in this instance comparison is possible. Although not a reason for the possibility of comparison, there are similarities between the four society examples and the populations under study. The Sanusi, the Swat Pathans, and the Saints of the Atlas are Muslim societies, as are Bedouin and rural Arabs. The Nuer are not Muslim but like the Bedouin they have a tribal structure. They live under ecological conditions that require them to move from place to place several times a year, and in this respect they are similar to the Bedouin.

So far only the mediation of disputes, especially blood disputes, has been discussed; but there are many different types of mediation situations. Some mediation is done by women, but it is usually kept on as low a profile as possible.

Case History XXIII

In 1979, in a village in the Triangle, a teacher reprimanded a pupil and accidentally broke the boy's hand. Apart from the resulting inquiries made by the education authorities, this event created tension between the families of the boy and the teacher. The father of the teacher, as would be expected, sent an emissary to the boy's father in order to make amends. The boy's father rejected this and other requests to bring about a reconciliation. A *ṣulḥa* was achieved only when the father of the teacher turned to an influential woman in the village, who spoke to the injured boy's mother. What several men could not arrange in weeks of negotiations, the women achieved by quickly arranging a meeting between males and females of both concerned families. The *ṣulḥa* took place in the evening. As the teacher's father pointed out to the author it was the women themselves who decided to have the ceremony in the evening so as not to demonstrate, in the words of the teacher's father, "What man with big moustache could not achieve." This unfortunate occurrence was not settled through set ideological ways of going about effecting a *ṣulḥa*, but by cooperation between women who recognized the importance of keeping their active role on as low a profile as possible.

It will be rewarding to step momentarily outside the framework of mediation discussed here and to cite other examples. Mediation can also be on a grander scale. On the morning of December 30, 1982, just as the talks between Israel and Lebanon were getting under way, I heard a correspondent on the BBC World Service News describe the United States as a mediator between Israel and Lebanon. The correspondent concluded his discussion by noting that sources stated that America would not play a passive role in the negotiations, but on the contrary would be an active mediator. The Camp David Accords, which led to the signing of the Israel–Egypt peace treaty, is another example of mediation at the state level.

Mediation can also be on a more humanitarian level. In November 1985, Terry Waite, a special envoy of the Archibishop of Canterbury, acted as a mediator in the attempt to seek the release of four American hostages held by Muslim extremists in Beirut. There are a number of interesting facets to Waite's mediating mission as regards the role of mediators discussed in this volume: it is not Waite's first mediating mission; he has been called upon now because of his previous experience and successes; he is an outsider not only in the sense that he is not a party to the conflict at hand, but also he does not share the same religious faith as the Muslim kidnappers with whom he has to negotiate. Waite has been described as "charismatic and enigmatic," and that he "has no political point of view whatsoever. He carries out his missions from a strictly humanitarian point of view."[18]

There are many other different types of mediation such as mediation between man and God (Gellner 1969, 8); mediation to establish and maintain political influence; and mediation in finding a bride (Farsoun 1970, 269–70). So far the emphasis has been on the "mending of relationships," but mediation is also used to create relationships (Huxley 1970, 10). It often happens that a young man will have his eyes on a particular girl with a view to marriage. The first step is to find out, through the services of a mediator, whether the family of the girl will entertain exploring the possibilities of a marriage union between the two families. The mediator approaches the family of the girl in such a way as to give the impression that it is *his* idea for the daughter of the family meet the "young man whom I happen to know." If the mediator's advances are rejected it is rarely the presentation of the mediator that is at fault; the family might feel that the proposed young man is not suitable for their daughter, or reject the approach because of some other reason. By using the mediator as an intermediary the chance of animosity developing between the families is lessened. If the approach had been direct, a rejection might result in hurt feelings on one or both sides. Failure in the preliminary stages of establishing a new relationship, as exampled above, does not in any way harm the status of the mediator.

Mediation to establish new relationships is not fraught with the difficulties that mediation to mend relationships is. Successful mediation in a dispute contributes to the mediator's honor and power. But an unsuccessful mediation might mean that the mediator is on bad terms with both disputing parties, perhaps through no fault of their own. A second or third failure following the first will make the public wary about contracting his mediating services rather than those of another mediator who is seen to be successful. It also reduces his honor somewhat, with its consequent loss of status and power.

CHAPTER FOUR

The Outcast

Among rural Arabs, outcasting is practised so infrequently that no set rules can be delineated. Outcasting is mainly a Bedouin norm. Common to all Bedouin tribes is the burden of collective responsibility — each member of a co-liable group knows that if he murders someone, or even if he kills him unintentionally without any premeditation, he creates a conflict with the injured co-liable group that might lead to blood revenge. When the co-liable group is convinced that one of its members acted without due consideration for collective responsibility, he is likely to be expelled from the group.

The formal expulsion of an individual from the group is to declare him to be a *meshamas,* which literally translated means "one who is exposed to the sun." Formal expulsion *(tashmīs)*, in contrast to various forms of ostracization, is very rare in Bedouin society (Ben-David 1981, 34–35). Since the foundation of the State of Israel in 1948, up to the beginning of 1980, there were only two cases among the Bedouin of the Negev where a member of a co-liable group was expelled from his group. Recently, however, there has been a spate of outcasting cases, all involving a sheikh's co-liable group, and all for reasons other than protecting the welfare of the tribe. This aspect will be dealt with after describing the two cases of traditional *tashmīs*.

Where the perpetrator of violence is a *meshamas* and continues to live in the same area, the avenging group cannot renounce its duty of blood revenge. Blood money will not be received by an injured group from any individual pronounced a *meshamas*. No *'aṭwa* can be arranged, and not even the compulsory three-day term of *'aṭwa* may be imposed on the injured group. Because no negotiations can be held (in cases of blood dispute) with a person unattached to any group, the avenging group is left with no alternative but to try to kill the *meshamas*.

An individual initiates the outcasting of a member of the group by first meeting with several of the elders of the co-liable group to find out if there is any support for his proposal. If there is support the issue will be discussed in a general meeting of all members, which would begin after nightfall. The reason for the meeting beginning after dark is that no stranger can be present at such a meeting and it is most likely that unless it is an emergency, no guest will show up after dark. Such a meeting can last for many hours, and minor differences of opinion may cause three or four consecutive meetings to be held before a decision is made. Even though a majority of the co-liable group may have already personally decided for the *tashmīs,* there is an obvious reluctance to make this view known without hearing the opinion of others. It is then a majority decision as to whether the individual in question remain a member or whether, for the sake of the group as a whole, he should be cast out. (It is usual for the potential outcast individual to attend the meetings, where he can speak up for himself; sometimes others will speak on his behalf.) Where the decision is made to outcast an individual, group members immediately notify their decision to neighboring tribes as well as to members of other co-liable groups within the tribe. The notification, in the form of a verbal declaration, indicates that the group is not responsible for the actions of this individual and no longer bears the burden of collective responsibility for him. Only after the notification has reached all the tribes with whom they have relationships and interactions is the act of outcasting valid.

THE TRADITIONAL *TASHMĪS*

Case History XXIV

Jedū'a Abū-Ṣulb was the first case of a Negev Bedouin expelled from his co-liable group since the establishment of the state in 1948. The *tashmīs* took place in 1957 after his co-liable group, on three occasions between 1951 and 1957, had to pay blood money due to Jedū'a's excessive behavior. (Jedū'a's case has been analyzed from the blood revenge point of view in case history II.) After the first two incidents Jedū'a's uncle had a long conversation with him, pointing out the possible repercussions if he did not behave with more care and responsibility in the future. But this warning was to no avail and in 1957 he accidentally killed a Bedouin from northern Sinai.

Jedū'a's uncle, who was the head of the co-liable group, felt that the group should not have to bear the burden of his nephew's bad luck. Even though the uncle was very close to Jedū'a (who described him as being like a father to him) he nevertheless called all the male members for the meeting and proposed that Jedū'a be cast out of the group. This decision was justified when, two years later, in 1959, Jedū'a killed a man (although the case was defined by the police as self-defense.) The elders of the tribe stated that this was the first time in their living memory that a *meshamas* was involved in fight that resulted in a killing.

Emanuel Marx (1967, 240–41) relates that the injured group "began to suspect that Gadū's agnates were still maintaining relations with him, and that therefore their announcement of expulsion had been deceptive." Even though the injured group suspected that the *tashmīs* was not a real one, they could not do anything about it because the act of outcasting had been conveyed by the Abū-Ṣulb co-liable group in the proper way. Jedū'a faced a doubly difficult situation. Not only was he a *meshamas* with its concomitant social stigma, but he was also a target for revenge. Under these circumstances one can imagine Jedū'a wishing for the protection of collective responsibility. In 1960 Jedū'a asked the authorites to help him find a shelter away from the Negev, and for some time he stayed with a small tribe close to the Israeli–Lebanese border where I visited him on several occasions. In case of a blood dispute between two co-liable groups, an individual, his nuclear family, or the entire co-liable group can ask for and receive shelter in a neutral tribe.[1] The fact that most other tribes would be willing to help a fellow Bedouin who is in trouble results from the framework of reciprocity in Bedouin life. Every Bedouin knows that one day he might face the same situation and that he might also be in need of shelter. In the case of a *meshamas*, however, it is most likely that no one will give him asylum.

In this case the northern tribe with whom Jedū'a stayed chose to overlook the fact that he had been declared a *meshamas*. It helped that there was no contact between Negev Bedouin and Bedouin of the Galilee.[2] A more compelling reason was perhaps the fact that a member of this northern tribe had taken shelter among the Negev Bedouin in 1959 and it was he who served as Jedū'a's host. Being in the north, Jedū'a had conflicting feelings: He knew that he was safe but missed the Negev. Eventually he left the Galilee and came back to the Negev. Jedū'a was well aware that his life was in constant danger and he never remained in one place for all the night. He used to tell me when I visited him in the creeks where he hid: "I know that one day I will get it. I know that my fate is not to die a natural death. But only God knows the day. It is written up there when, where and how I will die." Eventually Jedū'a was killed, but not by the group who had sworn revenge. He became involved in an argument with a different group, over a separate dispute that had nothing to do with the blood dispute in question, and members of this group killed him.

Jedū'a's murder was not, however, the end of the blood dispute. As mentioned above, the injured group that planned to take revenge and kill Jedū'a claim that he was not really a *meshamas* and that the announcement to all the other groups in the tribe was a fake, especially since they learned later that Jedū'a had married a member of his tribe who had borne him a son. Additionally, although I do not believe that the revenging group knew this, Jedū'a's uncle had visited him secretly when he was staying in the Galilee. When Jedū'a returned to the Negev, however, the uncle cut off all relations with him. For many years the issue lay dormant, but since 1984 members of the Ṭawāra co-liable group have proclaimed in public that now Jedū'a's son is a man, they will take revenge by killing him. They now (1984) wish to determine the truth about Jedū'a's outcasting. As related in case history XXII, the Bedouin have several methods that purport to determine whether a man tells the truth or not. In this case the revenging group sent a message, through a third party, to the elders of the Abū-Ṣulb co-liable group, that they want to determine whether Jedū'a was really cast out from his group using the *bish'a* method. To my knowledge there has so far been no response to this request. If they find out, what they suspect, that he was not in fact cast out from his group, they might take the matter before Bedouin judges.

The case of Jedū'a's outcasting is a unique one. Nevertheless, it was done according to the social norms. It is a representative case of an individual who was cast out because he was a threat to the security and well-being of the group. There were no political or other motivations involved in the expulsion.

Case History XXV

In the mid-1960s a son of a sheikh of a large tribe was involved in several incidents concerning relations with women. Although in most cases of illicit sexual relations it is the woman who is punished, the co-liable group of the male offender may be "punished" as well, in the sense that the act brings dishonor on the group. Also, the group as a whole may become involved in Bedouin legal proceedings that might result in payment of some form of compensation. The involved man, called here Na'im, was in his early twenties and married. After previous rumours concerning his illicit sexual relations with various women, one relationship became public knowledge. The father asked two male relatives, a brother and a cousin of Na'im, to discuss the matter with his deviant son, but they did not manage to elicit a promise from him that he would change his behavior. Even when his uncle, whom Na'im greatly respected, approached him to change his ways, he did not make any commitment. Sometime later, another cousin of Na'im (another uncle's son) talked to him about the affair, but was cooly received and told to mind his own business. This was especially aggravating because the cousin was considerably older than Na'im. When the sheikh, Na'im's father, heard the report from his nephew, he thought carefully about declaring his son a *meshamas*. The phrase "Mind your own business" has a much deeper meaning than just an impolite approach. It contradicts the entire concept of the collective responsibility structure of the co-liable unit. Na'im knew very well that in the case of a dispute resulting from his behavior, all the males of his co-liable group would immediately become involved. The sheikh asked his nephew to keep the conversation with Na'im secret. And when Na'im became involved in yet another illicit amorous encounter, even though the female was a member of his co-liable group, the sheikh decided to outcast him.

Even though the *tashmīs* can be classified in the traditional framework, in the pattern that the *tashmīs* was culturally adopted for, it seems that there was another more important factor that made Na'im's father push for the outcasting. As a result of the upheavals of the War of Independence in 1948, many tribes previously resident in Palestine moved to territories that were under Jordanian rule. In many cases only subtribes, or fragments of a co-liable group, or even just a lineage left for Jordan. There were instances where first cousins and brothers became dwellers in two different countries — Israel and Jordan. Many members of the tribe, some of whom belonged to the sheikh's co-liable group, moved to the Hebron mountains (the West Bank) and to the fringe of the desert northeast of Amman in Jordan. Those members of the tribe who stayed in Israel came under the jurisdiction of the Military Government, which decided to join several subtribes to one of the largest tribes, the Ībn-Karīr — the tribe of which Na'im's father was sheikh. However, the sheikh did not have the charisma or the power of leadership necessary for so large a group, and the subtribes that unwillingly came under his umbrella did not show any desire for integration in the larger unit. Each subtribe emphasized its own identity. In the late 1950s and beginning of the 1960s some of the leaders of these subtribes applied to the Military Governer asking for recognition as independent tribes, and requested that they be officially declared as sheikhs in their own right. Although the requests were later granted for some of the subtribes, no request had yet been granted when the following circumstances took place.

In the spring of 1962 Na'im's father took the initiative to expel his son. He first had informal talks with several of the elders, as well as with some of the young members of the co-liable group. Na'im's *tashmīs* was a very short process. Within a single meeting, although a long one stretching from sunset until dawn, the co-liable group decided upon the *tashmīs*. Two days later this decision was communicated to all Bedouin of the Negev.

By casting his son out of the co-liable group the sheikh diverted attention from his internal problems relating to his lack of authority over the tribe. By taking such an action the sheikh accumulated honor and prestige. Even though it was only for a short period, the sheikh's *shiq* was full of tribal members who came to congratulate him for his courage in proclaiming his own son a *meshamas*. Although this case may be classified in the traditional framework, we see here the beginning of the use of *tashmīs* as a political weapon. There is no doubt that the *tashmīs* was promoted not just to protect the tribe or as a warning to other tribal members, but was used as a means to gain political power. There was no direct threat of blood revenge, albeit that Na'im's behavior reduced the reputation and honor standing of the co-liable group.

Bedouin in Transition

The Bedouin of the Negev are in an advanced stage of sedentarization. This process began in the 1960s and became more intensified during the late 1970s. The change was from a more nomadic to a less nomadic way of life, from a nomadic to a more sedentary way of life. In discussing various assumptions about the nature of change, Salzman says that:

> One such assumption is that socio-cultural change is irreversible, directional, and cumulative. Irreversibility is understood in two sense: that what has happened cannot be undone, and that a return to a previous state is impossible. Directionality is the sense that things change in a particular direction and continue to change in that direction, sometimes in an accelerating fashion. The cumulative nature of change means that previous change has an impact on all that comes after, and each new change feeds into the following developments. (Ibid., 1)

The fact that Bedouin society in the Negev is surrounded by Jewish settlements and has limited pastoral areas because of Jewish development of the Negev, seems to indicate that the changes taking place in their social and economic life will not be reversed. Changes and developments in the *tashmīs* norm are just one manifestation of the whole gamut of change that the Bedouin are undergoing. A period of sedentarization is a transition period where the older generation, particularly sheikhs and heads of co-liable groups, try to keep the traditional customs. In particular they are most anxious to maintain cohesiveness within the group. The younger generation, however, pushes toward economic and social integration with the wider society. Although both generations fear losing their identity as Bedouin and of becoming fully assimilated, for the older generation this is an overriding concern.

In the past a member of a co-liable group could be cast out if his behavior caused, or there was reason to believe that it might cause, a breakdown in the solidarity of the group. For example, an individual who paid no heed to the burden of collective responsibility would be a candidate for outcasting. Even under such circumstances the decision to instigate a *tashmīs* would not be taken lightly nor in a hurry, as witnessed by the fact of so few reported cases prior to 1980. Since 1979, however, there have been four cases where individuals were cast out from their group and one case where this action was threatened. Those outcasted belonged either to a sheikh's co-liable group or to an important co-liable group of the tribe. In all these cases no individual was cast out because of traditional considerations. In contrast to its previous function, outcasting has now become a device to counter the disruptive influences on tribal organization resulting from the rapid changes in the socioeconomic and sociocultural life of the Bedouin, as reflected in their rapid pace of sedentarization.

Outcasting is now deliberately used, in an unprecedented fashion, as a tool for increasing unity and solidarity among co-liable group members. It is also used as a warning to members not to disrupt the cohesiveness of the group. Such warnings are considered very necessary by the elders of the tribe because some of the young generation, especially those who have permanent jobs, feel that the collective responsibility system is a burden from which they should be relieved. The threat of being cast out is a strong pressure to conform to the wishes of the elders. The use of outcasting as a warning to group members has parallels in other aspects of Bedouin life, especially in the issue of illicit sexual relations (see chapter five). The killing of a girl or a married woman who has had illicit sexual relations serves as a deterrent to other girls who might think of breaking the chastity code. As stated by an informant, "If she is murdered, the others will think twice before losing their virginity" (Ginat 1982, 180).

The need to make a decision on a *tashmīs* proposal focuses the group on a problem common to all members. The exercise of formal politeness when the group meets and the recognition in seeing all the members of the group together that the group comes from a common heritage, helps promote the idea that the group is bigger than the individual. Group cohesion is reinforced in such decision making in much the same way that it is reinforced in cases of revenge. In a revenge case the head of a co-liable group will try to find the best political

The late Sheikh Salmān al-Huzayel.

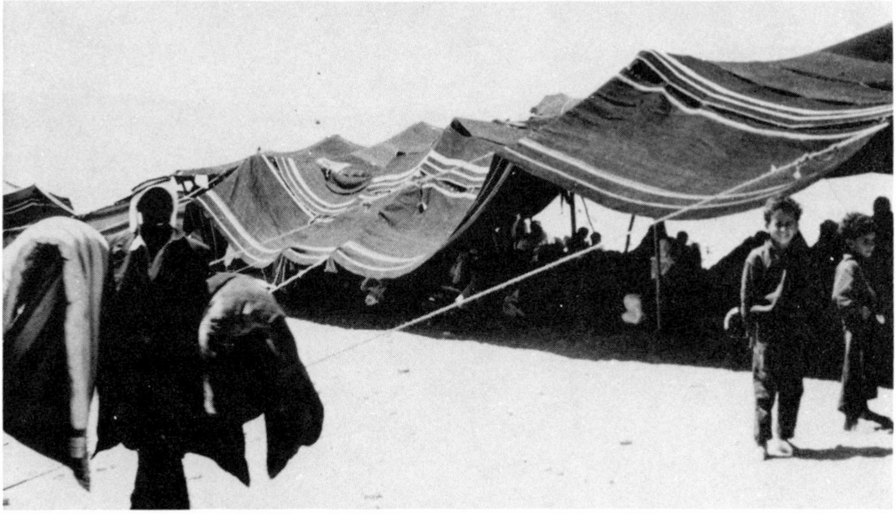

Negev Bedouin prepare the *shiq* for a *ṣulḥa* ceremony.

Jedū'a Abū-Sulb, the outcast.

The late Israel Yeshayau, Chairman of the Knesset, and the late Sheikh Ṃuhammad J'abari, Mayor of Hebron, at a *ṣulḥa* ceremony.

situation to reunite the group members. He will turn down the mediator's request for *'aṭwa*, and take advantage of the situation to congregate all the co-liable members for consultation and discussion. These gatherings contribute to the unity of the group for exactly the same reasons as given for a meeting concerning an outcasting proposal.

The Sheikh's Co-liable Group

All outcasting instances since 1979 have been within a sheikh's co-liable group. A sheikh's co-liable group is the main link of the tribe; it is the focus of all the inter- and intratribal activities. All sheikhs are at pains not to lose the cohesiveness of the group, for if this happens members would lose their group identity (and the sheikh would of course lose his authority). Outcasting in this new situation of sedentarization is a mechanism for building-up cohesion within the group. Outcasting is no longer a punishment of the individual, but increasingly serves as a warning for others. In this latter way it is a social defense.

The new mechanism of outcasting fits Durkheim's theory regarding punishment. "But today, it is said, punishment has changed its character: it is no longer to avenge itself that society punishes, it is to defend itself. The pain which it inflicts is in its hands no longer anything but a methodical means for protection" (1960, 86). "Its true function is to maintain social cohesion intact, while maintaining all its vitality in the common conscience" (ibid., 108). The two factors analyzed by Émile Durkheim, the weapon for social defense and the importance of social cohesion, are the primary motivation in all the outcasting case histories that follow. The individual is no longer the *causa causons* of the outcasting process. The change in outcasting is part of a wider ongoing process of dramatic change in the social life and organization of the Bedouin. In the past the Bedouin themselves would determine the most suitable form of punishment for any wrongdoing that took place within the co-liable group. In the past it was a common norm to tie a misbehaving member of the tribe to the peg of the tent. If a father or a cousin did this today the individual against whom such an act took place would in all likelihood file a complaint with the police.

Case History XXVI

Jamīl was the sheikh of the Ībn-'Abada tribe. During the 1948 War of Independence some members of the tribe moved to the Hebron mountain area in Jordan, while others remained on the Israeli side of the cease-fire lines. Jamīl had three wives and quite a large extended family. He also owned several hundred acres of land and two buildings in Beersheva.

In the 1970s the Israeli Government mapped the entire Negev for land settlement. The Bedouin were asked to indicate land they claim to have possessed prior to 1948. Such claims had to be accompanied by information relating to the names of their neighbors with whom they had had common boundaries. As there was no land settlement at all in the Negev prior to the establishment of the State of Israel the Bedouin did not have any documents that could prove ownership or possession.[3] The Government's proposal was that 50 percent of the land claimed by any individual, assuming that there were no conflicting claims, would be recognized as land that belonged to that individual. Each individual would receive 20 percent of the land in kind and the remaining 30 percent in money. The land to be received in the terms of the proposal would be close to settlements that were already being built by the authorities as part of a sedentarization plan for the Negev Bedouin. The proposal also included the possibility to exchange land for irrigated land. One hundred dunams (one quarter of an acre) would be deemed equivalent to one dunam under irrigation; the maximum amount of land that could be exchanged for irrigated land was four hundred dunams.

Collectively, the Bedouin refused to sign any agreement. Although they agreed to the proposal regarding the 50 percent claim, they wanted at the same time to receive all of the land owing to them under the proposal, and not part of its value in money. They also turned down the proposal of exchanging one hundred dunams for one dunam under irrigation. Although most of the Bedouin refused the proposal, some individuals came to an agreement with the Land Authorities concerning all or part of the proposal insomuch as it related to land owned by that particular person. Sheikh Jamīl Ībn-'Abada, however, even though he urgently needed money, refused to sign an agreement under the above mentioned proposal. When he died in 1978 his oldest son 'Oda succeeded him and became the sheikh of the tribe. In the summer of 1979 'Oda found out that Salīm, his half brother, had secretly signed an agreement with the Land Authorities. Although at first 'Oda thought that the agreement related to the half brother's share of the inheritance only, he learned later that his half brother had signed for the entire land left to them by their father. 'Oda hired a lawyer to stop the transaction and at the same time decided to outcast Salīm from the co-liable group.

At the first meeting in the *shiq*, 'Oda told members of the co-liable group that several years earlier Salīm had not obeyed his father over some matter, and that the father had thoughts about outcasting him at that time. He pointed out that in Bedouin society land is a very sensitive subject, equivalent in importance to the sensitivity accorded to a man's honor. 'Oda argued that Salīm's action was worse than stealing from one's own family and proposed that the strongest sanction be imposed. There was no objection by the other members and the *tashmīs* document was drawn up. The document stated that "Our father, the sheikh [had previously] outcasted his son [Salim],"[4] and that their current action was to continue the wishes of their father. A notice to this effect was also printed in an Arabic newspaper. Some dignitaries questioned the truth of this statement. They claimed that if Salīm had really been cast out by his father, what need was there now to repeat the *tashmīs*. Furthermore, when a *tashmīs* takes place, everybody knows about it. How come, they asked, that nobody knew of Salīm's outcasting by his father.

The outcasting in this instance was pure punishment. Salīm was a wrongdoer and was punished for his crime. The question arises as to whether such a severe punishment was appropriate in the circumstances. The punishment could not be said to stand for any kind of warning to others and Salīm 's behavior was not a threat to the co-liable group. But it *was* a threat to the sheikh's own family and this last point provides a clue to 'Oda's insistence on the outcasting. 'Oda had only recently succeeded his father as sheikh, and he was still young in years. The important consideration in determining his decision to outcast his own brother might have been that he knew that his personal esteem within the group and beyond would be raised by the taking of such a drastic step.

Case History XXVII

Samīr was a member of the Ībn-Karīr co-liable group. He worked in a variety of jobs such as picking oranges and working in an industrial plant in Beersheva. Working in the city he met people from the criminal underworld and became friendly with some of them. He began to take loans from different Bedouin who did not belong to his co-liable group or even to the Ībn-Karīr tribe. Samīr never returned the money and people complained to his older brother about his behavior. Samīr played this game of loaning and not returning so much that it became public knowledge, as was his association with criminals.

Musa, Samīr's brother, then decided to outcast Samīr. As Musa was a member of the sheikh's co-liable group, any meeting concerning a *tashmīs* proposal would have to take place at the sheikh's *shiq*. However, Musa was not on good terms with the sheikh and did not want the sheikh to have the opportunity to call a meeting in his *shiq* on Musa's behalf. So, instead of asking for a meeting of his co-liable group all together, Musa spoke to members of the group individually. He first went to the elders of the co-liable group and told them that his brother's behavior constituted a potential danger to the group and that Samīr should be declared a *meshamas*. The majority of co-liable group members whom Musa approached agreed with his interpretation of Samīr's behavior and with the concomitant sanction that was suggested.

Musa wanted to cast out his brother as fast as possible but he was faced with a problem. There was no real unity in the Ībn-Karīr co-liable group. For many years there had been a latent competition for leadership between three subgroups of the co-liable group, and this competition had increased after the death of the former sheikh (Na'im's father in case history XXV). The authorities appointed the late sheikh's nephew as successor, but one of the brothers of the deceased sheikh felt that he should have become the head of the tribe. There was also another possible contender, although he had never expressed the wish to become sheikh. This individual, another nephew of the late sheikh, worked in an important public position through which he had concentrated power. Because there was no political unity in the group Musa decided not to bring the issue of outcasting his brother to a formal co-liable group discussion. In particular he knew that the late sheikh's brother and the nephew who had accumulated power harboured so much animosity toward the sheikh that they would not attend any *shiq* meeting in the sheikh's tent, not even one concerning a *tashmīs*.

So, instead of bringing the issue to a formal discussion within the co-liable group, Musa invented a new system of outcasting. He went to his brother Samīr, tied his hands, and forced him to go with him to three different tribal leaders. At the same time Musa invited five (carefully chosen) members of his own co-liable group to join him. He first brought Samīr to the *shiq* of one of the most famous judges and mediators in the Negev, a sheikh who was head of a related tribe — a tribe from the same subfederation of tribes that the Ībn-Karīr belonged to. (Thus it could be interpreted that Musa went to an outsider who was not really an outsider.) Musa declared that Samīr had been cast out and he asked the judge to be a witness to this proclamation. Musa then continued to do the same at the *shiq*s of two other tribal leaders. Again, he carefully chose the sheikhs to whom he took his brother. In both cases the sheikh's tribes had for many years been subtribes within the Ībn-Karīr tribe, and only recently had they been recognized as independent tribes. One of the tribes is the al-Aṭram (see case history XXX). Once again, in both *shiq*s, Musa proclaimed that his brother Samīr has been cast out, and asked the sheikh in question to serve as a witness. Note that Musa always took his brother to sheikhs with whom he had some connection. Because the sheikhs knew Musa they did not question him too closely about the outcasting action. Other sheikhs may not have been so compliant.

Musa's action was prompted by a feeling of shame concerning his brother's behavior. He had warned his brother about borrowing but not returning prior to his decision to outcast him, but Samīr had taken no heed of this warning. It is common in Bedouin society to grant a loan without interest. The understanding is that the loan will be returned at the first opportunity. Samīr had taken advantage of this custom to steal money. Apart from this obvious wrongdoing that had to be punished, Musa also concluded that his brother's contact with the Jewish criminal underworld would worsen and would lead to a further deterioration in his behavior, a deterioration that might in the future have serious consequences for the group as a whole. There were, however, more compelling reasons why Musa acted as he did. Musa knew that sooner or later the different individuals from whom Samīr had taken loans would come to ask Musa himself for the money. By outcasting his brother Musa protected himself from being approached regarding his brother's loans. The act of outcasting meant that Musa was no longer responsible for Samīr's actions.

Musa may well have concluded that the outcasting procedure was not in fact so stringent as was held by common custom and that the outcasting of his brother, albeit under unusual circumstances, stood a good chance of success. The question to be addressed is whether Samīr's *tashmīs* was really necessary. In fact, Samīr was very careful. Within the Bedouin circle he played it according to the rules of the game. Although he took loans, there is no specified time stipulated before one has to return the loan. If Samīr was going to get into trouble it would most likely be with his Jewish criminal companions and the police, and not with any Bedouin group, which was the *prima facie* reason for casting him out of the group. As the Bedouin become more economically independent they are increasingly exposed to the influence of the wider society. As this trend continues cases are bound to arise where Bedouin individuals become involved with criminals and come under the influence of criminal behavior. Nevertheless, the promotion of lineage loyalty by the elders of the tribe will go some way to prevent situations arising where non-Bedouin criminal influence might jeopardize the safety of Bedouin tribal members.

Case History XXVIII

Prior to the establishment of the State of Israel the al-Ṭamma tribe pitched their tents in the western Negev. After the establishment of the state the Military Governor moved them, as well as other tribes, to the eastern Negev, close to the cease-fire line with Jordan. About half of the tribal members chose to move to Jordanian territory, where they repitched their tents on the southern slopes of the Hebron mountains. In the late 1950s and early 1960s many of the Bedouin who had moved to Jordan became sedentarized. A brother of the sheikh of the tribe (the sheikh lived on the Israeli side of the border) had previously been employed by the British Mandate government and continued to hold his position as a Jordanian employee. He built a nice home in a West Bank town, south of Jerusalem.

After the June 1967 war the cease-fire lines between the West Bank and Israel ceased to exist, and everyone could cross freely in both directions. There were many reciprocal visits from tribal members on both sides of the ex-border, and also some marriage unions between families that up to the time of the war had been separated by a border.[5] Although these meetings and marriages created new alliances and renewed old ones, the tribe did not unite. Even on the co-liable group level, tribal members felt at a distance from their relatives from the other side of the old border. Nevertheless, they were all aware of the fact that from the collective responsibility point of view there were no differences between them and any other Bedouin co-liable group. The fact that for more than thirty years the tribe had been split between two different countries, and where a hostile border had prevented any official contacts, did not change the basic rules of collective responsibility of the co-liable group.

The sheikh of the tribe, who was from the Israel proper side of the ex-border, tried to strengthen the bonds between the members of his co-liable group. Such a move was important for his status in a number of ways. Apart from the general status of being head of a united, rather than disunited tribe, there were other status-linked reasons. Those living in the West Bank had, for the first time, to deal with an Israeli administration. Such dealings could often be made easier by those who had lived on the Israeli side of the border during the hostile border period. Apart from personal contacts they knew the ins and outs of dealing with Israeli bureaucracy. The help afforded by the sheikh in such matters to members of his co-liable group from the other side of the previously closed border added much to his status and power. However, there were ups and downs in the relationship between the two sides. One much talked about crisis occurred as a result of a marriage. The sheikh's brother, the government employee in the West Bank, refused to give his daughter to the sheikh's son. He preferred to marry her to a villager of peasant origin. The sheikh wanted to outcast his brother for this insult — not only did his brother refuse to marry his daughter to her first patrilateral parallel cousin, but he married her out to a peasant. The sheikh consulted with several of the elders of the co-liable group as well as with other sheikhs of other tribes. But everyone advised him not to expel his brother and the sheikh decided not to bring the issue for a formal discussion. This event, and the bad feeling that developed between the two brothers because of it, did not contribute to the unity of the co-liable group. In the fall of 1981, however, another case concerning the al-Ṭamma co-liable group led to a real *tashmīs*.

Yusūf grew up in a town in the West Bank. His father, 'Abdalla, was getting on in years but still worked as a mediator among the local tribes and rural communities. Yusūf used to sit a lot in the coffee-houses of his hometown, and in the regional centers of Hebron and Beersheva. He was lazy, had no desire to work, and adopted the system of borrowing money from different people and never returning it (like Samīr in case history XXVII). One of his cousins determined that his behavior was unbecoming to the tribe, and initiated to outcast him. But before the matter reached a formal discussion in the *shiq,* Yusūf's father became very sick. His illness lasted some six months and then he died. During the period of 'Abdalla's illness the cousin did not pursue the *tashmīs* idea. After 'Abdalla's death many Bedouin, including co-liable group members from both sides of the ex-border, came to the *shiq* to pay their respects. This sad event served as a good opportunity for building up cohesiveness among the co-liable group, and one of the older members took advantage of the circumstances to arrange a reconciliation between the sheikh and his brother over the marriage affair.

As soon as the forty days of mourning was over the outcasting of Yusūf came to the fore. The formal discussion was short and there were no objections to the *tashmīs*. Every member of the co-liable group signed the paper on which the discussion notes were summarized. The outcasting, however, must be viewed in the light of additional facts. The six months' period of 'Abdalla's illness had a profound influence on the behavior of Yusūf. He turned over a new leaf and no longer frequented the coffee-houses as before. Nevertheless, even though the reason for outcasting Yusūf was now no longer valid, the *tashmīs* still took place. Usually the head of the co-liable group is concerned with cohesiveness within the group. But on this occasion, because several co-liable groups had previously been prevented from interacting with each other due to the closed border, the *tashmīs* contributed not only to inter-group cohesiveness but also to inter-tribal cohesiveness. It seems that some decisive event was needed to cement the group unity that had taken place as a result of 'Abdalla's death. The mourning served as a fusion between the two sides of the tribe; the *tashmīs*, albeit of the son of the deceased, strengthened this fusion of the different co-liable groups of the al-Ṭamma tribe.

Case History XXIX

In March 1983, Sheikh Ḥusain died. According to Negev Bedouin tribal custom no initiative for succession should take place within the mourning period, which lasts in Muslim societies for forty days. However, five days after the sheikh's death two members of the co-liable group, opponents against each other, began to recruit support in order to gain leadership of the tribe.

One of the opponents, Daūd, was the late sheikh's uncle. The second individual who began recruiting was Khalīl, a cousin of the recently deceased Ḥusain. In the 1960s, at the time of the previous succession, there had been competition between Ḥusain and Daūd, and Daūd had lost the nomination. Daūd was convinced that because he was a candidate in the 1960s, co-liable group members would automatically support him in his application to the authorities to receive the sheikh's seal of nomination. The situation, however, turned out very differently. The majority of members signed a petition supporting Khalīl, Daūd's opponent. Khalīl, who is in his late forties, and who has worked in a public position for the last 20 years, has established a wide network of relations with many Bedouin and with many Jewish people, especially the authorities.

Daūd (who is Khalīl's uncle) told Khalīl that he did not want to become the sheikh. Khalīl, of course, knew that this was untrue because he found out that Daūd had sent an emissary to convince members of the co-liable group to sign a petition supporting Daūd. Apart from promoting his own candidacy, Daūd's petition stated that the other candidate for leadership, Khalīl, had told him that he did not want to serve as the head of the tribe because of his longstanding involvement in public life. When Khalīl found out about his uncle's underhand way of recruiting support he gathered his followers and together they decided on a course of action. Khalīl's followers calculated the support for each of the two candidates and concluded that Khalīl was supported by about 83 percent of the co-liable group. Some of Khalīl's followers were concerned about the possibility that the authorities might grant the nomination to Daūd on account of his previous unsuccessful nomination in the 1960s and the fact that he was older than Khalīl. In order to prevent Daūd's nomination they conceived the idea of "threatening" him with the possibility of declaring him a *meshamas*. The reasoning and purpose behind this proposal was that Daūd would then cancel his application to become head of the tribe, or in case he received the nomination they would actually outcast him. This act would put the authorities in a situation where they would have to change the nomination.

In his capacity as sheikh a leader has two functions. He represents the tribe to the authorities and vice versa. If the nominated sheikh is declared a *meshamas* he cannot, from the Bedouin point of view, continue to serve as a sheikh. This is because the Bedouin would no longer recognize his authority, even though the authorities recognize his standing as leader. Such an action places the individual concerned in an intolerable situation. The followers of Khalīl calculated that once rumours of the threat reached Daūd, he would withdraw his candidacy. In late 1984 Daūd was nominated as sheikh. Although the *tashmīs* was not implemented, Khalīl and his followers still threaten this action. The very fact that a formal meeting of co-liable group members discussed its possibility under the circumstances outlined above is indicative of the sharp change in its usage. The possibility of outcasting has no connection whatsoever with a threat to the group — it is a clear social pressure on Daūd. Once again the case is within the sheikh's co-liable group.

Case History XXX

Before proceeding with the particulars it is necessary first to provide the tribal background of the actors involved. Until the War of Independence in 1948, the al-Aṭram was an independent tribe. After the establishment of the State of Israel the Military Governor attached members of the al-Aṭram to the Ībn-Karīr tribe. From 1949 onwards the elders of the al-Aṭram continually requested to again become an independent tribe. In 1978 the authorities granted the group their desired independence and a sheikh was appointed. Most members of the tribe belonged to the al-Aṭram descent group that over time split into two co-liable groups. The sheikh's co-liable group, however, remained the largest of the two co-liable groups.

In 1980 Ḥabīb al-Aṭram was pronounced a *meshamas* even though he was not a threat to the security or well-being of the co-liable group. Ḥabīb was a member of a different lineage than the sheikh belonged to, but within the same co-liable group. At the time of his *tashmīs* Ḥabīb was 25 years old, married, and had a baby daughter. His father had died when he was thirteen, and he was the eldest of three brothers. His mother came from a large co-liable group, which formed a subtribe in the Ībn-Karīr tribe. Ḥabīb's mother, Jamīla, did not return to her natal family after the death of her husband. She preferred to raise her children among the al-Aṭram co-liable group, although she kept close contacts with members of her family of origin. Jamīla has a strong personality and through her contacts and influence Ḥabīb, as well as his younger brothers, married close relatives of their mother.[6] Ḥabīb serves in the Israeli army,[7] and the uniform and the personal weapon contribute much to his status among members of the tribe. Even though Ḥabīb was quite young he was much respected in his lineage, his agnates would often wait until he returned from his military duty in order that he participate in discussions and decision making. Many of the young people from the other lineages of the co-liable group liked him and respected him.

In the fall of 1979 women from the al-Aṭram claimed that women from the co-liable group to which Ḥabīb's mother and wife belonged had encroached on their territory and grazed on al-Aṭram land. The accused women denied this and a quarrel developed. The situation quickly grew more serious and the men of both sets of womenfolk intervened in the affair by calling in a mediator. After studying the details of the altercation, Ḥabīb expressed the opinion that his mother's co-liable group were in the right and that the women of his own descent group were in the wrong. The sheikh of the al-Aṭram summed up the situation for himself as follows: His tribe had been recognized as independent for only a short period and there was a real need to promote cohesiveness among tribal members. In the normal course of daily events this was very difficult because most members worked for wages outside the tribal area, and the sheikh's *shiq* was not used very often for discussions and meetings that could help promote cohesiveness among tribal members. The sheikh determined that the circumstances of the quarrel could be used to promote cohesiveness and to this end he spoke to co-liable group members privately. He persuaded them that Ḥabīb's behavior could not be tolerated and that he should be cast out. Under no circumstances, he said, can a co-liable group member publicly support another co-liable group with which one's own group is in dispute.

The *tashmīs* took place on January 12, 1980. Neither Ḥabib nor his brothers were invited to participate in the meeting concerning his outcasting. In the process of the decision making the sheikh took notes that were then summarized as an official document,[8] signed by the elders of the co-liable group and by several witnesses. The paper was shown to sheikhs and heads of subtribes all over the Negev, as well as the contents of the document being conveyed by word of mouth among the tribes. The sheikh decided that even though it was his initiative to cast out Ḥabib and his brothers, it would be more suitable if the official *tashmīs* did not take place in his tent. He felt that his *shiq* should remain neutral. The reasoning behind this is that the sheikh was not only the leader of the co-liable group, but was also head of the entire tribe. He therefore requested that the official *tashmīs* ceremony take place at the *shiq* of the sheikh of the Abū-Karīr tribe (to which the al-Aṭram had been attached before they received independent status as a tribe). This request was granted to Sheikh al-Aṭram, who signed the document as a witness of the outcasting and not as a protagonist. Those signing in the name of the co-liable group were of Ḥabib's own lineage: two of his paternal uncles and Ḥabib's father's uncle. In this case the sheikh also decided to outcast Ḥabib's brothers as well. Their "crime" was merely supporting Ḥabib. This was a very unusual circumstance, however, and normally any individual (even a close relative) who does not agree to the outcasting proposal would not be cast out himself.

The meetings prior to the *tashmīs* and the gathering for the decision making involved all the males of the co-liable group. Never before or after the *tashmīs* did the sheikh see such an attendance of members of his co-liable group in the *shiq*. Clearly, the event added much to his personal status. Further, it indicated to all those present that the unity of the group was of paramount importance and that serious consequences would ensure if this unity was disregarded. The *tashmīs* was used not only as a punishment for Ḥabib, but it served as a warning to others, especially to the younger generation. In the course of the discussions in the *shiq* some of the young members of the group claimed that they too thought that it was the women of the al-Aṭram who were originally at fault. The sheikh, as well as other elders of the co-liable group, emphasized that the unity of the group comes first and that this unity should have the highest priority in determining the actions and speech of any individual co-liable member. The point being made here is that there must be a distinction between private knowledge and public knowledge,[9] and a concomitant action must arise from this distinction. In taking the outcasting course of action, Sheikh al-Aṭram succeeded in delivering his "unity" message to the members of the tribe, especially to the younger group members who might have felt inclined to act in the future as Ḥabib had done. Ḥabib acted as if he did not mind being outcast and he never left his home. But in private talks I had with him he admitted that it was difficult to live among the Bedouin with the stigma of being a *meshamas*.

After Ḥabib's outcasting became known among the tribes the legitimacy of the sheikh's action was a point of discussion and argument in many *shiqs*. Several well-known judges and mediators told me that the concept of the *tashmīs* was invented in order to *protect* the group from any possibility that as a result of misbehavior of one of its members, another member of the group be killed or injured as a revenge. In order to prevent such an occurrence, the group can expel any irresponsible member by casting him out. Some judges and mediators expressed the opinion that the outcasting of Ḥabib was a misuse of the *tashmīs*.

At the end of 1981, about six months after the *tashmīs* took place, several dignitaries from other tribes came to the sheikh's tent and asked him to abolish the *tashmīs*. The sheikh agreed and after some delay he eventually went with two mediators to Ḥabib's home to tell him that the *tashmīs* was abolished. To demonstrate his decision he took the *tashmīs* document from his wallet, tore it up and threw the pieces of paper into the open fireplace. However, no effort was made to notify other tribes that Ḥabib and his brothers were accepted back as full members of the co-liable group. Many elders and dignitaries feel that once a person is declared a *tashmīs* it can never be undone. According to many Bedouin this is the first time in the Negev that a *tashmīs* was abolished.

Changes in Ideology and Group Structure

Studies of non-Bedouin societies that are undergoing sedentarization shed light on social and political changes in group structure. Daniel Bates (1980, 137–38), in his discussion of the Yoruk settlements, states that "Political factions developed which even though they were phrased as genealogically-based groupings, encompassed non-descent members in internally hierarchic relatively stable coalitions." Bates mentions that in recent years brothers and cousins took sides against one another in village politics. In one case "one of the factions has come to ally itself more closely with the non-Yoruk section of the village, and has thereby gained control of the headmanship." Abu Jaber and Gharaibeh (1981, 300), in dealing with various aspects of Bedouin settlement in Jordan, state that "The fruits of progress brought with them the loosening of tribal bonds and the weakening of the sheikh's position. A new breed of leaders has emerged, who are educated and more aware of the Bedouin role in the national scene."

The loosening of tribal bonds, the emergence of newly established political factions, and the decline of in-group solidarity are the reasons for the spate of outcasting in recent years. As a result of sedentarization and the close contacts the Bedouin now have with the surrounding Jewish society, there are more and more conflicts between the law of the state and the "law" of the social organization of the co-liable group. By adopting the new mechanism of outcasting the ideology of the *tashmīs* has been changed. This new ideology now has to be adopted within the social behavioral pattern of the Bedouin. Salzman (1978) refers to this issue in the context of complementary opposition:

> The actual pattern of behavior found must not only be compared with the pattern asserted by the ideological norm, but it must be placed in the range of possible behavior patterns. This is because it may be quite as significant that certain patterns do not emerge as it is that others do emerge.

We would expect some differences between ideology and behavioral norms in every society, but if the gap between ideology and behavioral norms becomes too wide, then the ideology must change. The gap between the value norms and the behavioral norms regarding the *tashmīs* have become very wide. The Bedouin, thus, now give a new interpretation to the concept of the *tashmīs*. In times of stability, they now say, the co-liable group can tolerate some deviation of an individual's behavior from the group's ideology; but in times of instability, in times of the current rapid changes in the economic, social, and political structure and tribal organization, the group and especially its leaders are very sensitive to any deviation that might influence the behavior of others in the group.

Emrys Peters (1967) argues that we should not accept Bedouin ideology as an accurate picture of their political system. For where their interests are not in accord with lineage solidarity, their loyalties also are not to their lineage. Peters notes that conflicts often arise in cases where alliances are based upon matrilateral and affinal networks. For example, Ḥabib's alliance via his mother and wife were based upon matrilateral and affinal relationships and interactions (case history XXX). But once there was a conflict between the two levels of loyalties (the co-liable group's patrilateral loyalties, and the matrilateral and affinal loyalties, which in Ḥabib's case lay in the same genealogical line), the sheikh, because of in-group considerations, felt that he had to protect co-liable group interests in order to reach a higher degree of cohesion within the group as a whole. The *tashmīs* in Ḥabib's case was a safety valve for protecting the co-liable group in the sense that if more members of the group did as the *meshamas* had behaved, the co-liable group would disintegrate as a corporate group.

Earlier on I stated that various assumptions concerning sociocultural change, referred to by Salzman (1980, 1), are valid in the case of the new developments in the outcasting process of the Bedouin of the Negev. The large increase in outcasting instances outside of the traditional value norms framework; the recognition that the outcasting procedure can be changed to suit individual circumstances; and the stated change in ideological thinking of the purpose of the *tashmīs* — all indicate that this particular social aspect of Bedouin life has changed. This change is irreversible because the Bedouin themselves can never go back to viewing the outcasting procedure only in a value norms framework, thus a "return to the previous state is impossible" (ibid., 1). The case histories indicate that a change in the procedure is taking place in a particular direction, namely that outcasting is becoming more and more a political weapon, and that changes in the procedure are taking place cumulatively as witnessed by the invention of outcasting procedures in response to the particular requirements of the case in hand.

This conclusion must be tempered, nevertheless, with a word of warning. Salzman states that "a shift [in customary practices] in one direction does not by any means preclude a shift back as the circumstances change, on the contrary, . . . a shift back is necessary and to be expected" (ibid., 6). Nevertheless, we see in the changed procedure of outcasting a certain discreteness and absoluteness in the sense that "a boundary has been crossed and a new nature of the phenomenon now appears." The points made in this concluding section concerning the irreversibility of change in the outcasting process must also be considered in the light of the general changes taking place in the social and economic structure of Negev Bedouin as they become sedentarized at an accelerated pace.

Within a period of two years there were four cases of outcasting (and one case where this action was threatened) against two cases that took place within a period of 37 years prior to this two-year period. One may speculate that if other co-liable groups are to adopt outcasting in order to protect the group and increase cohesion whenever there is a threat of decline in co-liable group loyalty, the social effects on the individual of being *meshamas* will change as well. In other words, the stigma of being an outcast will diminish as the group begins to recognize the real reasons behind the increase in outcasting.

CHAPTER FIVE

Family Honor

When the media announce the murder of a young Arab girl or woman in a village or among a Bedouin tribe, it is usually seen as an act intended to remove the stain of shame from the name of a family due to illicit sexual relations by a daughter or sister. Such female deviant behavior, which has been documented by many scholars,[1] is considered shaming and affects family honor. There is no one pattern of punishment and sanction against deviant sexual behavior, despite a general condemnation of unlawful sexual relations. The deviant may be killed, sent away, ostracized, or just left to suffer the gossip of neighbors.

Honor and Shame

"Honor in the Arab world is a generic concept which embraces many different forms." "That the sexual conduct of women is an area sharply differentiated from other areas of the honor-shame syndrome is reflected in the language" (Patai 1976, 90, 120). *Sharaf* is a type of honor that fluctuates according to a man's behavior. If a man looks after the needs of his guests and is seen to be generous to those in need, his honor standing is high. If a man's daily intercourse with others is lacking in politeness, then his honor standing is considered low. This type of honor can be accumulated or lost according to a man's behavior. *'Irḍ,* on the other hand, is a type of honor that is used "only in connection with female chastity and continence" (Abou Zeid 1965, 256). A woman cannot by exemplary conduct add to her agnates' *'irḍ,* though by misbehaving she can detract from it. This renders a male vulnerable and dependent on a female's conduct. In fact, it is surprising that a woman should have the power to detract so much from male honor when Islamic tradition stresses her frailty. Bedouin and rural Arab societies are "shame cultures" in the sense that "individuals are controlled by public threats to personal reputation and honor. Public shame reflects not only on the individual, but on his family and kin, and there are, therefore, strong familial sanctions on deviation from communal norms" (Abercrombie, Hill and Turner 1984, 190).

Dishonor and shame are due to "sexuality and the most serious breach of the modesty core is an illicit sexual act regarded as sinful in the Koran . . ." (Mason 1975, 649–50). The definition of such an act, however, is any unseemly contact with a male; to have been seen in the company of one in doubtful circumstances is enough to stigmatize a female and to reduce the *'irḍ* of her agnates. Julian Pitt-Rivers says that "honour and shame are synonymous."[2] He defines shame not as a disgraceful act, but as the feeling of a person, usually a female, that prevents her from committing an act deemed shameful. He makes this point explicit by saying that "shamelessness is dishonourable" (1965, 42). I use the term "shame" in both the above mentioned meaning: as a feminine quality preventing shame through chastity on the one hand, and as an act staining honor on the other.

The questions to be addressed are: When is deviant sexual behavior punished by death? What sanctions are used? And when does such conduct meet with leniency? One general feature stands out — whenever there is a possibility of hiding shame (through marriage with the person responsible, for example), the woman is not punished.

An important dimension in family honor cases is mate selection: fathers controlling mate selection, versus daughters initiating their own relations. The ideology is such that the daughter is viewed as an integral part of her natal family. The father makes the decision who she should marry (though many times it is the mother who has the greater hand in the decision).[3] Once married, the daughter serves as a connecting link between her natal family and her family of reproduction. Neither in Bedouin nor in rural Arab society do members of the bride's family attend her wedding ceremony. The symbol of the bride's family not attending the wedding ceremony expresses itself in the ritual abduction of the bride practised by Negev Bedouin.

> It takes place only after the marriage arrangements have been completed and the marriage-payment paid over, and is carried out not by the bridegroom himself but by one or more of his close agnates, among them usually a brother or a first cousin. It operates not only when the bride is of another co-liable group, but also when she is of the bridegroom's own group, and even when she is a patrilateral parallel cousin . . . The insistence of the bride's group on performing the capture rather indicates that it has given something beyond what it was morally entitled to; it has given a woman to another family or section, whereas a woman ideally remains all her life also a member of her group of origin . . . The woman has been captured by force, as it were, and therefore she ought to be allowed to return to her father's tent. (Marx 1967, 103–104)

The non-attendance of the bride's family at the wedding ceremony symbolizes that she has not left her home and that she continues to belong to her family of origin. It also means, in effect, that she is still under the control of her father. The ritual abduction described above is just one category of abduction. Maya Melzer-Geva (1983) states that the two most important categories of abduction *(hatīfa)* are (a) a real kidnapping, and (b) where the female cooperates in her own abduction (what in the West we would call an elopement). The issue of elopement is dealt with in the Surviving Offenders section of this chapter.

Some scholars claim that a girl is not harmed if the circle of acquaintances who know of the sexual encounter is limited, but insist that once there is public knowledge the girl is killed (Antoun 1968, 684, 687; Black-Michaud 1975, 218). The argument presented here is that murder occurs only when there is public accusation by an injured party, because "public opinion will gossip, but not demand any harsh punishment" (Malinowski 1959, 80). An injured party is always a member of her co-liable group or the spouse of her father (i.e., either her mother or her father's wife). The reasons for public accusation by an injured party vary. Accusation and murder cannot be explained as normative behavior alone. Usually there is personal motivation and often it is of a political character.

Accusation is always based on the violation of the norm that a girl or single woman who has "sinned" must be punished by death unless she marries her partner in intercourse. If a marriage takes place between the offenders, no sanction is carried out. If marriage does not take place for some reason (the male refuses to marry, or his or her parents prevent the marriage, for example), the death sanction on the girl is determined by whether, as stated above, there is a public accusation by an injured party. If the offending girl is to be punished according to the norms, it is always the obligation of her natal family to punish her. Although the killer himself might be inclined to instigate some lesser form of sanction, in order to preserve family honor he has no other alternative but to kill. In effect he is pushed to kill by the person who made the public accusation. In most cases it is a brother who "punishes" the sister. Gideon Kressel (1981, 146) found that "The largest group of attackers by relationship to those attacked is that of brothers, and the second largest is that of fathers. In third place are father's brothers and their sons, of the latter three were, at the same time, the husbands of those attacked. All husbands accused of attacking their wives were their agnates: three were their father's brother's sons."[4]

There are two reasons why the girl's father (or brother) is the one who has to inflict a sanction against her. First, it symbolizes the control that the natal family has over the daughter. This control has already been referred in terms of the non-attendance by the natal family at Bedouin weddings; the same principle applies to rural Arab society. Thus, even though the daughter lives with her family of reproduction far away from her family of origin, this fact does not reduce or take away the element of control exercised by the woman's natal family. The second reason is related to shame. A woman's important socialization period takes place within her natal family.[5] By breaching the chastity norm she brings shame on those with whom she grew up.

Violation of the sexual norm by a married woman automatically calls for her death. Abner Cohen (1974, 116) states that "An adulterous woman, even an unmarried woman having a sexual affair with a man, must be killed by her brothers or her father's brother's sons. If she is killed the group not only reasserts its position but also rises in prestige scale. If she is not killed they suffer loss of prestige." Fredrik Barth (1968, 83) says that "Fornication or adultery with a woman, if it becomes the subject of a common gossip, reflects on the honour of her male relations; her kinsmen, particularly brothers and sons, and her husband, can only wipe out the stain by avenging themselves on the seducer." Thus, even in case of adultery, it is not the family of reproduction that carries out the sanction, but the family of origin.

The accusation against the sexual offense is often made in the form of a dramatization of the actual stigmatization. Howard Becker (1973, 15) points out that "the degree to which an act will be treated as deviant depends also on who commits the act and who feels he has been harmed by it. Rules tend to be applied more to some persons than others." Sometimes the accusation is neither politically motivated nor premeditated, but spontaneous — an outburst due to accumulated frustration and a sense of unbearable humiliation. This happens more frequently to women, whose traditional role has conditioned them not to castigate their male relatives in public and with whom provocation must be very strong to overcome restraint imposed by upbringing. In this context it should be remembered that the social organization of both rural Arab and Bedouin communities is in a process of change: Family ties are no longer the only ones and the political structure too is no longer dominated by groups organized on family lines. Thus it may be speculated that effective accusation will in future also be made by persons possessing political or economic influence on the man whose daughter, sister, or wife has violated the norms ruling the sexual behavior of females.

Case History XXXI

This case occurred in Jewish society though the family involved was of Yemenite origin.[6] A rabbi who had two wives, a situation legalized in his country of origin and also in several other Middle Eastern Jewish communities, lived in a moshav (cooperative settlement) in Israel and had fourteen children. One of his daughters, a particularly beautiful woman, was married to another member of the same settlement, who was weakly and unprepossessing. Her husband made friends with a young man who worked in the village but did not live there. The husband sometimes invited the stranger to his home and later intimate relations developed between this stranger and his wife.

The affair soon became public knowledge in the moshav, and both the woman's father and her husband were aware of what was going on. Their exhortations to discontinue the affair were rejected; the woman told them that she had no intention of breaking off relations with the other man. She said that Israel, unlike their country of origin, was a modern society and she had no desire to perpetuate outworn traditions. This situation was particularly hard on her father whose congregation did not hide their disapproval of the woman's conduct and of his own reaction (or lack of reaction) to it. It was even insinuated that he should not preach virture, including chastity, while at the same time disregarding his own child's immoral conduct. After a prolonged period during which the husband again unsuccessfully tried to induce his wife to give up her affair, the unhappy man turned to his father-in-law asking him to intercede, expressing disapproval of the rabbi's tolerance of his daughter's unseemly behavior in the presence of numerous witnesses. Soon after the husband's accusation the father strangled his daughter, declaring subsequently that his conscience was clean and that he had done no more than fatherly duty, adding that he preferred imprisonment to shame.

The rabbi's reaction was motivated by a conception similar to that in rural Arab and Bedouin societies regarding honor and shame. As long as the affair was public knowledge (but no public accusation by an injured party had been made), he could ignore it; once an injured party had made an accusation he had to act against the further flouting of norms. The rabbi's action must also be seen in its political and economic context. He had already been criticized in front of others before his son-in-law's public accusation; his status in the community and his political influence on the local plane had been threatened, as well as his continuation in office. This would have had economic consequences. Although he claimed to have acted to preserve morality, he did not act before his position in the village was seriously jeopardized.

ACCIDENT OR MURDER?

Kressel (1981, 147) states that, especially among the Bedouin, there are "attempts to give murders the appearance of suicide or accident." There have been several cases where a girl has been found dead at the bottom of a well and the family have claimed that the death was due to suicide or to an accident. Postmortem examination has revealed no incriminating evidence. In case histories XXXII and XXXIII, however, I received information that the girls were pushed into the well for having broken the sexual propriety code. Informants are surprisingly candid when questioned about the number of cases of girls found at the bottom of wells. They point out that *if* a brother wants to murder his sister for some reason, then pushing her down a well is a way of doing it that will not leave any sign of injury or evidence of homicide.

Case History XXXII

In this case four villagers, who at that time were present in the village, told me of a murder that took place in the early 1940s. A man who was born a considerable distance from the village where the incident occurred, moved to this village. His first wife, a Bedouin by origin, bore him four daughters; later he took a second wife from one of the most respected families in the village. One of his daughters from his first wife had illicit sexual relations with a ploughman who worked in the village but did not live there. Rumour spread before the father learned about it, but when he did hear of it he took care to ensure that the ploughman was no longer employed in the village.

His second wife was not satisfied with this solution and reproached her husband for having failed to protect the family honor. She expressed resentment in the presence of members of her natal family who were visiting at the time and indicated that both her and her husband's status was reduced by his inaction. In reaction to her accusation the father ordered his other daughters to push their sister into the village well at their next daily trip to draw water. This was done and represented as an accident. But when the girl's corpse was recovered one of the man's rivals informed the police, a most unusual step to be taken in a rural village. An autopsy was ordered, which the girl's father wished to prevent, anticipating the result. He tried to convince the police that such a procedure offended religious custom, and pretended to be outraged when suspicion of murder was mentioned. However, as he was also interested in establishing the truth, so he said, they could make an experiment that would provide the answer. Virginity could be tested by inserting a hard boiled egg into the vagina. If this was possible, intercourse had taken place; if not, the girl was innocent and consequently her father would not have a motive for killing her. An old woman was entrusted with the task and made a great show of unsuccessfully trying to push the egg into the dead girl's vagina. A policewoman who was present accepted the "proof" and the file was closed.

This case shows how accepted the killing of a daughter who had violated the norm was, and how easy it was to stage a deceptive maneuver that hoodwinked the police. The father did not kill his daughter when he learned that she had offended the norm. It was his wife's accusation, made in public, that prompted him to take steps. In addition, his wife's prestige in the community was higher than his own; this made it easy for her to prevail on him, especially because she involved her natal family in the matter. She cannot be said to have acted spontaneously. She may have staged her accusation knowing that it would be most effective in the presence of her natal family, particularly as she mentioned status from which she derived her superior position toward her husband. Furthermore, the girl's father had only daughters from his first wife, but she had two sons. Thus the ascribed status of her natal family plus her own superior position due to her being the mother of sons, gave her the power to influence her husband's actions decisively.

Case History XXXIII

In 1977 some Bedouin tribes left the Negev because of drought conditions; they camped close to a moshav located in the center of the country. One day a Bedouin woman found an infant close to death in the fields. She thought that the child was one of the moshav babies and rushed him to the nearest hospital. but the baby died a few hours later. Police investigation revealed that another Bedouin woman and her daughter had been working in the field where the baby was found. Both women had disappeared but were later traced to the Negev. After questioning it was discovered that a Bedouin of peasant origin of another tribe had been the daughter's lover and that the two families knew each other, having been on the move together for several years. The man in question did not deny having intercourse with the girl. All involved were arrested, and in order to ensure their speedy release both sets of parents agreed that the young people should marry immediately.

Some time later, however, the young man's family objected to their son marrying, arguing that he had confessed only in order to gain the release of all concerned as quickly as possible. The boy was requested to swear an oath that he had not had sexual relations with the girl. The oath taking was to have taken place at a well-known sacred place, Abraham's cave in Hebron, a procedure recognized as binding by all Bedouin. Lying to the police does not offend their social norms, nor perjury at a trial, but an untrue oath at a sacred place is out of the question for Bedouin. (Bedouin believe that something bad will befall them if they tell a lie under these circumstances.) It is indicative that the young man evaded the actual oath taking.

The girl's family returned to the Negev, while that of the young man remained in the center of the country. The girl's uncles were obviously dissatisfied and one of them repeatedly accused the father of neglecting the problem, insisting that he clear the family name. Not much later the girl's body was found at the bottom of a well. An autopsy failed to establish any signs of violence so the question of whether she committed suicide or was murdered remained open. In this case close relatives accused the father of neglecting to preserve the family honor, and he acted. The relatives probably did not foresee the outcome of their accusations. Rather, they expected that the father would take steps to force the male responsible to marry his daughter, which would restore the injured family honor. The intention might even have been to prevent a killing rather than to bring one about. The young men's peasant origin was a further aggravating factor, for unless there were special circumstances a Bedouin girl would not marry someone with a peasant background.

At the prompting of some tribal dignitaries who wished to prevent bloodshed in which the young man's agnates might have been the victims, a *ṣulḥa* was arranged. But not all the dead girl's agnates attended and one of her uncles who enjoyed particularly high status was conspicuous by his absence, while the young man's family was fully present. Several Bedouin remarked that "everyone has his own way of settling a problem," but no one said openly that murder had been committed; others insisted that Bedouin women do not commit suicide. Political motives also enter the picture in that the girl's uncle who appeared eager to defend the family honor had an ulterior motive. He wished to use the girl's murder as a means of uniting his co-liable group, the sheikh of which had died several years previously. Since that time the cohesion of the co-liable group had been on the decline. A murder would thus rally them together. The uncle wished to prevent the *ṣulḥa*, which would have ended the conflictual situation and removed the cause of unification of the group.

Several informants disclosed to me that the girl had been murdered. Kressel (1981, 147) states that "the file was closed for lack of evidence, but fieldwork revealed the true situation."

Case History XXXIV

In the Spring of 1977 a young girl was observed in the company of a young man of another corporate group, in a creek not far from the Bedouin encampment of her tribe. After the rumor of her escapade had reached her co-liable group, the male members assembled to decide on what steps had to be taken to defend their *'irḍ*. After several meetings were held it was decided that the girl should not be killed but would have to undertake the hardest menial tasks. At the same time negotiations were to be held with the young man's family regarding payment of indemnification. Opinions were divided as to the right of the girl's family to claim anything from the young man and his agnates, as in cases of offense of the sexual norm Bedouin tradition maintains that the female is guilty. At the beginning of 1978 the girl disappeared and a search party discovered her body at the bottom of a well. Her parents were arrested but said that she had committed suicide. A postmortem showed no signs of violence on the body and the parents were released as no definite proof as to the cause of death was found.

Two significant aspects suggest themselves in an analysis of the case. Even though the event was public knowledge the girl was not killed immediately. Secondly, this is the first time to my knowledge that several meetings of the offender's agnates took place to determine the outcome. This in itself shows that the norm is not obeyed automatically and that there is scope for deliberation when it is offended. It is also significant that once a resolution not to kill the girl was adopted, it was contested. As a result a fission took place within the co-liable group. In the six months following the decision not to kill the girl there were constant conflicts between the two sections of the co-liable group. Her death only took place about two weeks after the struggle between the two sections had reached a climax. This was demonstrated on the occasion of the visit of an important guest. Two of the agnates who were known to oppose the decision to kill her absented themselves from the reception in the *shiq* and also tried to persuade others to abstain from attending.

If I had not been informed of the deliberations I might have analyzed the case incorrectly. I could well have surmised that public knowledge alone condemned the girl to death. But this was not so. A dramatization was required. There were two stages to this dramatization. The absence of the two agnates from the meeting honoring the important guest was noted by everybody in the encampment and became a focus for gossip. Secondly, a group member who supported that faction which wanted to kill the girl, openly discussed the case, and noted the reason why the two members had absented themselves. To do this in the presence of an outsider guest amounted to a public accusation. Unlike the previous three case histories, where the injured party was a very close relative, in this case the accuser was a co-liable group member (a third cousin of the girl's father). An additional factor was that some members not only accused the girl of deviant behavior, but also accused the male. This double focus, instead of a single one, was a contributing factor in not killing the girl immediately.

Case History XXXV

In a village closer to the Syrian–Lebanese border, the wife of a much older man was said to be having an affair with a married neighbor. Her paternal uncle sought out her half brother and informed him of the situation. The half brother did not know the children of his father's second wife well, his own mother having died when he was young. His childhood had been unhappy, he had had to beg for bread and often resorted to petty theft. He did not even possess the minimum of clothing and wore the *thob*, the long gown traditionally worn by Arabs, without undergarments. Because his stepmother completely neglected him he used to be covered with lice; the only way he could rid himself of the vermin was to place his gown in an ant nest for the ants to devour the lice.

The young man had had to do all sorts of menial jobs in his youth, including minding the flocks, which is more highly regarded among Bedouin than villagers. Despite these difficulties he married, saved some money, and set himself up in business together with his wife's brother. Thus the young man had little reason to take an interest in his half siblings or to protect the honor of the family that had neglected him. Furthermore, all the children in his father's house were from the second wife. Yet, Arab society being patrilineal, the fact that they all had the same father imposed obligations on him.

The young man received further information from his uncle that shocked him. The man his half sister had committed adultery with was his own brother-in-law and business partner, a man considered by the community as law abiding, and a good father and husband. So incredulous was the young man that he set up an ambush; on discovering the accusation to be true he let his father and brothers know. He met with strong resistance from the woman's mother, his stepmother. When her husband told her the news she insinuated that her stepson had acted with malicious intent and had maligned her daughter. The young man asked his brother-in-law to cease relations with his half sister. When the brother-in-law refused, the young man dissolved the partnership. In the meanwhile he had to decide how to continue as he was under pressure from his uncle, who had not only warned the guilty couple himself but had also approached the father of the young man.

Six months passed since the matter was first raised and the uncle became impatient as rumors continued to be spread in the village. Other people observed the clandestine meetings, causing the affair to become public knowledge before news of it reached members of the woman's natal family. A younger brother decided to join his half brother in another ambush to convince himself that the rumour was true. All this time the uncle was increasing pressure, claiming that he could no longer show his face in the village unless drastic steps were taken. When this was known it would confirm the gossip and demonstrate his despair at the inactivity of those whose duty it was to punish the "sinner." The uncle's action was akin to a public accusation. His threat convinced the woman's brothers that they had no alternative but to murder her, which they did, going also to her lover's house and murdering him as well. To escape revenge from the dead man's family they went to southern Lebanon, taking advantage of the political situation there.[7]

The facts support the theory that it is public accusation by an injured party (close relative or co-liable group member) that eventually leads to murder in reaction to illicit sexual relations by a female. Knowledge of the act is not enough, public accusation by an injured party is the dominant factor. The fact that the persons involved had been warned and disregarded the warning also indicates that the norms were not a substantial obstacle and could be flouted so long as there was no public accusation by an injured party.

Political motives should also be borne in mind. The young man who had grown up as an orphan was very close to his wife's natal family, as was understandable under the circumstances. His paternal uncle had aimed at severing or at least weakening these links and the first step his nephew had taken was to dissolve the partnership with his wife's brother. But this was not enough: there must be a killing. This was the uncle's true objective, which he justified by concern for family honor and his own prestige. As his nephew did not feel any obligation to his natal family, his uncle had to make the young man aware of his collective responsibility obligations.

Case History XXXVI

In November 1983, a man who was married to his first patrilateral parallel cousin *(bint 'amm)* came home from work and found his wife together with her *ibn khal* (mother's brother's son). The lover hit the husband, who ran away. The wife and her lover then went to the police and explained what had happened.

The woman claimed that she was in her third month of pregnancy, and that she was pregnant from her lover. The police, fearful that the girl would be harmed by her husband or her agnates, arranged for her to take shelter with a local sheikh. Later, the woman's father came to the sheikh and asked to speak with his daughter, promising not to harm her. In the presence of the sheikh and two members of the sheikh's family, the father met his daughter. The young woman told her father that she loved her *ibn khal* and that it was his child that she was carrying. The father was shocked at her words, especially that she openly admitted these facts in the presence of the sheikh and his relatives. The father left saying that he had to think about how he should handle the affair. After hearing about the visit to the sheikh's tent, the husband told his father-in-law (who was also his uncle) that he would divorce his wife at the earliest opportunity. He also publicly accused his father-in-law of not protecting the family honor. In particular he noted the fact that his wife had publicly claimed (in the presence of the sheikh) that she was pregnant from her lover and that she wanted to marry him.

A week later the woman was found dead in a hut that had been burned down. Postmortem examination revealed that she had been stabbed twice prior to the "accident" of the fire. The police immediately arrested the husband. Three different informants told me that the wrong man was held in custody. They state that it is always the father or brother who is responsible to protect the family honor. In this case the young Bedouin woman did not try to deny her relations with her lover, on the contrary, she claimed that the husband was not the father of the child she was carrying. And she publicly stated that she wanted to marry her lover. The woman, and probably her lover as well, thought that by going to the police they would protect themselves from any dangerous sanction by her husband or agnates. This was to no avail. Even though her killer knew that the police had knowledge of her circumstances, family honor was avenged by someone.

Case History XXXVII

This case history has been previously outlined in chapter one, where my role as anthropologist/mediator in helping Sa'id and his father to be released from prison is explained. The detailed circumstances of the case are given here.

In the Spring of 1970, a girl residing in a small hamlet situated in the

Triangle was hospitalized and found to be pregnant. She admitted to her family that she had had intercourse with a young man of her lineage. This young man was about to be married to his first patrilateral and matrilateral parallel cousin in a *badal*. (A *badal* is an exchange marriage where siblings marry siblings, the two unions being linked — if one union breaks up, the other union automatically breaks up too.) The future wife of the guilty young man was the daughter of his paternal uncle. Thus the "culprits" could not legalize their act through marriage without considerable difficulties, nor its consequence — the birth of a child. If this course had been chosen it would have meant cancelling the *badal* arrangement, which would have left the paternal uncle's daughter, already in her mid-twenties, with scant prospects of marriage.

The uncle took the matter up with the young man's father (the uncle's brother), suggesting that a younger brother of his future son-in-law marry the pregnant girl. Obviously, such a conversation can only take place where there are very close family relations.[8] The girl's father was the paternal uncle of the young man's father and had previously been married to the widowed maternal grandmother of the young man. After this woman's death, the girl's father married again and the pregnant girl was his second wife's daughter. The pregnant girl therefore had half siblings who were also half siblings of the young man's mother. One half sibling of the young man's mother was married to another of the young man's paternal uncles.

The uncle suggested that once the *badal* ceremony was over, the second marriage could take place. The girl's father was advised that because some time would elapse before she could marry, an abortion should be arranged, and this was carried out soon afterwards. After the *badal* wedding, however, the young man who was supposed to marry the girl refused to play his role, explaining that he had not been consulted about the arrangements. He was a school teacher, economically independent, and could thus defy his elders. In the wake of this development, relations between the girl's parents and the parents of the *badal* couples deteriorated. Another brother, married to the girl's half sister, also stopped speaking to his two brothers, who were the fathers of those involved in the *badal*. Moreover, he spread the rumour of the girl's "sin" among his co-villagers, which led to public knowledge of the affair. When this did not produce any results, he physically attacked his nephew (the young man who had had illicit sex relations) while he was working in the fields and, in the presence of numerous witnesses, accused him for all to hear.

Although this inevitably increased tension between the two hostile groups of relatives, six months passed and no action was taken. Then the same uncle, together with the girl's brother, let it be known within a strictly limited circle made up of members of the lineage only, that they would strangle the girl after having arranged for her death to look like gas poisoning. In order to give plausibility to their story they even mentioned to neighbors their intention of acquiring a new gas stove. But a respected dignitary of the lineage pointed out that the true cause of death would be revealed by a postmortem, which would doubtless be required by the authorities.

About a year after the field incident the girl's father was busy preparing for the wedding of one of his sons. He planned to construct a new building for the young couple next to his own house. Because the plot suitable for this purpose was registered in the name of several heirs, including the young man's mother, a go-between was sent to her home in order to obtain the required permission. The answer to this routine request was that the woman would give her consent only against payment, so unusual a reply and so inappropriate in the special circumstances that it shocked the go-between who, passing the message on to the girl's parents, left without drinking the traditional cup of coffee.

The girl's mother reacted to what she considered an insult added to injury with a hysterical accusation of her husband, calling his handling of the whole affair incompetent and charging him with indifference. She shouted that "First they lay our daughter and then they want to devour us," and so loud was her voice that she was heard by some of the neighbors. The upset father's reaction was immediate. He picked up a hoe, entered the room where the girl was sleeping, and hit her over the head until she was dead. He then went straight to the house of one of the elders of the village and made a full confession.

After the husband had killed their daughter, the girl's mother ran away to the home of her natal family. Her son, Sa'id, who had been sitting in a local cafe, heard his mother's screams and rushed home. Not realizing that his sister was dead, he picked her up and took her to an Arab physician who, on examining her, pronounced her dead and told Sa'id to take her away because he did not want to become involved. Sa'id brought the body back home. When the police arrived he determined to spare his father the imprisonment and claimed that he was the one who had killed his sister. The father, however, had already confessed. Later, Sa'id retracted his confession, but both father and son were arrested and both were sentenced to life imprisonment. Whilst in prison both father and son, with my help, petitioned President Navon for a pardon. After several years the president reduced their prison sentences. Subsequently there were other petitions, especially concerning the father who by this time was old and sick. Some Arab dignitaries pointed out that the old man should not be allowed to die in prison. In March 1983 the father was released. The innocent son, however, remained in prison. In May 1983 a television documentary was shown concerning the entire case. On the night of the program President Navon signed papers reducing Sa'id's prison sentence. Because of previous reductions in his prison term due to good behavior the President's additional reduction allowed Sa'id to be released immediately.

Although murder followed immediately after the public accusation, there was more than a sudden feeling that things could not go on like this much longer. A special event prompted the accusation and led the girl's mother to an assessment of all that had happened so far. It was then that she analyzed the father's handling of the affair, being aware that his inability to find a solution had reduced both his and her prestige so much that the insulting request for payment in return for a signature was made. The father's credulity when he was promised another husband for their daughter seemed a fatal error. He should, she now knew for certain, have insisted on immediate marriage instead of agreeing to the abortion; the person who had caused the pregnancy should, according to custom, have become the daughter's husband. Once the girl's mother thought the matter over seriously, she also realized that the suggestion that another brother marry the girl had not been realistic. After all, the daughter would be the former lover's sister-in-law if she had married his brother as proposed. Whenever a quarrel broke out between her and his wife, the past would be brought up and the girl would never have been allowed to forget her "sin." Also, her husband (if she had married him) would have faced contempt from his peers, for the whole affair was public knowledge. The same uncle who had attacked his nephew before witnesses would certainly do his best to publicize the incident and its consequences. This was only to be expected for it was known that he wanted the young man's position and standing in the community, and even more the position of his father, to be reduced for political reasons. This, of course, had nothing to do with the girl and her conduct. The aim of the uncle was to ostracize them and to oust them from the group, the motivation for which dated back to an earlier time when there had been antagonism between himself and the young man's father. Thus latent hostility was fanned by what had happened and an opportunity used to settle old accounts.

In this case public knowledge was inevitable. In a small village where intermarriage is frequent and where neighbors are relatives, the only chance of keeping the affair secret would have been immediate marriage between the two culprits. Once this opportunity was missed, chances for a satisfactory settlement of the case were much reduced.

As related in the Introduction, Sa'id was released from prison by presidential decree after a televison documentary detailed Arab norms concerning illicit sexual relations and family honor. The following postscript not only details Sa'id's reintegration problems, but is indicative of the "political" nature of life in an Israeli rural Arab village. While Sa'id was in prison his older brother began preliminary negotiations for a prospective wife for him and this activity caused some difference of opinion in the family. The older brother's daughters are married to the two sons of the head of the *ḥamūla*. The older brother had become very close to his daughters' father-in-law and wanted his newly-freed brother to marry the *ḥamūla* head's daughter. Sa'id's brother felt that marriage would help Sa'id reintegrate back into society. The girl's father has much influence in the village, he sits on the Regional Council and has good contacts with various governmental departments. It is these latter facts, rather than Sa'id's reintegration back into society, that probably explain the brother's readiness to marry Sa'id off — especially into a family where he, the elder brother, would benefit in influence and prestige from the marriage arrangement.

The head of the *ḥamūla* also tried to promote the marriage arrangement, but Sa'id was firm in his refusal. Sa'id's mother frowned upon the negotiations. She felt that Sa'id deserved a better wife, one more educated and more beautiful. Sa'id protested symbolically against his brother trying to marry him off by not going out from his home and having his mother bring his meals there, in this way indicating that he still felt himself to be in prison. The message was received and no more pressure was put on Sa'id.

Sa'id's wish regarding his not wanting to marry the *ḥamūla* head's daughter was not indicative, however, of his being against settling down into normal family life. When the filming for the television documentary took place I interviewed a young woman from a nearby village, a secretary at the local high school, about her feelings on family honor killings. Sa'id, who was on leave of absence from the prison that day, stood nearby when the film interview took place. He noticed the attractive young woman and thought about her a lot when he returned to prison. Some time later Sa'id's mother arranged for a mediator to approach the family of the secretary. The family gave their consent to the marriage and at the insistence of the groom's mother the engagement took place immediately.[9]

A Bedouin listens to a case while a group member prepares coffee for the participants.

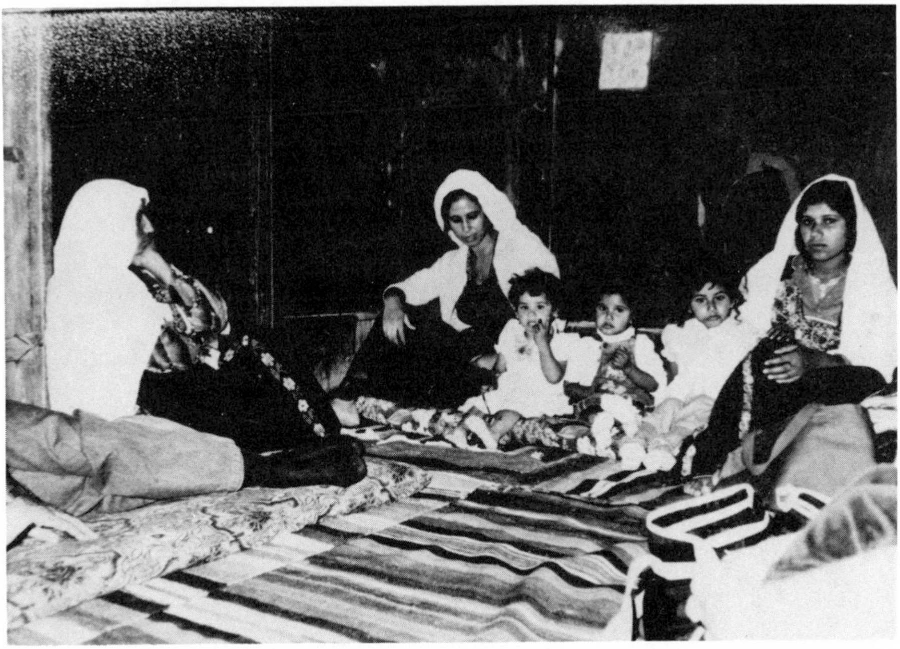

The author's Bedouin "sister" and her daughter-in-law, grandchildren, and daughter.

The injured party is about to tie knots in the flag (chap 3, n. 8).

The shanties of the families of Isma'il and N'ama (case history XLVIII).

The following two case histories of family honor killings differ from the pattern outlined earlier on in this chapter in that the focus of attack for revenge is in some way different. Usually it is the woman in family honor affairs who is the target for physical attack but sometimes, as the following case history illustrates, it is one of the male actors who is the target.

Case History XXXVIII

'Adel married Ṣafa, who came from a mixed Jewish–Arab city in the north of the country. 'Adel lived in a Triangle village to where Ṣafa moved after her marriage. Many years later, after their union resulted in four children, 'Adel discovered that his sister's husband, Salām, was having an affair with his wife. Salām and Ṣafa's relations not only became public knowledge, but Salām publicly mocked 'Adel by discussing out loud how he enjoyed having sex relations with Ṣafa. 'Adel divorced his wife, and his parents took care of the children. After the divorce Ṣafa moved to the small house of her parents.

Despite the divorce, Salām continued in his pretension to greatness by detailing his sexual encounters with Ṣafa, in the presence of 'Adel and others. 'Adel felt very humiliated, wherever he went in the village he felt that people were talking about him. 'Adel was well aware that by her behavior Ṣafa had brought shame on her family members, and he knew that it was custom for them to deal with the matter. Nevertheless, he also felt that his honor was at stake and that his family was offended against. One evening 'Adel murdered Salām, using Salām's illegally possessed submachine gun. As they were brothers-in-law, 'Adel could easily go to his sister's home, from where he took the gun. It is not known whether this act was carried out with 'Adel's sister's compliance, but she certainly had good reason to assist him. Perhaps she just did not warn her husband that his brother-in-law had taken the gun.

Salām was known to mix with criminal elements, hence his possession of the submachine gun: it would not have been too difficult to stage the circumstances of his shooting so that the police thought that it was Salām's accomplices in crime who had murdered him. But instead, 'Adel went to the village square; holding the gun aloft he proclaimed to everybody he met that he had just killed Salām. He then gave himself up to the police. As he himself expected, and according to Israeli law, 'Adel was sentenced to life imprisonment. In June 1984, five years after the murder, I visited 'Adel in prison. He emphasized that he was proud that he had restored his honor and that of his family. To 'Adel this was more important than the difficulties he faced as a long-term prisoner.

In this case the public pronouncements of having illicit sexual relations with the wife of the injured party was injurious to both the honor of the man and his family. The situation is different when somebody meets secretly with a married woman; public knowledge of the affair may bring forth doubt as to the husband's manhood, but it does not put into question the fatherhood of his children. In cases, albeit rare, where the sexual competency of the father is put into serious question by the explicit nature of the proclamations by the guilty male, the question arises as to whether the father is really the progenitor or just a social father. In such an instance the adultress occupies only a secondary role in the husband's priorities regarding honor.

Case History XXXIX

After his first wife died in the late 1960s, a Negev Bedouin sheikh proposed to marry Khaḍra, who became his third wife. Khaḍra was a widow whose husband had only recently died; she belonged to the same tribe as the sheikh, but was from a different co-liable group. After the customary year of mourning the sheikh approached her family to negotiate the marriage. The marriage proposal caused a split in Khaḍra's family. Her father and her elder brother agreed to the proposal, but her father's brothers and their sons opposed it. Their opposition to the marriage was not directed against the sheikh but was due to personal reasons resulting from an in-family dispute several years before. In order to prevent the marriage they kidnapped Khaḍra. The sheikh, however, used the authorities, with whom he was on good terms, to make the kidnappers return her to her father. The marriage then took place on the background of the passive objection of most of Khaḍra's agnates. Their objection was passive because they were under threat of a kidnapping charge; the sheikh hinted that if no further objections to the marriage were made he would arrange that the criminal charges relating to the abduction be dropped. In the event no prosecution took place.

Three and a half years after the marriage took place, during which time Khaḍra bore two children, relations between the couple looked ideal. However, one day the sheikh's teenage son from one of his earlier marriages saw Khaḍra go to her *sandūk* (a box where Bedouin women keep their jewelry and money) and take out a small bag, which she emptied into the coffee pot. After being told of this the sheikh took the coffee pot to the department of health in Beersheva where he was informed that the coffee contained a fatal poison. The sheikh immediately divorced Khaḍra, who returned to her agnates. In accordance with Bedouin custom the two children stayed with their father.

Khaḍra's explanation of the affair was bizzare to the extreme. She explained that her uncles had told her that they had been wrong to object to her marriage and that she had established relations with them again. The uncles, who lived in the same encampment, kept close contact with Khaḍra. Whenever the sheikh was away she always went to visit them. And when the sheikh moved to one of the new settlements built especially for the Bedouin, Khaḍra's agnates also sedentarized in the same neighborhood of the town. Khaḍra claimed that her agnates told her that the sheikh intended to marry another young woman, and that they gave her the "spice" telling her that if she puts it into his coffee the sheikh would concentrate only on her and would forget about any other woman.

From time to time Khaḍra sent messages to the sheikh that it was never her intention to harm him. And toward the end of 1979 the sheikh decided to remarry her. This action elicited a strong response from the sheikh's eldest son, Khaled, who felt that Khaḍra had deeply hurt the family honor not only by attempting to poison his father but also by her previous behavior of spending too much time with her agnates. This neglect of her family life during the time that the sheikh was away from the tribal area had been the subject of gossip, especially the fact that she neglected her young children in favor of her natal family. Neither did Khaled believe Khaḍra's story regarding the poisoning. He was embarrassed at the gossip leveled at his father, namely that the sheikh had been blind to Khaḍra's faults during their first marriage, and wanted to endure them again by remarrying her. Khaled knew that talking to his father would get him nowhere. In Bedouin society a son does not dare to argue with his father. Being the oldest son he decided that in order to save the honor of the family he would have to kill Khaḍra. On the third day after the second marriage, Khaled killed Khaḍra by assaulting her with an axe.

The family fully supported Khaled. His father, the sheikh, periodically visits him in prison and has applied to the ministry of justice and to the President in order to obtain a pardon for his son. Khaled's sentence has already been reduced from life imprisonment to a sentence that entitles him to visit his family on special occasions. At the end of June 1984 Khaled visited his family for the Muslim holiday of *'Id al-Fiṭ*er, which follows the month of the Ramaḍān fast. I visited Khaled at his home, together with his wife and two children. Khaled maintains that he feels that he did the right thing and does not regret the murder deed. He claims that it would have been easier for him if the circumstances had involved a more regular breach of family honor (i.e., if he had had to kill his sister or his daughter). "Emotionally it was difficult for me to kill my father's wife," he explained, "but family honor must come first."

Cases of family honor killing that do not involve a breach of sexual modesty are rare. In this case Khaḍra's not putting the interests of her family of reproduction first was a contempt to family members. Although the sheikh himself did not see the disrespect, other family members felt it strongly. This feeling of despisement was obviously enhanced by local gossip. By marrying her a second time the sheikh viewed her as innocent of the poisoning charge, but the public and family knew the facts of her honor-reducing behavior as far as family interest was concerned. Khaled viewed the attempt on his father's life not only with personal feelings for his father, the head of the family, but also in recognition that he was head of the co-liable group. Thus his action may also be seen in terms of protecting the honor of the co-liable group.

It is argued here that murder is not committed in rural Arab or Bedouin society for reasons of breaking the chastity code unless there is a public accusation by an injured party. (An injured party is always a member of the offending girl's co-liable group or the spouse of her father.) As it is direct, it cannot be shrugged off and requires a reaction. Direct accusation often serves a political aim. Max Marwick (1965) says that the attempt is often made to expel a person so accused from his group by these means.[10] The objective is not so much to punish the offender as to stigmatize a political opponent, to undermine his position, and wherever possible to isolate and oust him from the group.

When an involved person voices a public accusation, emotional stress may have prompted the outburst, especially if something has happened that brought resentment and a feeling of injury to a head. Here too political considerations may contribute, but above all there is a need for an emotional letting off of steam, for relief through saying what is troubling one. Of course, such an outburst may be staged, but on the other hand it can be a genuine attempt to give vent to pent-up feelings. If the accusation is true it usually has a strong impact on those present, impressing itself and awakening their empathy. In many cases the accusation produces a chain reaction, stirring up enough strong impulses to result in murder if the person judged guilty is at hand. Often there is a climax at the end of a prolonged process during which tension has steadily been on the increase. Strain has reached such a degree that violent action becomes inevitable.

Explanations involving suicide should be accepted with caution. Émile Durkheim (1966, 77) argues that "suicide has most victims among the most cultivated and wealthy classes." Traditional communities have a much lower suicide rate than affluent societies. In traditional communities life is much more regulated by a "body or practices minutely governing all the details of life and leaving little free room for individual judgement" (ibid., 161). Thus the fact that rural Arab and Bedouin societies are highly integrated, makes suicide unlikely. This is confirmed by Marx (1976, 12), who reports that "in human memory no case of . . . suicide has occurred among the tribes of the Eastern Negev nor have I heard of suicides in other Negev tribes." Marx's observation of the Bedouin and Durkheim's argument indicate that few instances of suicide should be expected in the societies under discussion here.

Surviving Offenders

So far, only examples of girls murdered after having offended the sexual mores of their society have been given, but there are also cases of surviving offenders. Unmarried girls or married women are killed only when there is an accusation by an injured party. Sanctions against offenders where there is no accusation by an injured party are structured according to prevailing circumstances. Sanctions include being married off to an older man or to a man of a lower status, or made to do menial tasks (i.e., to become an unhappy "helper" to her natal family).

In a symposium held in Beersheva, in December 1983, on out of wedlock pregnancy among Negev Bedouin girls, Captain Michael Baz of the Negev District Police told the audience that Bedouin girls who become pregnant are often sent to live with Bedouin dignitaries whom the police trust and in whose custody they place these girls for a limited period. The police attitude is that because of the uncertainty as to whether an injured party will make a public accusation of the affair, and hence increase the chances that the girl will be killed, they have to take some action to protect the possibility of a homicide. The girls thus still reside within the Bedouin circle, but at the same time are protected from any homicidal sanction being carried out against them. Police officers at the symposium explained that in such cases they have to navigate between Israeli law and Bedouin custom.

Recently, Bedouin girls who are pregnant out of wedlock have begun reporting their condition to the police. The girls do this in order to prevent their agnates taking any sanction against them. The girls reason that if they are harmed, the police will have clear suspects to investigate.

It is most likely that this new attitude of the girls is due to the rapid sedentarization of the Negev Bedouin. As Bedouin girls attend schools and come into contact with Jewish girls, they begin to recognize that Bedouin norms can be circumvented now that they live within a wider society.

Case History XL

It was common knowledge among a northern Bedouin tribe that two of its unmarried members, Yūnis and Jalīla, were having illicit sexual relations. Jalīla's father severely admonished his daughter for her shaming behavior; nevertheless the couple continued to meet, albeit with more circumspection. None of the tribal members thought that the union would end in marriage, for there had long been animosity between the two different co-liable groups to which each of the offending young people belonged.

Since the late 1960s and early 1970s, most of the male tribal members have worked for wages in Jewish settlements; some worked in agriculture in the local kibbutzim, and others in local industry. Previously, most of the Bedouin owned goat herds and some cattle. But the development of Jewish settlements in the area meant that there was less and less grazing areas for their animals. Settlement development brought with it job opportunities, and within a short period of time the greater part of their income was derived from wage labor outside the day-to-day tribal life. In consequence, there was a marked decrease in economic interaction between tribal members.

In the mid-1970s the authorities put strong pressure on the Abū-Ḥusni co-liable group to join the rest of the tribe, which had previously sedentarized in an established settlement about two miles east of the hill where the Abū-Ḥusni group currently dwelled in shanties. In the course of negotiations between the land authorities and the Bedouin, a dispute developed between the various members of the co-liable group. Some agreed to the conditions laid down by the authorities, others said that they wanted more money from the government before moving. One of Jalīla's father's cousins, Faiṣal, together with two others, led the faction that refused to move before receiving more financial compensation. Jalīla's father, however, was a strong proponent for making the move. Eight months after the rest of the co-liable group moved to the settlement, the three nuclear families that made up the opposition faction moved to the settlement too.

In 1978, Faiṣal publicly accused Jalīla's father of bringing shame on the co-liable group. He voiced his accusation at a time when neighbors from the other co-liable group, and even some outsiders, were present. The occasion was a gathering to celebrate the pouring of concrete for the roof of a new building in the settlement. (It is customary on such occasions for all family members of the builder, and friends and neighbors, to come to help and watch.) Faiṣal began by jokingly referring to Jalīla's father as a person who has forgotten that he was a Bedouin and that he was too much influenced by the Jewish environment. This elicited no response so Faiṣal said that some tribal members had not participated in the celebration because of the shame that Jalīla brought on the co-liable group. Faiṣal dramatized his accusation by leaving immediately and not partaking in the communal meal for all those who took part in the day's work. That night the Abū-Ḥusni co-liable group held a meeting where it was decided to kill her. Jalīla's eldest brother, Ṣubḥi, was approached to carry out the deed. But Jalīla's father was not at ease with himself over the decision, especially over the way he had been manipulated by Faiṣal. He realized that Faiṣal's accusatory outburst, which had led to the decision to kill Jalīla, was aimed to hurt him. For ever since Faiṣal had led the opposition faction against the land authorities' proposal, he had been his political rival.

Even though there was a public accusation by an injured party, the girl who breached the sexual norms was not punished. (In this case, Faiṣal must be viewed as the injured party in terms of the dispute about moving to the settlement.) The facts reveal that prior to the public accusation, Jalīla's family was not prepared to take action against her, apart from pointing out her dishonorable behavior. Only after the public accusation did the matter of killing Jalīla come to the fore. Jalīla's father disobeyed his co-liable group and kept his daughter alive.

That this solution could be implemented was due to two reasons: Bedouin interactions with the wider society and the security of permanent work. By working in local kibbutz settlements and being invited to different homes there, the individual Bedouin is given the opportunity to discuss issues and ideas that he can never openly discuss with his relatives or neighbors. This outside influence has a strong impact on his socialization. When Faiṣal provoked Jalīla's father by saying that he was no longer a Bedouin, he referred to the influence of the father's outside social life on his attitude toward the behavior of his daughter. As more and more settled Bedouin obtain permanent jobs there will be a shift of social focus from the co-liable group to the nuclear family. Where the individual is no longer dependent on the maintaining of a common herd, or on an inheritance of land or animals, it is likely that he will drop some of the customs and attitudes that were prevalent in the time of his earlier economic mode. Sedentarization does not change the distinction between the relationship of the co-liable group to other groups, and between individuals within the co-liable group. A dispute with a different co-liable group will still bring the group as a unit together. But disagreements between members within the group now often result in a more individual approach. In this case, although a certain action was agreed upon by the co-liable group, the father chose to protect his daughter, a decision that even ten years ago would probably have never crossed his mind.

Case History XLI

In 1980, an 18-year-old girl of the 'Azagra tribe had illicit sexual relations with a Bedouin of African origin, called 'Abed.[11] 'Abed is Arabic for slave,[12] as originally Bedouin of African origin had been the slaves of the tribe. Although today they are technically free, their status is still negatively affected by their past and most Bedouin will refuse inter-marriage with them.

After Hagar complained of body pains, the Bedouin promised to marry her but first took her to some "experts" in the West Bank town. Hagar was found to be in a late stage of pregnancy so she tried to abort the birth by taking various concoctions of weeds. This traditional Bedouin remedy was unsuccessful and Hagar gave birth at the home of a friend of her lover. She was told that her baby was born dead at birth. The circumstances of the case did not remain a secret and were openly discussed among tribal members. A 17-year-old cousin of Hagar was chosen to murder her by pushing her down a well. But the water of the well was not deep enough to drown her and a young shepherdess heard Hagar crying for help. Hagar then went to the police and told them the whole story. Obviously, any further attempt on Hagar's life in the future would bring with it a thorough police investigation.

Case History XLII

In 1972, in a Triangle village, a young girl was discovered to be pregnant; after the child's birth she continued living with her natal family and the baby was given out for adoption. So far she has remained single. In an argument between the girl's father and a neighbor, the father was accused of not keeping the norms. The neighbor went so far as to tell him that he had no right even to participate in an argument with his co-villager. Even though this accusation was publicly made, because the accuser was not an injured party the father did not feel compelled to kill his daughter.

Case History XLIII

In Spring 1977 a Bedouin girl from the central Galilee was married. The morning after the wedding night the groom sent the girl back to her father's home, claiming that she was not a virgin. The frightened girl confessed that she had had sexual relations with a Christian man who lived close to the Bedouin encampment. This Christian man belonged to a *ḥamūla* from a rural Arab village six miles away from where the Bedouin were situated. Thirty years ago the family of this Christian man, which now constituted some 46 members, had moved to an area close to the Bedouin encampment where they cultivated land irrigated by natural springs.

By mid-morning of the day after the wedding ceremony the circumstances of the girl's rejection was known by all. That afternoon a neighbor of the bride's father laughed in public at the father's misfortune. This act may be viewed as a public accusation of his daughter's breach of the chastity norm. The accusation prompted a retaliation, but its focus was different from what might have been expected. That night members of the bride's co-liable group attacked the local Christians, physically injuring them. The Bedouin told the Christian community to leave the area of the springs and return to their village. The focus of the public accusation was thus diverted away from the offending girl and onto the family of the Christian man involved in the illicit affair. The Bedouin father manipulated the circumstances to the ethnic level. He claimed that the Christian male wanted to humiliate the Bedouin inhabitants by seducing his daughter.

Being told to leave the area that provided them with their income, and which they had inhabited for thirty years, was an extreme repercussion for the Christians. With the help of Christian dignitaries they sent a famous mediator to the Bedouin to negotiate an agreement whereby they could return. Six months later a *ṣulḥa* took place; all the Christians returned to their dwellings, except the male offender. He returned three years later, after his lover was married to an older man from another Bedouin tribe. In this case there was public knowledge and a public accusation. But the accusation was not made by an injured party. The ethnic difference between the offenders provided the father with a way of "protecting" family honor without killing his daughter.

Case History XLIV

The following circumstances took place in a settlement where Galilean Bedouin have been sedentarized since the early 1960s. In 1980 an unmarried Bedouin woman, who worked as a cleaning woman in a nearby Jewish settlement, became pregnant. Her pregnancy was visible to all and in her fifth month her family arranged for an abortion in a private hospital.

In Autumn 1981 the woman married a villager (not the man she had relations with previously), who lived some forty miles away from the Bedouin site. According to custom, the Bedouin bride moved to live with her husband in his village. The husband, however, did not work at a regular job. His wife therefore suggested that they return to her matrilocal residence and that she would continue working as a cleaning woman in the nearby Jewish town so as to provide them with a regular income. The husband agreed, and so they returned. Gossip concerning the woman's out of wedlock pregnancy did not stop when she married. On the contrary, returning to the settlement where the breach of sexual modesty took place only increased the snide remarks directed at her and her natal family. Two points are particularly worth noting in this surviving offender case. The woman's natal family did not take any sanction against her, instead they helped matters by arranging for the abortion. Secondly, as far as I could ascertain, no descent group members had any motive to accuse the father of not protecting the family honor, hence the girl was not harmed.

Case History XLV

In 1985, in a security search by Israeli soldiers in a West Bank city north of Jerusalem, a young woman was found locked up in a basement; she was living there in subhuman conditions. The wife of the man whose house it was told the soldiers that the woman was a mute. But the young woman spoke haltingly to the soldiers, who made further inquiries about her. Neighbors explained that some 14 years ago her father had claimed to have killed his daughter after she had had illicit sexual relations. Some Arabs came to the father to suggest that he send the young woman for a check-up in the hospital and the local military commander ordered him to appear with his daughter before the authorities so that it could be determined what social and medical care could be given to her. Before the girl was presented, however, her father killed her and then admitted his deed.

Immediately after the girl had broken the chastity norm she had been the subject of gossip in the neighborhood. But her father had taken no action against her. Soon afterwards the father divorced his first wife and immediately remarried. His second wife, fearful of neighborhood gossip that might be directed toward her because of her stepdaughter's previous shaming behavior, pressed the father to find some solution. The father, instead of killing the girl as custom prescribes, chose to keep the girl locked up in a basement. The girl's real mother suspected that her daughter had not been killed, but did not know of her whereabouts. According to informants, although there was public knowledge of the girl's misdemeanor, no public accusation was voiced against the father by any co-liable group members. Not having been shamed in public the father could look for a solution other than killing the girl. Although the father might have been inclined to allow the girl to continue her life normally, his second wife's position was vulnerable to the extent of her pressing for a more direct action; hence the compromise solution of keeping the girl locked up.

This is a most unusual surviving offender case in that the girl was punished and murdered. Analysis must focus on the role of the man's second wife. The pressure put on the father by his spouse (which must be viewed as an accusation), was not done in public. Because the father was not publicly accused he could look for a solution, other than a killing, that would satisfy his honor. As the case histories cited here have shown, there is many times a reluctance by fathers or brothers to undertake to satisfy family honor, which they only do when publicly accused.

The class of surviving offenders includes not only single women, but also those who have committed adultery, as the following case histories illustrate.

Case History XLVI

In Spring 1977, in a village with a mixed Druze, Muslim, and Christian population, a Druze woman had illicit sexual relations with a Muslim. Her husband, who was acquainted with the Muslim, discovered the affair and divorced his wife, sending her back to her natal family in a neighboring village. The incident, however, had consequences outside the family sphere and caused the outraged Druze villagers to assault their Muslim neighbors, who fled for their lives. Not a single Muslim family remained, all preferring to take shelter in a neighboring village. Later the woman in question became engaged to an aged widower in another village, and no harm came to her. The escalation of this incident may be ascribed to special causes peculiar to the Druze community, which does not accept converts, and yet is so small that there may be hesitation in putting any member of the community to death, especially a woman in the most fertile period of her life. In this case the anger felt by the woman's agnates did not entirely focus on her — the male was accused and there was a transfer of attention to his community. A purely private conflict became an intergroup and interfaith conflict.

Case History XLVII

In the late 1950s, in a Triangle village, a married woman had an affair with a member of her lineage who lived on the other side ofthe border. (This man used to cross illegally the boundaries between Jordan and Israel in order to see his lover.) The woman was born in the village, and thus lived close to both her natal family and her family of reproduction. According to rumour the affair was carried on for several years, when one day the woman's husband was found with his skull smashed by a large rock. Local gossips said that the act had been committed by the woman and her lover, but the police file was closed for lack of evidence.

Although the killed man's family must have been bitter toward the adulteress, they did not make a public accusation against any member of her natal family. Even if they had done so, it would not have led to a sanction against the woman. For the sanction of a killing to take place, there has to be an accusation by an injured party. Members of the family of reproduction have, in this case, been injured only by the assassination of their member; they have not been injured by the shaming behavior of the woman. They can take revenge from the killer's family, but are not considered as an injured party as far as the adulteress is concerned. Two years later the widow married a much older man in a neighboring village after the usual negotiations.

In another case of an adulteress remaining a surviving offender, the police succeeded in establishing that both the lover and his mistress were guilty. They were sentenced to life imprisonment but released after eight years. The woman's children, who had been entrusted to the care of the dead father's family, refused to have anything to do with her, but this was the only sanction carried against her. Later, her natal family arranged for her to marry again and she moved to another village after the wedding.

Case History XLVIII

The following surviving offender case is a story of elopement. As the younger generation becomes less and less prepared to accept what they consider the outmoded mate-selection manipulations of their parents, they will have to find ways to circumvent them without breaking off relations permanently. Elopement, and its consequent *fait accompli*, may well become a popular method. This case history is unique in that it exemplifies the interrelatedness between all four main topics of blood dispute: blood revenge (in this case, threat of), mediation, outcasting, and family honor.

During the 1970s Isma'il's family settled in orchards, near Ramle, which belonged to Jewish farmers. They lived in a shanty, and both Isma'il's father and brothers worked for the orchard owners or for wage labor in local agricultural towns. In 1980, N'ama's family, which was from the same tribe but from a different co-liable group, settled in the same orchard. The distance between the two family dwellings was less than one hundred yards. The 19-year-old Isma'il was immediately attracted to the 15-year-old N'ama. After meeting secretly for a few months they agreed that Isma'il would request a mediator to approach her father to ask for his consent to their marriage. N'ama's father, being a newcomer to the area, was anxious to obtain assistance in the form of obtaining jobs for his sons. He felt that the family of Isma'il, long established in the orchard area, would enable him to do this. He therefore quickly agreed to the proposal. The two families then met and together read the *Fatiḥa* (the first chapter of the Koran). This symbolized that N'ama would become Isma'il's future wife. However, a distant relative of N'ama's family opposed the union and encouraged N'ama's father's brothers to cancel the marriage arrangements. The opposer used the ideology of the preference of first cousin marriage. He pointed out that there were four cousins available to marry the girl. The uncles were persuaded and began putting pressure on N'ama's father. As a result the proposed marriage arrangements were cancelled. Distressed at their situation, Isma'il and N'ama realized that their only hope for a life together would be to elope. An eloping girl realizes, of course, that she might pay with her life for breaking the norms. 'Āref al-'Āref (1933, 63) says that if a girl elopes she is killed unless her abductor marries her (a situation similar to the general case of protecting family honor); but the fact that there is public knowledge of the elopement does not induce her agnates to murder the offending female.

Isma'il and N'ama continued to meet secretly, but one day they were discovered by her mother who passed the information on to her husband. Isma'il realized that quick action was necessary to secure their future. At his cousin's suggestion, Isma'il approached a Negev Bedouin dignitary, 'Aqel Abū-Ṣabūl, who agreed to give the couple shelter and to act as a mediator. On a certain day, agreed in advance, Isma'il and Abū-Ṣabūl met N'ama outside the high school where she studied. They took her to the mediator's encampment in the Negev, where she was housed in the women's section of the guest tent. As a wise precaution and according to custom, the mediator brought with him witnesses who could testify that the young man and abducted girl were not alone.

The following morning Abū-Ṣabūl visited N'ama's father and told him the events of the previous day. He explained that he was acting as a mediator and asked N'ama's father for his consent to the marriage. It is customary under such prevailing circumstances for the girl to return to her father's home under the promise that she will not be harmed; later, the marriage arrangements can be negotiated between the families. Returning home symbolizes that the norms were not breached and that no act of rebellion took place. Abū-Ṣabūl hoped to obtain such an agreement. His services as a mediator had not been much sought after as of late and he was anxious to obtain good publicity and an increase in his prestige. N'ama's father did not give an immediate answer, only that he would think about the mediator's proposal. As soon as the mediator had left, the father told his wife, his other (elder) daughter and two of his sisters-in-law to visit N'ama in the Negev and persuade her to come home. When N'ama refused to accede to their persuasion the four women tried, unsuccessfully, to kidnap her. N'ama's father then tried another tactic. He hired a lawyer who went to the police and demanded that they bring back the daughter because she was a minor. This use of the legal system of the state to get back his daughter also ended in failure. After the police consulted with Bedouin sheikhs, who expressed the opinion that the girl would be killed if she was returned to her father, they decided that N'ama should take shelter with a different tribe, one of the largest and strongest tribes in the Negev.

N'ama stayed with the family of the sheikh of this tribe for almost a year. A court decision then gave guardianship over N'ama to a social worker. The court's decision[13] not to return N'ama to her natal family took into consideration the fact that the couple might have had sexual relations. This meant that, according to Bedouin norms, her life was in danger from an attempt to satisfy family honor. The guardianship period was to be up to N'ama's 18th birthday, at which time the state would consider her an adult, able to decide for herself which home to choose.

During the period that N'ama stayed at the tribal encampment chosen by the police, Isma'il visited her regularly. On several different occasions her father came. These visits always took place with advance notice to the sheikh host and were always conducted in his presence. At these meetings N'ama's father tried to persuade his daughter to return home, sometimes he even threatened her. Upon N'ama's pleading he pronounced that he would never allow her, under any circumstances, to marry Isma'il. After this particular outburst N'ama's sister came to visit her secretly. The elder sister warned N'ama not to be tempted to come home. This warning revealed that the decision to kill her had already been made. The sister's warning was all the more eloquent for the fact that she was unwillingly engaged to her father's brother's son and was somewhat envious of her sister's rebellion against marrying within the family. Her envy was such that previously she had been the main instigator among the four women who had tried to kidnap N'ama. But now that the decision to kill her had been made, sisterly loyalty overtook personal feelings relating to her sister's rebellion.

After the decision of the authorities to give N'ama shelter rather than return her to her natal family, tension arose between the respective families. At first there was just avoidance of each other, but later considerable verbal aggression took place. In order to avoid confrontation, Isma'il's family left their dwelling in the orchard and moved to another location about seven miles away. Some time after the move a group from Na'ama's co-liable group ambushed Isma'il's brothers, injuring two of them. The police, anticipating revenge, succeeded in preventing a retaliation by surprising the revengers from Isma'il's co-liable group, who were in the last stages of planning an attack. Undoubtedly the police prevented bloodshed, which most certainly would have occurred without their intervention.

At the behest of the police, and in the light of the deteriorating relations between the two families, several famous mediators were asked to attempt some form of reconciliation. N'ama's family would agree to *ṣulḥa* under two separate preconditions: Either Isma'il would proclaim that he has no intention of marrying N'ama, or that he be declared a *meshamas* by his co-liable group. Isma'il's relatives were afraid of the recent developments and put pressure on him to make the necessary proclamation, but he refused. The co-liable group then decided to outcast him, but at the same time they agreed to help him, albeit secretly. Isma'il was cast out of his group and to the best of my knowledge N'ama's family suspected that the *tashmīs* was not a real one. After his *tashmīs* Isma'il lived and worked in Tel Aviv; once a week, during the hours of darkness, he visited his parents. He also maintained contact with his co-liable group through his mother's relatives, who reside in Lod.

At the beginning of May 1984, when N'ama reached her eighteenth year, the couple took shelter with a Bedouin tribe in the Galilee. Despite being far away from the center of the country where possible antagonists from N'ama's family lived, Isma'il was careful about where he went. In order to protect himself from any attack he bought a stolen gun from a soldier. A military investigation revealed the purchaser and Isma'il was arrested. After Isma'il's prevailing circumstances were explained the authorities agreed to release him on bail. His father's brother's son paid the bail fee and signed the papers at the court. If the *tashmīs* had been a real one, no member of the co-liable group would have assisted him in this way.

Instances of elopement, especially where the honor of all concerned is protected, are usually settled quickly. A sense of *fait accompli* prevails, and providing there has been no damage to honor the matter ends in a negotiated agreement. In this instance, however, matters were more complicated. So complicated in fact that the case history highlights all the major issues relating to blood disputes. N'ama's rebellion against her parents' wishes was akin to breaching the norms of sexual behavior. In this case the rebellion led to a situation where they lived together; this breach of the norm demanded a reaction.

The tension between the two families could easily have led to a murder and a consequent revenge. In order to prevent such an occurrence the mechanism of outcasting was used. The proposal that Isma'il be declared a *meshamas* was an "insurance policy" for the rest of his family. Both families lived outside their natural environment. Some lived in the center area, while others remained in the Negev. Under these conditions an attack could easily have been perpetrated. The *tashmīs* meant that tension between the families would be reduced and the possibility of a homicide avoided. In contrast to all other *tashmīs* cases cited earlier, where the *tashmīs* proposal was indigenous to the *meshamas*'s co-liable group, in this instance it was suggested and promoted as a solution by the opposing group.

There were several different mediations in this case history. The first was when Isma'il sent a mediator to ask for N'ama's hand. After the elopment Abū-Ṣabūl came to mediate, albeit unsuccessfully, with N'ama's father. Later still, other mediators were called in to prevent a blood dispute between the two co-liable groups. One can also predict another stage of of mediation. Isma'il and N'ama were married in August 1984, although the girl's family did not know this at the time. At some time in the future Isma'il will have to request a mediator to arrange a *ṣulḥa* and to obtain N'ama's father's blessing for their marriage. The success of this mediation will depend upon whether the rebellion can be forgiven. As the matter stands at the moment the father has undergone a certain loss of prestige through his daughter's rebellion. He may well be inclined to accept his daughter in her new role, but he also has the rest of his family to contend with, especially those who supported the cousins in line to marry N'ama. It is probable that the outcome of internal family relations will be the determining factor as to whether or not N'ama's father will agree to a *ṣulḥa*.

The story of Isma'il and N'ama's marriage affords an opportunity to see how far collective responsibility pervades Bedouin everyday life. It was not easy for Isma'il and N'ama to get married. When they came to register their intentions, the registrar asked N'ama where her father was, for it is usual for the father's consent to be given. N'ama was 18 years old, an age at which she can legally make her own decision concerning mate selection. Nevertheless, the registrar consulted a religious judge (Qaḍi), who told him not to conduct the marriage. The Qaḍi said that they must make an application to the court. Because the young couple were afraid to go to the court for fear that N'ama's family might ambush them, they returned to their shelter in the north.

On behalf of the couple a mediator approached a different Qaḍi, who invited N'ama's father to appear before him. The father stated that he had no objection to the marriage, but insisted that N'ama should first return home and only then would the marriage take place according to Bedouin custom. The Qaḍi rejected the father's proposal and decided that the couple could marry. In order for them to be married it was necessary to obtain signatures on an official form stating that neither of them had been married before. Isma'il went to members of his co-liable group, but they told him to approach his mother's co-liable group, because officially he was cast out of his own. One of Isma'il's cousins accompanied him to his mother's relatives, who signed the paper.

But now a new problem arose. After the date for the marriage was set, the mediator approached several Bedouin to act as witnesses at the marriage ceremony. On the morning that the ceremony was to have taken place, the Bedouin who had been approached did not turn up at the registrar's office. Two other individuals who were asked to appear as witnesses refused. They explained that some time in the future their role in the affair might become known. They were afraid that N'ama's family would frown upon their action and this could create tension between their respective co-liable groups. The mediator set about locating a new set of witnesses. Two more individuals were approached, both of whom said that it would be difficult for them because of the collective responsibility factor, but that they would nevertheless come. It goes without saying that the mediator chose these latter two individuals because they were indebted to him for previous mediating services. On the appointed day neither the one nor the other showed up. Later, one of them explained that he had to take his wife to the hospital and therefore could not make it on time. The other individual did not offer an excuse. He said that the request had caused him so much anguish that he could not sleep the night before the ceremony. In the morning he explained the whole affair to his brother who insisted that he stay at home.

Isma'il and N'ama's wedding ceremony preparations reveal how the collective responsibility element exerts itself on each and every step a person takes. All actions have repercussions that focus, and are seen and felt to focus, on the entire co-liable group. In this case two individuals were invited to repay a debt by acting as witnesses. Normally it was correct that they fulfill their obligation to the mediator, but their decision not to attend was based on how their attendance might reflect on the entire co-liable group.

Another important dimension to this case is N'ama's father's application to the court to force his daughter to return to her natal family. If his application had been successful he would then have behaved according to the customs and norms of the Bedouin society by killing her; by so doing he would, of course, have breached the norms of the legal system he used as a tool to get her back. The return of his daughter under the Bedouin code would have had a completely different outcome. No authority entrusted with the care of N'ama would hand her back without a guarantee in the form of an honor obligation, such as a *ṣulḥa* or promises made in front of mediators or witnesses, that no harm would come to her.

Bedouin now face two disparate sets of laws and customs: their traditional tribal ones and the legal system of the state. N'ama's father could, in effect, choose. He had a chance of "manipulating" the two systems to his advantage. He would not have hesitated, as determined by the sister's warning, to have his daughter killed (Bedouin custom) after getting her back (through the state system). As Bedouin and rural Arabs become accustomed to living under this duality it is probable that they will consider using the apparatus of the state to settle conflicts, and use less the services of mediators and judges. What is sure is that they will use the dual system to their best advantage by choosing and supporting the codes of that system which, at that time, best promotes their goal. Such manipulation, which could perhaps be described as conforming to their generally pragmatic nature, can only lead to a situation where the formal organizational framework of their society will exert a diminishing authority on the actions of its members.

Code of Chastity

There will be varying approaches to the question of norms and the degree to which they should be observed. Some will advocate killing, while others will tend toward a more merciful and forgiving attitude. Others again, perhaps influenced by the wider, non-Arab environment, will condemn as barbarous the killing of anyone offending the sexual norm.

Sometimes the reason for violent and vociferous defense of murder in case of violation of the code of chastity springs from personal motives. A man may raise his voice with the intent that his womenfolk overhear him and be deterred, especially his teenage daughters. It is not only moral indignation that makes a father wish to warn his daughters or wife not to "sin," but the wish to discourage the choice of a marriage partner other than through negotiations between families. If a girl is found to be pregnant or "disgraced," the customary way of arranging for marriage with the person who has had illicit sexual relations with her may lead to a situation where marriages are forced on the parents — the partners being chosen by the young people themselves, instead of by the family, especially the father. To ensure that social control by the paterfamilias is maintained a mechanism of sanctions and punishments has been created of which the killing of a girl or woman who has trangressed is one.

Chastity is both moral and ideological. It formalizes and sanctions certain moral values, which do not easily adjust to changing conditions. With some people the ideology of chastity tends to be rigid. When they realize that the practice of chastity is no longer the stringent norm that it was, they try to promote even further the outdated norm; others reject the ideology and accept the reality, and yet others compromise in some way. The following Bedouin stories illustrate two extreme positions. Both are frequently related and enjoy much popularity.

The first tale is of a man married to his patrilateral parallel cousin. Due to their blood relationship he was her agnate as well as her husband, and thus had obligations toward her that were far greater than if he had been married to someone to whom he was not related. This man heard that his wife was having unlawful sexual relations and decided to kill her, but wanted to commit the murder some distance from the encampment. When his family and caravan of camels was about to cross the river Jordan, the head camel refused to budge. His 13-year-old daughter turned to her father saying, "O father, do you see the young female camel over there? She is the daughter of the one that used to cross the river first, and all the male camels followed her. Let her go first . . ." The father looked at his young daughter, pondered over what she had said, and then took a sword and cut off her head. When the mother started screaming he turned to her and said, "It was for you I kept this sword in readiness and you who I intended to kill. That girl is your daughter, just as the young female camel is her mother's daughter. She resembles her mother as your daughter resembled you. It is better she should die before committing a sin such as you have committed."

The second story is that of a Bedouin whose sister hated his young and beautiful wife. One day while he was away she told her daughter to put on male attire and enter her aunt's tent. The girl did as she was bid and her mother made sure that there were witnesses around to see what was to all intents and purposes a young man entering the young wife's tent in her husband's absence. When the husband returned his sister told him the trumped-up story of his wife's faithlessness, and there were enough eyewitnesses to make him believe in her betrayal. Public knowledge convinced him of the truth of his sister's accusation. Now the Bedouin loved his wife and could not find it in his heart to kill her, so he took her with him when he went to tend his flocks and one night when she lay fast asleep he left her.

The young woman took shelter in another Bedouin encampment and as the years went by remarried and bore her new husband several children. Her first husband did not take another wife but lived a lonely and unhappy life. One day he was about to enter his sister's tent when he heard raised voices. He stopped to listen and was amazed to hear his niece accuse her mother of having made him, her uncle and her brother, miserable. The man walked in, demanded to hear the truth, and killed both women on the spot. Then he quickly left to search for the woman he had deserted. Learning where she was, he entered the encampment of the tribe where she was now living. He was led to the *shiq* and coffee was prepared for him. The Bedouin asked to be permitted to crush the coffee with a pestle and mortar, a job reserved for men, and which everyone performs according to his own personal rhythm. As soon as the woman heard the sound of the pestle and mortar she rushed to the tent and found the man she had loved when she was young and who had loved her. The sheikh of the tribe, asked to decide to whom she belonged, left the decision to the woman. "She can go or stay as she pleases," he said. She chose to leave all behind and go with the husband of her youth. "He showed great mercy," she explained, "he could not but believe I had sinned and yet he did not kill me . . ."

Two entirely opposing attitudes are revealed in these stories. The man in the first story does not only not hesitate to put his wife to death, but even kills his daughter lest she follow in her mother's footsteps. The individual is insignificant where such a view prevails, justice must be done and above all family honor be kept whatever the price. The second story is a very human one. Even though the husband sees no possibility of doubt in the tale he has been told, his love is stronger than his devotion to family honor. He cannot kill his wife but neither can he go on living with her in his society. Her removal from the encampment doubtless saved her from the ire of agnates, who might have killed her had she remained where she was.

It is perhaps an indication of the ambiguous attitude to the issue that both tales are equally popular and are narrated time and again whenever the subject of sexual shame and family honor come up. They seem to represent two possible reactions; they show the extreme ends of a scale of possible attitudes. There are, of course, many other approaches of varying degrees, and punishment may be much lighter than in the first story and yet a man may not be as lenient as the one in the second tale. Girls who have violated the code of chastity are not necessarily put to death, but neither do they inevitably escape punishment. Unless they marry the man with whom they have had sexual relations they are often doomed to spinsterhood, which in their society means low status and often hard menial work. As Dodd (1973, 45) says: "The penalties for violation of the norms surrounding *'irḍ* are severe and may include death".

The case histories presented here show that the ideology which insists on female chastity and female shame as a basic value is by no means invalid. On the other hand, ideology does not rule supreme and reality creates its own patterns, which are often variations of ideology and compromise solutions. A killing, which does not take place unless there is a public accusation by an injured party, is one form of reacting to the violation of sexual norms, but an extreme one. Sometimes no punishment is imposed nor any sanction; then again, various modes of punishment and sanction may be applied.

Concluding Remarks

Every society is dynamic. Even where a society has little or no outside influences impinging on it, there will still take place indigenous social changes. Where a society does have contacts, and especially in cases where these contacts are "side-by-side," as in the Bedouin and rural Arab cases with the wider Jewish society, there will be dynamic changes on all levels.

Recently there has been a polarization of attitudes between individuation and group unity as a result of Bedouin and rural Arabs working for wages in the Jewish sector. The far reaching changes in economic structure have caused changes in the social and political structure. Working for wages gives individuals a sense of independence, which simply did not exist when the economy was based on the raising and grazing of herds and flocks. The collective responsibility that grew out of the consideration to assist each other in a hostile environment is less and less considered an asset by the younger generation. The individual has accumulated more power, while the group leaders have lost a certain amount of control over their co-members. Changes in the patterns of blood disputes, outcasting, and killing for family honor are a reflection of the changes in social organization, which are a result of dramatic changes in the economic structure of these societies.

Three patterns of resolution of blood disputes can be discerned. The first is where revenge is taken; although the avenger knows that he might face life imprisonment, a revenge is taken in order to satisfy honor. The second pattern is where blood disputes are settled through *ṣulḥa* negotiation and payment of *diyya*; in such instances honor is also restored, with the additional benefits of a cash compensation and perhaps some political leverage as a result of the indebtedness that remains on the side of the group to which the killer belonged. A third pattern of resolving blood disputes can be foreseen — their resolution through use of the legal apparatus of the state.

The particular pattern conducted by the actors depends on the economic and political structure in which the disputing parties live, and the cohesiveness that the respective leaders can generate over the issue.

On the one hand, within the context of sedentarization, there has arisen a tendency to solve disputes by negotiating a *ṣulḥa* and accepting blood money compensation. On the other hand, because many Arabs now work for wages and are no longer economically dependent on the group, there is less cohesion within the group. If an injured group suffers from a lack of cohesiveness, as a result of members being scattered far and wide in their various wage labor jobs for example, the leader of the co-liable group will call for revenge as means to unite his group. The visits of mediators who come to request *'aṭwa* contribute to the group leader's power, as does the general focus of a co-liable group exercising its most stringent collective responsibility norm. The cohesiveness factor operates in a similar fashion in outcasting instances.

The solution of blood disputes through using the legal apparatus of the state has not been used so far. But there are a number of indicators that this pattern will, increasingly, become an important mode. As more individuals of any particular group enter the wage labor market and build up ties and commitments outside the collective responsibility framework of the co-liable group, they will prefer ways of settling disputes that (a) will not put them or their families in danger, and (b) will not disturb their outside working relations by them having to return to the encampment to attend a co-liable group meeting. It is probable, therefore, that the resolution of blood disputes will increasingly be achieved through *ṣulḥa* negotiations and payment of blood money. If the negotiations are not successful, the leaders of both the injured group, and the group from which the killer comes, may well come under pressure from tribal members to put the matter into the hands of the police. Perhaps even the threat of such action will be used to catalyze into action a settlement via *ṣulḥa* negotiation and payment of *diyya.*

The connecting links between the subjects discussed in the chapters are power, exchange and honor. In blood disputes, power is a function of relations between individuation and group unity; similarly, in outcasting. When a member of a descent group accuses somebody publicly that he does not behave according to the value norms by not killing his daughter (or sister) who engaged in illicit sexual relations, he actually weakens that person. The motivation behind his action is power: If the person he pushes to kill becomes weaker, the pusher becomes stronger.

A mediator's power is not so much direct power, but rather the power of influence. Although mediation will probably remain a hallmark of social conduct in Arab society, due to the indirect way they conduct their social and political affairs, the power of individual mediators will, perforce, be reduced somewhat. The contemporary pattern of *ṣulḥa* committees in the Galilee is indicative of this. Where several mediators act as a committee, the individual mediator is more limited in his manipulations. Even on the non-dispute level, other ways of arranging affairs may increasingly be used as the Arab population becomes more strongly integrated into the Jewish, western-oriented society. One interesting new development is the setting up of a committee (in a Bedouin settlement in the Galilee), the task of which is to determine whether disputes be solved internally or be solved by due process of law. Mediators and elders sit on the committee as a means to prevent Bedouin from using western-type methods, such as litigation, to solve disputes. Establishment of the committee means that the leaders have a greater control over the actions of individuals. This obviously limits the individuation process.

Family honor, as regards the propriety of female offspring, will continue to be closely guarded. The increase in personal mate selection as against arranged marriage is likely to be a source of conflict between the younger and older generations. Fathers will continue to promote the established norm for fear that loss of control over the daughters will result in loss of control over sons and the implications of this as regards honor standing and economic ties, and the power these imply. In the last few years there are many more cases of elopement than in the past. An individual who works for wages can allow himself to run away with a woman. In other words, he can do it if he does not depend on his group for his welfare.

A long term change can be predicted. The shame mechanism of social control explained here can only operate among small groups, such as comprise rural villages. In the future, as more Bedouin and rural Arabs enter a more urban way of life, the shame mechanism will not operate in such a stringent manner. Because a public accusation will not so easily effect a response, there may well be a decrease in the number of girls killed for family honor. It may be speculated that effective accusation will in future also be made by persons possessing economic and political influence on the man whose daughter, sister or wife has violated the norms ruling the sexual behavior of women.

Bedouin and rural Arabs are in process of transition. It is impossible to calculate the degree to which their norms regarding blood disputes and related issues will change in the coming decade. Nevertheless, the case histories presented here indicate that changes have taken place, in some respects at an unprecedented rate, and some of these changes have even been institutionalized to some extent. But there is also a possible reversal to this pattern. Many of the Bedouin and workers from the rural areas are the first to lose their jobs in times of economic crisis. They then return to their tribal encampment and villages where they become reoriented back into the group structure, and of course its ideology. Thus changes in the economic structure influence the equilibrium between individuation and group cohesiveness. Although factors such as a downturn in the economy or political instability might slow down these changes, the perspective offered here is one of a radical change in the handling of blood disputes and related issues. But this is just one aspect of a whole range of changes that are taking place in Arab norms throughout the Middle East.

Notes

All biblical references are taken from *The New Scofield Reference Bible* (Authorized King James Version). *Yediot Aharonot* and *Maariv* are daily Hebrew newspapers.

Chapter one: INTRODUCTION

1. The Triangle is a strip of territory that was under Jordanian control after the War of Independence, 1948. This area was given to Israel in exchange for other territory as part of the Rhodes Cease-fire Agreement, 1949, between Israel and Jordan. The strip of land itself does not form a triangle, but the three major cities in the Samarian region of the West Bank form a triangle, of which this strip of land was a part.

2. For details of the settlement of Negev Bedouin in the center of Israel, see Ginat (1970, 240–80; 1984b, 13–33), and Kressel (1976).

3. Specifically, *shiq* (guest tent) refers to that part of the tent reserved for entertaining guests. In Bedouin society there is no *shiq* in members' tents; there is a *shiq* only in the tent of the head of the tribe, the sheikh, and in the tents of the heads of different co-liable groups within the tribe. In rural society the guest room in a building is the *diwan*.

4. The situation is different among the Bedouin in Sinai. "Jobs are not secured, and a Bedouin may be dismissed without notice. The unpredictable political situation adds another element of insecurity. As a result, Bedouin consider their work to be temporary . . ." (Marx 1980, 113).

5. In 1983 a new Oman law for *diyya* (blood money) distinguished between Muslims and non-Muslims. The *diyya* for a non-Muslim male is $4,830, and for a non-Muslim female half this amount. *Yediot Aharonot,* 28 February 1983.

6. I would like to thank Dr. Wahib J. Ayache of Lebanon for his explanation of Lebanese law as it relates to blood revenge and family honor.

7. Criminal Law, *Law Book*, No. 864, Article 300A, 4 August 1977, p. 271.

8. Judgment of the Israeli Supreme Court, vol. 9, 1955, p. 1051.

9. Appeal judgment of the Israeli Supreme Court, vol. 34, part II, 1980, p. 608.

10. Personal communication from State Prosecutor Jonah Blatman, and from Haifa District Judge Malkiel Slutzky.

11. Criminal Law file No. 374/80, Haifa District Court.

12. Criminal Law file No. 102/73, Haifa District Court.

13. Beersheva District Court, June 1984.

14. The interview was given to Jonathan Randal of the *Washington Post* and was published in *Maariv* on 20 September 1982.

15. Based on Randal's article, see note 14.

16. It is up to the president, in consultation with the minister of justice, to reduce the period or grant a pardon, or do both. In most cases the family applies to the president

who, if he sees merit in the application, reduces the sentence by a few years; he may also further reduce the sentence a few years later. If the prisoner shows good behavior one third of his sentence is deducted.

17. There are no set rules for how far an anthropologist should become personally involved with the people he is studying. An interesting example of involvement is cited by Marx (1967, 106), who became involved in the "ceremonial" abduction of a bride.

Chapter two: Blood Revenge

1. Professional literature abounds with analysis of blood disputes by various scholars, among them Smith (1966 [1907]); Kennett (1925); Hardy (1963); Peters (1967); and Black-Michaud (1975). In addition, many travelogues refer to such disputes and textbooks have at least partly dealt with some of the issues. Investigation has focused on procedure rather than on ethnographic findings. Barth ([1959] 1968), Marx (1967), Colson (1953 and 1962), and Kressel (1982) have presented field data as the basis of their analyses.

2. Gideon Kressel has written a book in Hebrew titled *Blood Disputes Among Urban Bedouin: An Anthropological Study* (1982). In the book the title is translated into English as "Blood Feuds Among Urban Bedouin."

Peters (1967, 269) distinguishes between types of feud that should follow from the segmentation model developed by Evans-Pritchard. According to Peters, revenge is impossible within a tertiary group (parallel to the co-liable group in the Negev). Between two different tertiary groups blood revenge or payment of blood money may take place. At the level of secondary sections (parallel to the subtribe in the Negev — a co-liable group with some individuals or families who for one reason or another left their original groups and joined the tribe), there is feud; at the level of primary sections (practically the same as any tribe in the Negev), there exists a reciprocity of hostilities leading to raids. Hostility at the level of tribes (which are very similar to subfederations of tribes or a federation in the Negev), generally expresses itself in warfare.

Black-Michaud (1975, 234–35) has this to say about feud: "Since feud is an essentially diachronic phenomenon it is usually impossible to observe a whole feud at first hand. Much of the material on feud presented by anthropologists has consequently been gleaned from conversations with tribesmen from stories told about great deeds in the past. Such material is naturally wrought with contradictions stemming from the desire of the opposed individuals and groups to exonerate and justify their position in a feuding relationship. But in the absence of written records this is the only possible method of investigating feud." In the literature the term feud is generally applied to all types of hostility. There are no feuds in Bedouin or rural Arab society; there is only blood revenge or warfare.

When this book was in the last stages of production I was introduced to Christopher Boehm's *Blood Revenge: The Anthropology of Feuding in Montenegro and Other Tribal Societies*. At that stage in the book's production I was not able to address Boehm's thesis on blood vengeance. However, in regard to blood feud, Boehm takes issue with Peters and Black-Michaud. Boehm (1984, 203) states that "feuding is best understood as a pair of indigenous ideas: (1) *homicide calls for lethal retaliation,* and (2) *such retaliation may call for further retaliation, so that a chain of such incidents becomes predictable"* (italicized in original). Blood revenge is retaliation, but there is no "further retaliation" in Bedouin and rural Arab societies. Thus, one case of retaliation is blood revenge; where there is a subsequent retaliation for the first retaliation, this defines feuding exactly.

Blood revenge and feuding can therefore be distinguished; they are not synonymous.

3. Ernest Gellner (1969, 126–27) explains the rules governing blood disputes, and the payment and distribution of blood money among the tribes of the Atlas mountains in Morocco. The "culprit pays one half and the rest of his [ten closest agnates] the remaining half, whilst the sons (or failing any the brothers) of the murdered man receive one half, and the [ten closest agnates] the other half." This is in marked contrast to Bedouin society, where the blood money payment is collected and distributed equally.

4. In Atlas mountain society, after a murder, the killer's ten nearest agnates flee until the dispute is settled. The "eleventh" agnate should have no reason to fear for his life. However, "it would be a most unwise Berber who placed his trust in such arithmetical considerations" (Gellner 1969, 127). This state of affairs resembles the difference between the fifth and sixth generations in Bedouin society.

5. If the *'aṭwa* stipulations are broken, this provides a legitimate excuse to take revenge. The *'aṭwa* agreement often stipulates areas where one side is forbidden to go. If an individual trespasses a forbidden area he may well forfeit the life of a member of his group.

6. The late Avshalom Shmueli, in a personal communication to me, relates an instance of a formal settlement of blood disputes between distant groups. He states that there was a formal settlement between the Ta'amra tribe and a group in Nablus. Such a settlement may perhaps be explained by the fact that in dry seasons and drought years Ta'amra Bedouin need to graze their herds and flocks on the eastern slopes of the Samarian mountains, not far away from Nablus.

7. According to al-'Āref (1933, 180) two versions exist regarding *'aṭwa mafrūda.* One version claims that it lasts one day, another version that it lasts three days. All my informants claim that the period is three days and three nights, and one third of a day.

8. Every member of a group that is granted shelter is called *ṭanīb*. The word *ṭanab* means literally the cord of the tent connected to a peg. Those seeking the protection of the tent-dwellers pitch their tents by continuing the line of tents of the group that is to play host to the refugee. The cords of the first tent of those asking for shelter are tied to the last tent of those who offer shelter. When anyone comes to ask for shelter for himself he is called *dakhīl.* He holds on to the central pole of the tent and asks for asylum. (The verb *dakhal* means to enter.) The person seeking asylum only for himself is seated in the *shiq* and there he spends the night. He is thus taken into the host's home and enjoys his protection (see also chap. 3, n. 17). Robertson-Smith (1966, 48–49) provides additional information regarding *dakhīl* and *ṭanīb.*

9. The Qla'iyya marriage patterns are different from those of the Ẓullām Bedouin. The percentage of in-group marriages among the Ẓullām amount to 30 percent, while the corresponding figure is 70 percent for the Qla'iyya Bedouin peasants (Marx 1967, 112). The Bedouin of the Ẓullām tribe endeavor to establish as many relations as possible through marriage among the groups of the three tribes residing in the district (ibid., 143). The Qla'iyya, on the other hand, try to cope with their landless situation through marriage within the group (ibid., 223–24). In Spring 1983 the Qla'iyya, which previously camped in the airfield area, were moved to a nearby settlement (see chap. 3, n. 7).

10. A *Waqf* is an Islamic property endowment to be held in trust and used for a charitable or religious purpose.

11. See Coser (1956, chap. 7) for the theoretical basis of this remark.

12. Another factor to be considered is the verbal insults that preceded the physical violence in the first attack. Marx, in the preface to Kressel's *Blood Feuds Among Urban*

Bedouin (1982, 4), says that whereas physical aggression is limited, verbal aggression is an attempt to hurt deeply the honor of the opponent. Where the hurt is made manifest it can be compared to a rape in which the winner is an active male who humiliates his opponent, who is symbolized as a passive female. Kressel (ibid., 34) makes this idea explicit by quoting a conversation between opponents where one person said: "In God, I will fuck you like a woman."

13. For the granting of shelter, see note 8.

14. For an analysis of advantages afforded by out-group marriages, see Ginat (1982, chap. 4).

15. Among the Rwala Bedouin there is more emphasis on three generation co-liable group responsibility than on five generation responsibility. Minor disputes are dealt with in the framework of three generation responsibility. Only in cases of murder is the five generation unity involved. Personal communication from Fidelity Lancaster.

16. In Israel, arrest follows murder if the suspect is known; release against bail cannot be arranged until termination of the trial. The court, according to the law, cannot but impose sentence for life on anyone found guilty of murder. In this case the fact that the man was released was indicative that the authorities saw the manslaughter as an act of self-defense.

17. During wedding and circumcision ceremonies the Bedouin customarily fire shots into the air while singing and dancing takes place. They explain that this is a way of expressing joy. The sound of shooting whips up enthusiasm, and many more people feel impelled to join the circles of singers and dancers. On such an occasion a man holding a licence to keep a weapon may permit relatives or friends to use it in order to fire some shots.

Chapter three: Role of the Mediator

1. Ayoub (1965, 11–17; 1966); Black-Michaud (1975); Farsoun (1961, 127–40); Hottinger (1966); Huxley (1978); Khalaf (1968, 234–69); Khuri (1968, 898–906); Nadar (1965a, 394–99; 1965b, 18–24). Most of the literature deals with different types of conflict, mainly political and economic issues that were solved through the services of a mediator. The emphasis of these studies is on the issue (i.e., the conflict itself). Marx (1967), Colson (1953 and 1962), and Kressel (1982), however, describe and analyze the conflict.

2. The roof organization of Bedouin society is a federation of several tribes (known as *qabīla*, pl. *qabā'il*). Marx (1967, 11) calls such an organization a tribal confederation. Each federation is subdivided into several tribes that have common descent. Organization of grazing territories is according to subfederations of tribes. See also chap. 2, n. 2.

3. In Arab society power contributes to status but there are instances where an individual has a higher status than others without having power. For example, although many mediators are heads of tribes and of co-liable groups, there are instances where a mediator has status in the sense that he is honored for his mediating qualities but does not have an economic or political power base. A second example is where a man passes his property rights on to his siblings in his lifetime in order to avoid being responsible for the whole amount of income tax dues. (Once the property is distributed each individual inheritor is responsible for his share of the dues.) The sons no longer have expectations from their father. They will honor and respect him, but the father will no longer have power because the inheritance, now distributed, was previously the focus of power.

4. Not only is the meeting referred to as a *malām,* but also the man to whose tent they retire to is known by the same name.

5. For the organization of Bedouin tribes see note 2, and chap. 2, n. 2.

6. Personal communication from Muḥammad al-ʻAsam, a well-known mediator and judge among Negev Bedouin.

7. There is a new dimension to problems of land settlement in the Negev as a result of the Camp David agreement, which stipulated the giving back of Sinai to the Egyptians. One of the airfields built in the Negev is in an area where the tribes of this subfederation of tribes were located. The regular procedure for land settlement among the Bedouin was suspended as a result of the urgency of building this airfield by the passing of a special bill by the Knesset. The dispute referred to in this case history is the result of these special circumstances regarding the land settlement of the area where the airfield is sited.

8. Culture is determined by values, beliefs, signs and signals. On this occasion the tilting of the *ʻaqāl* was a sign of rudeness. On other occasions the waving of one's headdress signals danger. The *ʻaqāl* also plays a part in the *ṣulḥa*s of the Bedouin of the Negev. The murderer, or his co-liable representative, comes to the closest relative of the man who was killed with the *ʻaqāl* on his neck and the *kafīyya* (headdress) in his hand. The mediator says: "Here, you can do whatever you want to this man." It is then customary for the closest male relative of the deceased to signify a satisfactory ending to the dispute by placing the *kafīyya* on the head of the man. He then takes the *ʻaqāl* from the man's neck and replaces it on his head, thus restoring the man's dignity. The above custom applies only to Bedouin society in the Negev.

In rural Arab society a white headdress is put on a stick, which they refer to as a "flag." In the *ṣulḥa* ceremony the representative of the killer's family holds the flag while someone from the injured family, in the presence of the mediators, makes several knots. This signifies that the dispute is now over and a new link (knot) of relationship is established. In one case I witnessed the man holding the flag was so shaking with fear that the head of the *ṣulḥa* committee had to help support him. After the knots were tied by the injured party, and the possibility that revenge would be taken had now disappeared, the man no longer had anything to fear, and stopped shaking. The difference in his outward appearance was striking and I told him later that I could see that he was happy to see the conclusion of the affair. He told me that there is "no insurance company" for these matters, and up to the time of tying the knots he had been afraid of what the injured group might still attempt. (See case history XVIII for an instance where a brother of the murdered man killed the brother of the murderer at the *ṣulḥa* ceremony.)

9. For information on the *ʻaṭwa mafrūda,* see chap. 2, n. 7.

10. *Maṣārwa* means Egyptians. The name *Maṣārwa* became a surname for many people, not necessarily related to each other, who are descendants of the peasants who came with Ibrahim Pasha when he conquered the country in the 1830s. These individuals settled in the region of the Triangle. See Cohen (1965, 11, 49).

11. For examples, see Kressel (1982, 125, 131).

12. Mediators are not officially paid for their services, although sometimes a small, and sometimes not so small, monetary gift is made. Usually, however, the payment is much more subtle. Apart from supporting the mediator/judge politically the indebted family will look for chances to repay the debt. For example, if the mediator is not well the indebted family will offer their help. If the mediator needs any kind of help, a hint is enough for all those persons indebted to the mediator to offer their assistance. As one Bedouin mediator told me: "It is always good that people owe you."

13. Within the context of the current land settlement situation in the Negev (see note 7), in September 1980 two groups were awarded independent tribal status. During the last 20 years six groups that detached themselves for one reason or another from the main tribal group were recognized by the authorities, and the head of the group recognized as a sheikh and given a tribal seal. In all cases where this occurred mediators were asked to promote the interests of the group involved.

14. Kressel (1982, 118) describes a case where the delegation of mediators were the *mukhtār* (the head of the local government council), the chairman of the Muslim Committee of Ramle, and a local community dignitary.

15. With regard to the expropriation of Bedouin land, see note 7.

16. Personal communication from E. Gellner.

17. An individual, or even the entire co-liable group of the individual who killed a member of a different group, can ask a neutral sheikh for refuge in his tent, or to pitch their tents in his territory. Such a refuge guarantees protection by the host group as long as the "guests" stay within the boundaries of the encampment (see also chap. 2, n. 8).

18. Quoted from *Time* magazine, 2 December 1985, p. 41.

Chapter four: THE OUTCAST

1. See chap. 2, n. 8 and chap. 3, n. 17 for information on the granting of shelter.

2. During the 1950s there were severe restrictions on movements from one part of the country to another due to the general security situation. These restrictions were lifted only in 1966.

3. Although Bedouin do not as a rule have documents proving ownership of land, they do possess documents relating to land ownership. In the past, when a Bedouin bought a piece of land, this fact would be documented by a contract signed not by the seller and the buyer but by several dignitaries who would act as witnesses to the transaction. Other written records that Bedouin keep concern weddings or circumcision ceremonies. If a present of a goat or a sheep is given on such an occasion it is sometimes documented so that later (perhaps years later) a similar gift can be returned at a similar occasion. For gifts in circumcision ceremonies, see Marx (1979). Yet other documents that the Bedouin possess are concerned with religious matters and marriage contracts. Aharon Layish and Avshalom Shmueli (1979) relate that in recent years the Bedouin use actual legal documents. Layish (1984) has analyzed the Islamization of the increasingly sedentarized Bedouin society by using the records of the Shari'a Court.

4. The translation of the *tashmīs* document in Arabic (originally written out on a page from a child's school exercise book!), and the notice of the *tashmīs* in an Arab newspaper, and fascimiles of them, are shown below.

The English translation of the *tashmīs* document:

> 28.12.79
> In the name of the merciful God. This document was prepared and signed in the home of ______. We, the signatories to this document, testify as a proof to what our father the Sheikh ______ did to his son ______. We [the four names of sons of the late sheikh] certify that our father cast out his son ______ in the presence of three men ______ at the dwelling of ______.
> As a proof to this deed we sign this document and certify that the man who is known by the name ______ is outcast, and we undertake not to intervene on his

behalf or to act against him. He is no longer of us. We shall not pursue his pursuers and we shall not be pursued by his pursuers; not by blood and not by a blow of a stick, and not by word of mouth. We undertake this by our signatures and by the signatures of the witnesses and God is our best witness.

Signatures of the four brothers | Signatures of 8 witnesses

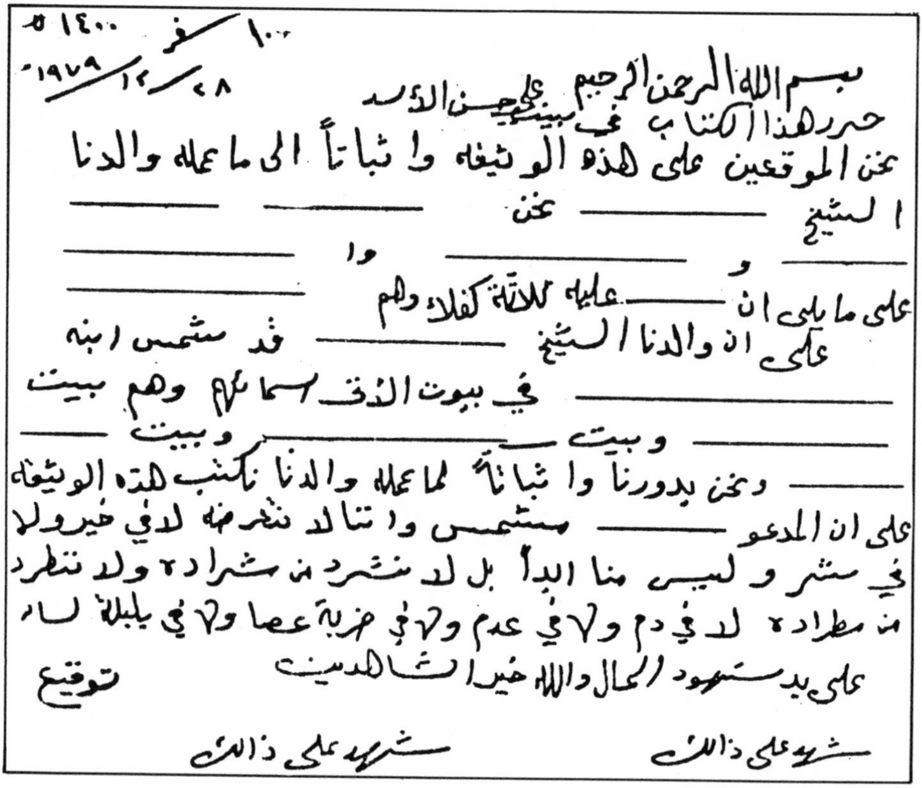

١٤٠٠ هـ صفر ١٠٠

٢٨ / ١٢ / ١٩٧٩ م

بسم الله الرحمن الرحيم

حرر هذا الكتاب في بيت علي حسن الأسد

نحن الموقعين على هذه الوثيقة واثباتاً الى ما عمله والدنا

الشيخ ____ نحن ____ ____

____ و ____ وا ____

على ما يلي ان ____ عليه ثلاثة كفلاء وهم ____

على ان والدنا الشيخ ____ قد شمس ابنه

____ في بيوت الذف اسمائهم وهم بيت

____ وبيت ____ وبيت ____

____ ونحن بدورنا واثباتاً لما عمله والدنا نكتب هذه الوثيقة

على ان المدعو ____ مشمس وانا لا نتعرض له لا في خير ولا

في شر وليس منا ابداً بل لا نشرد من شراده ولا نتطرد

من مطارده لا في دم ولا في عدم ولا في ضربة عصا ولا في يلبلة لسان

على يد شهود الحال والله خير الشاهدين

توقيع

شهود على ذلك

شهود على ذلك

The tashmīs *document*

The English translation of the *tashmīs* notice in the newspaper:

We the brothers ______ the sons of the deceased Sheikh ______ who was well known in the Negev in the Beersheva district, hereby announce that our brother, who is known by the name ______ does not belong to us, and neither to the tribal family. No legal or any other connections exist between us any longer. According to our tribal custom he has been outcast by our late father before his death.

Signatures of the four brothers.

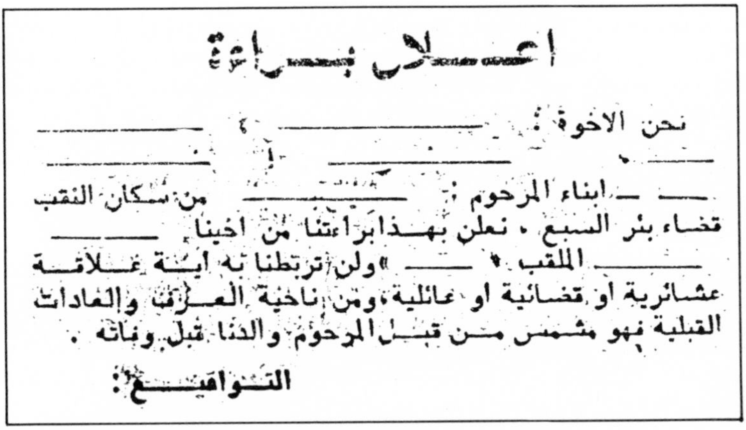
اعلان براءة

نحن الاخوة: ______ ______
______ ______
______ ابناء المرحوم: ______ من سكان النقب
قضاء بئر السبع، نعلن بهذا براءتنا من اخينا ______
______ الملقب ______ ولن ترتبطنا به اية علاقة
عشائرية او قضائية او عائلية، ومن ناحية العرف والعادات
القبلية فهو مشمس من قبل المرحوم والدنا قبل وفاته.

التواقيع:

The tashmīs *notice in an Arab newspaper*

5. See Ginat (1982, 131–32) for histories of marriage unions between rural Arab families previously separated by a border. "Furthermore, parents of the West Bank girls encouraged marriages with Israeli Arabs as they wished to establish contacts in Israel. They often depended on the connections of their new affines both for jobs and for smooth contacts with the authorities."

6. For women's power in decision making regarding marriage of their children, and mother-son relationships, see Ginat (1982, 170–72, 185–91).

7. The Israeli authorities do not draft Arabs to the army. There are, however, many Bedouin volunteers, most of whom are accepted.

8. The English translation of the *tashmīs* document:

> On this day, 21 January 1980, group No. 1 was at the home of Sheikh Abū-Karīr. [The names of the three relatives that signed the document are specified as having attended]. The members of Group No. 1 cast out the members of group No. 2 — Ḥabib and his brothers — according to the Bedouin tradition. Therefore from this day we (members of group No. 1) are not responsible for them (members of group No. 2) and they are not responsible for us. Not in any illegal event and not in any case of a killing of a person or even a baby.
> At the request of group No. 2 [those who were cast out], if a member of group No. 1 interferes in the matters of group No. 2, they will pay a fine of $2,700.
> The document is signed in the presence of members of group No. 1.
>
> Signatures of three witnesses
> 1) Sheikh al-Aṭram
> 2) Mediator of Abū-Karīr tribe
> 3) Mediator of Abū-Karīr tribe
> Signatures of the three members of Ḥabīb's lineage (who officially cast out Ḥabīb)

Comment

Ḥabīb told me that he and his brothers were never invited to attend any meeting concerning the outcasting, which was unusual in itself. Further, Ḥabīb claimed that he never asked for any money as a fine in case members of his co-liable group interfere in his affairs. He first knew of this clause only when he received a copy of the document.

9. Private knowledge are the real facts that the individual feels or knows are the right ones but which, for the interests of the group to which he belongs, he must not make public outside the group. Public knowledge is the revealing of these facts to others outside the group, which reduces the effectiveness of the group, or in this case weakens the group's position vis-à-vis the other group. The recognition of this distinction and acting in accord with it is part of the individual's collective responsibility to his group.

Chapter five: FAMILY HONOR

1. Canaan (1931, 199–200) says that a girl who is caught breaking the sexual norm will be killedby her agnates. Cohen (1966, 126) mentions a widow who became pregnant and was stoned to death by members of her natal family. Antoun (1968, 683–84) describes an instance of a girl who had unlawful sexual relations with a married man after her engagement. She too was murdered by her father.

2. Barth (1965, 81) says that among Swat Pathans the qualities of reputation and authority "are evaluated in terms of the polar opposites *izat* honour, and *sharm* — shame." This might seem to contradict Pitt-Rivers' assertion that "honor and shame are synonymous," but his later statement that "shamelessness is *dis*honourable" (italics added) clarifies the matter.

3. For women's power in decision making regarding marriage of their children, see Ginat (1982, 170–72).

4. Kressel (1981, 48) found that in 97 recorded cases of the killing of a female, there were 31 instances when the attackers were their brothers, 12 their fathers, and eight their father's brother's sons. Out of a total of 112 murderers imprisoned for family honor crimes, twenty-four were under the age of 20, and eighteen between the ages 21–40.

5. Granqvist (1931) states that early marriage has advantages for both families. The groom's mother does not want her daughter-in-law to bring with her manners and customs of her natal family. Rather, she prefers to "educate" (i.e., socialize) her daughter-in-law herself. The advantage for the girl's natal family in marrying their daughter off at a young age is that in this way possible illicit sexual relations are avoided.

6. The ethnographic data for this case are taken from a paper presented by Phyllis Palgi at the annual meeting of the Israeli Anthropological Society in Jerusalem, March 1979.

7. The murder took place in northern Lebanon, an area that is not accessible to me, but I was able to interview family members who took refuge in southern Lebanon.

8. The chart and explanation below details the complex family relations.
D6 is the oldest son of C4 and the elder brother of Sa'id (D4). D6, Sa'id's oldest half brother, wanted Sa'id to marry the daughter of the head of the hamlet. However, Sa'id's mother (C1) helped Sa'id (D4) to marry a woman (D1) from a nearby village. D3 is a full brother of D4, who did not like the idea of the television program. He thought that his future wife's (D2) family would cancel the marriage had they seen the program showing the story of his father (C4), who killed (D5) for family honor reasons.

C5 and C6 are brothers who married two sisters C3 and C2; C6=C2 and C5=C3. The husbands and wives are first cousins, being the offspring of the brothers B4 and B2. When B2 died, C4 married his widow (B1). The daughter (D9) of this union married C8, who is the brother of C6 and C5; thus the wives of C6 and C5 are half sisters of C8's wife. When B1 died, her husband (C4) married C1.

D12 is the young man who had illicit sexual relations with the girl (D5) killed by her father (C4). The *badal* between the cousins was as follows: D13=D10; D12=D11. D14 is the younger brother of D12. It was proposed that D14 marry D5 (the girl who had had an affair with D12). The marriage was supposed to take place after his brother (D12) and sister (D13) married their cousins (D11 and D10).

C8 is the uncle of D12. C8 threatened to kill his nephew (D12). C8 married D9, who is a half sister of D12's mother and a half sister to D5, with whom D12 had the illicit sexual relationship.

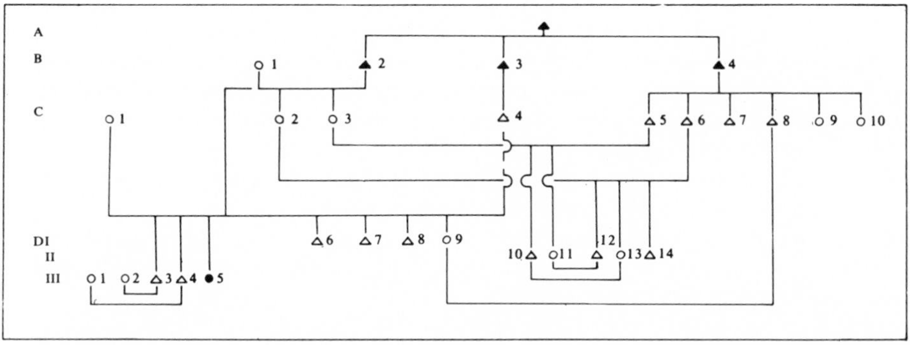

9. The groom's mother was anxious for the engagement to take place immediately. She was afraid that rumourmongers, using the events of the murder and the imprisonment, might destroy her son's chances of marriage. Furthermore, she realized that the head of the *ḥamūla*, motivated by personal revenge, might try to undermine the marriage because of the unsuccessful matchmaking between his daughter and Sa'id. See Ginat (1982, 102) for a case where wedding arrangements were cancelled due to fake rumours being spread about.

10. Marwick's experience is different from mine. In none of the case histories cited in this volume have the breaking of the chastity code been used to expel a female from the group.

11. This case history was reported in *Yediot Aharonot*, 3 August 1980. In conversation it is customary to call all Bedouin of African origin "'Abed" (i.e., slave). But there is no derogatory connotation in such name-calling.

12. Lancaster (1981, 13) explains: "[A] slave had no honour of his own except among other slaves. He only reflected the honour of his owner and it was because he had no honour that he was unable to marry a free Bedouin girl . . . Nowadays slaves are free and, in law, equal; they still have no honour and they have lost much of the reflected honour and the protection of the past."

13. Magistrates Court for Juveniles, Beersheva. File No. N.H. 31/82, dated 12 September 1983.

List of Case Histories

The names of the characters, and the tribes and *ḥamūla*s to which they belong, have been changed in order to preserve anonymity. Real names of individuals and tribes are used only in case histories I, II, XIX, and XXIV, and in the Political Assasination section of chapter one. Where the same (albeit pseudo) name is used in different case histories, this indicates that the actors belong to the same named group or tribe.

Chapter two: BLOOD REVENGE

I. A split occurred in the Qla'iyya after they were recognized by the authorities as a tribe. After a blood dispute between rival co-liable groups, the sheikh refused *'aṭwa* in order to consolidate unity of the tribe.

II. Jedū'a Abū-Ṣulb was expelled from his co-liable group after having several times become involved in bloodshed. Members of the Ṭawara claim that they will take revenge by killing Jedū'a's son. (See also case history XXIV.)

III. A building contractor of the Abū-Karīr tribe was killed by his father's brother's son. The father and brother remained in the region. A lack of economic cooperation between relatives impeded the promotion of *'aṭwa.*

IV. Two neighboring co-liable groups from the Abū-Karīr tribe were in dispute as to whose land a dam was situated on, and the dispute led to killing. *'Aṭwa* was not agreed to. Members of the responsible group, instead of seeking shelter in a neighboring tribe, continued to visit their close female kin with the connivance of relatives who lived nearby.

V. Ḥassan persuaded his co-liable group to expel a cousin whose conduct was likely to involve the group in disputes. After a fight incident involving group members, Ḥassan argued for a modification of the norms of collective responsibility.

VI. An owner of a combine harvester was charged with manslaughter after he accidentally killed a man. Both the killer and victim were from the Bani Ḥajar tribe. A quickly negotiated *ṣulḥa* required that the killer exile himself for seven years. The killer was pronounced innocent at the trial and now wishes to return to his encampment. (See also case history III.)

VII. A sheikh was arrested after a man was shot with the sheikh's revolver in ambiguous circumstances at a wedding celebration. Members of the injured co-liable group were of low socioeconomic status and sought a peace agreement with the sheikh's group, rather than take revenge.

VIII. In the encampment of the al-Ḥubshi tribe a stray bullet that escaped from a man's rifle while he was cleaning it killed a man. *'Aṭwa* was granted immediately and *diyya* refused. The weaker group sought to create a relationship in which the stronger group became indebted to it by refusing to let the latter pay their debt.

Chapter three: ROLE OF THE MEDIATOR

IX. A girl identified her attacker as the brother of the mayor of the local council. If the girl had been killed, the mayor, a political opponent of the girl's father, would have been asked to act as a mediator, for the public would have thought that the murder was for reasons of illicit sexual relations.

X. The head of tribe A accused the head of tribe B of selling land belonging to the first tribe. The first judge they chose suggested that he be an "active mediator." This offer was refused, but the judge said that he could not now act as a first judge.

XI. Some boys on bicycles demonstrated the supposed inferiority of women working in the fields by tilting their headdress. Relatives of the women ambushed the boys, who consulted a mediator in order to settle the dispute.

XII. A mediator was accused by those using his services of hardening the attitudes of the injured co-liable group.

XIII. The political motive behind the hasty organization of a *ṣulḥa* in case history VI is explained. The mediator could have arranged a long-term *'aṭwa* but by arranging the *ṣulḥa* quickly he showed his political adversaries that he had a strong influence over his tribe.

XIV. A mediator, who was also a political candidate, arranged a *ṣulḥa* at a politically advantageous time close to the elections, even though it could have been arranged earlier.

XV. The *ṣulḥa* committee of the Galilee was convened to arrange *'aṭwa* between a Druze and a Christian village. There were differences of opinion between the commitee members.

XVI. Prior to the 1977 elections there was a blood dispute in a Triangle village. Two mediators, both of whom wished to be nominated as candidates for the Knesset, recognized the potential gain to be made by acting as one of the mediators in support of the family to which his ascribed status was closest.

XVII. A *ṣulḥa* committee was convened and all members agreed that an early end to the blood dispute was best. One of the committee members suggested a clause in the agreement that meant that his mediating services would have to be used at some future date, thus focusing attention upon himself as an important mediator.

XVIII. At a *ṣulḥa* ceremony the brother of the murdered man killed the brother of the murderer by stabbing him, with obvious repercussions on the political standing of the involved mediators.

XIX. After Sheikh Abū-Rabi'a of the Bedouin declined to resign his Knesset seat in favor of Sheikh Gaber Mu'adi of the Druze (see the Political Assassination section of chapter one), mediators came on behalf of the Druze. Some of the mediators did not try to persuade Abū-Rabi'a to resign but on the contrary, encouraged him to remain in office.

XX. A distant relative of a murderer crawled into the tent of the family of the murdered man. He refused to be served refreshment until they agreed to a settlement of the blood dispute.

XXI. A man accused his nephew of stealing, but instead of going to the father of his nephew (who was, of course, his own brother) he filed a complaint with the police.

XXII. Two men consulted an Egyptian Bedouin mediator who conducted a *bish'a* ceremony in order to determine whether one of the men was lying about a certain event.

XXIII. A teacher reprimanded a pupil and accidentally broke the boy's hand, thus creating tension between the families of the boy and the teacher. The dispute was resolved only when the father of the teacher turned to an influential woman in the village, who arranged matters with the boy's mother. This case illustrates the important role that women play behind the scenes.

Chapter four: THE OUTCAST

XXIV. Jedū'a Abū-Ṣulb was expelled from his co-liable group because he was a threat to the security of other members, but the injured group suspect that the *tashmīs* (formal expulsion) was not a real one. (See also case history II.)

XXV. Na'im, a sheikh's son, had illicit sexual relations with various women. Because Na'im's behavior reduced the reputation of the co-liable group the sheikh decided to cast his son out of the group. This action also helped the sheikh in diverting attention away from internal problems relating to his lack of authority over the tribe.

XXVI. 'Oda, a recently appointed sheikh of the Ībn-'Abada tribe, found out that his half brother Salīm had secretly signed an agreement to sell land that did not belong to him to the Land Authorities. 'Oda hired a lawyer to stop the transaction and decided to outcast his brother from the co-liable group. The outcasting in this instance was pure punishment. But 'Oda's personal esteem within the group and beyond was also raised.

XXVII. Samīr took loans from Bedouin but never returned the money. Various people complained about his behavior to Musa, Samīr's brother. Instead of bringing the issue to a formal discussion within the co-liable group Musa forcibly took Samīr to the sheikhs of various tribes where he proclaimed him a *meshamas.*

XXVIII. Yusūf used to borrow money without returning it and it was proposed that he be cast out of the group. Before a formal decision was made, Yusūf's father became ill. The six months' illness of his father changed Yusūf's ways and he turned over a new leaf. Even though the reason for the *tashmīs* was not now valid the outcasting was still carried out. The *tashmīs* was a means to strengthen the cohesiveness of different co-liable groups of the al-Ṭamma tribe, which had only recently been able to interact with each other.

XXIX. Khalīl and Daūd were contenders for the candidacy of head of the tribe. Supporters of Khalīl threatened Daūd that they would declare him a *meshamas* (under which circumstances he could not, of course, serve as an authoritative sheikh) unless he withdrew his nomination.

XXX. In a dispute over territorial grazing Ḥabīb al-Aṭram expressed the opinion that women from his mother's co-liable group were in the right, and that women from his own descent group were in the wrong. The sheikh persuaded other members that Ḥabīb's behavior was detrimental to the cohesiveness of the tribe's descent group, and that he should be expelled. Later the *tashmīs* was abolished.

Chapter five: FAMILY HONOR

XXXI. A daughter of a rabbi was married but had intimate relations with a young man who worked in her village. Her father's and her husband's exhortations to call a halt to the affair were not heeded. The rabbi, under pressure from his son-in-law and his congregation, then killed his daughter.

XXXII. A father heard that his daughter was having an affair with a local ploughman. In reaction to his wife's accusations he ordered his other daughters to push their sister into the village well. A subsequent police inquiry involved "testing" the virginity of the deceased girl.

XXXIII. One day a baby was found in the fields. After a police investigation the parents agreed that the guilty young couple should marry immediately. Subsequently the young man's family objected to their son marrying, arguing that he had confessed only in order to gain release from police custody. The girl's uncles insisted that the father clear the family name; later the girl's body was found in a well. Political motives enter picture in that the girl's uncle wished to use the girl's murder as a means of uniting the co-liable group.

XXXIV. A young girl who offended the sexual norm was killed, although the family claimed that it was suicide. Before her death there were deliberations between various factions of the co-liable group as to the correct course of action. Public knowledge alone was not the reason for the death of the girl, additionally there occurred a dramatization of the affair in the form of a public accusation against the girl's family. Only after this dramatization was the girl killed.

XXXV. A man who as a child received very harsh treatment from his family was informed that his brother-in-law was having an illicit sexual affair. He later discovered that the lover of his brother-in-law was his own half sister. The man's patrilineal obligations were such that he tried to put an end to the affair, but without success. In the meantime his uncle refused to show his face in the village, an action akin to a public accusation. The man, together with his brothers, killed the lovers, and escaped revenge by going to southern Lebanon.

XXXVI. A man married to his *bint 'amm* (father's brother's daugher) found his wife together with her *ibn khal* (mother's brother's son). The woman not only told the police that she was pregnant by her lover, but openly told this to the sheikh of the tribe that had granted her protection. The woman's husband accused his father-in-law of not protecting family honor, and later the woman was found dead in her hut.

XXXVII. A girl was found to be pregnant and admitted that she had had intercourse with a young man of her lineage. This young man was about to be married to her cousin in a *badal.* It was suggested that a younger brother of the young man marry the pregnant girl at a later date, after the *badal* had taken place, and that in the meantime an abortion be arranged. The younger brother, however, refused to play his role. A year later the girl's mother was insulted by the family of the young man, and immediately accused her husband of incompetence over the affair. The husband then killed his daughter. (The continuation of the story whereby Sa'id, the dead girl's brother, confessed to the murder he did not commit and the efforts made to release him and his father from prison is related in the Anthropologist/Mediator secton of chapter one.)

XXXVIII. 'Adel discovered that his sister's husband, Salām, was having an affair with his wife, Ṣafa. 'Adel was much humiliated by Salām's public pronouncements of his sex relations with Ṣafa. He felt that his family's honor was at stake so he killed his brother-in-law with Salām's illegally possessed submachine gun, and then gave himself up to the police.

XXXIX. A Negev Bedouin sheikh married Khaḍra, who attempted to poison him. He divorced her, but later took her back. Khaled, the sheikh's son by a previous marriage, decided to save the honor of the family by killing his father's wife, which he did three days after the re-marriage ceremony. Khaled's action must be viewed in the light of Khaḍra's neglect of her family of reproduction in favor of her natal family and her disrespect to the sheikh, who was also the head of the co-liable group.

XL. Jalīla's father, a member of the Abū-Ḥusni co-liable group, severely admonished his daughter for her shaming behavior in carrying on a sexual affair. Faiṣal, a political rival of the father, publicly accused him of bringing shame on the co-liable group, which decided that she should be killed. Jalīla's father disobeyed his co-liable group and kept his daughter alive. In this instance the father's interactions with the wider society exerted a strong influence on his attitude to the broaching of the sexual norm.

XLI. After Hagar became pregnant by 'Abed she was pushed down a well and left to drown. Hagar was rescued by a shepherdess and told her story to the police.

XLII. After a young unmarried girl gave birth the baby was given out for adoption. The father was accused of not keeping the norms but because the accuser was not an injured party, no harm came to the girl.

XLIII. The groom of a Bedouin girl returned his bride, maintaining that she was not a virgin. The father of the girl was accused publicly of his daughter's breach of the norms, but maintained family honor by focusing attention on the Christian man who had deflowered his daughter.

XLIV. An unmarried Bedouin woman, who worked as a cleaning woman in a nearby Jewish settlement, became pregnant. Her family arranged for her to have an abortion and later she married a man from a different village. Although gossip continued concerning her out of wedlock pregnancy, the father of the girl was not accused of failing to protect the family honor.

XLV. A young woman was discovered living in subhuman conditions. Fourteen years previously her father had told acquaintances that he killed her for family honor reasons. Instead, he had kept her locked up. Upon discovery the father was ordered to present the girl to the authorities. But before doing so, he killed her. Analysis of the case focuses on the role of the father's second wife.

XLVI. In a village with a mixed Druze, Muslim, and Christian population, a Druze woman had illicit sexual relations with a Muslim. The outraged Druze villagers assaulted their Muslim neighbors, but no harm came to the woman.

XLVII. A married woman had an affair with a member of her lineage, and together they murdered the husband of the woman. Even if the killed man's family had publicly accused the woman's natal family, no sanction would have been forthcoming. Members of the family of reproduction were, in this case, only injured by the assassination of their member, not by the shaming behavior of the woman.

XLVIII. Isma'il and N'ama planned to get married. But a distant relative of N'ama's family used the ideology of first cousin marriage preference to thwart their plans. After the couple eloped a mediator tried to obtain consent for the marriage from N'ama's father, but this was refused. After unsuccessful attempts by the father to gain N'ama back through family persuasion and process of law, the authorities put N'ama under the protection of a famous Bedouin sheikh. Mediators were then called upon to attempt some form of reconciliation. Isma'il was declared a *meshamas*, but this was only a ruse to satisfy the demands of N'ama's co-liable group. The unreal nature of this *tashmīs* was demonstrated when his cousin put up bail for him over a misdemeanor and when he obtained signatures required for Isma'il's marriage papers. If he had been truly outcast co-liable group members would have afforded him no help.

Bibliography

Abercrombie, Nicholas., Hill, Stephen., and Turner, Bryan S. 1984. *Dictionary of sociology*. Harmondsworth: Penguin Books.

Abou Zeid, Ahmed. 1965. Honor and shame among the Bedouin of Egypt. In *Honor and shame,* ed. J.G. Peristiany. London: Weidenfeld and Nicolson.

Abu Jaber, K.S., and G.A. Gharaibeh. 1981. Bedouin settlement: Organizational, legal and administrative structure in Jordan. In *The future of pastoral peoples:* Proceedings of a conference held in Nairobi, Kenya, 4–8 August, 1980, ed. J.G. Galaty, D. Aronson, and P.C. Salzman. Ottawa: International Development Research Center.

Antoun, Richard T. 1968. On the modesty of women in Arab Muslim villages: A study on the accommodation of tradition. *American Anthropologist* 70:671–97.

______. 1972. *Arab village: A social structural study of a Trans-Jordanian peasant community*. Bloomington: Indian University Press.

al-'Āref, 'Āref. 1933. *Al-qaḍa bain al-badū* (Bedouin justice — in Arabic). Jerusalem.

______. 1934. *Tārikh Bir al-Saba wa-qabāilha* (History of Beersheva and its tribes — in Arabic). Jerusalem.

Ayoub, Victor. 1965. Conflict resolution and social reorganization in a Lebanese village. *Human Organization* 24:11–77.

______. 1966. Resolution of conflict in a Lebanese village. In *Politics in Lebanon,* ed. L. Binder. New York: John Wiley and Sons.

Barth, Fredrik. 1953. *Principles of social organization in southern Kurdistan*. Universitets Etnografiks Museum, Bulletin 7. Boktrykkeri, Oslo: Brodrene Jorgensen AOS.

______. 1961. *Nomads of south Persia: The Basseri tribe of the Kamseh confederacy*. Boston, Mass.: Little, Brown and Co.

______. [1959] 1968. *Political leadership among Swat Pathans*. London: The Athlone Press; New York: Humanities Press.

Bates, Daniel G. 1980. Yoruk settlement in southeast Turkey. In *When nomads settle. See* Salzman 1980a.

Becker, Howard S. 1973. *Outsiders: Studies in the sociology of deviance*. New York: Free Press.

Ben-David, Y. 1981. *Jabaliyya: Shevet Beduii betzel haminzar* (Jabaliyya: Bedouin tribe in the shadow of the monastery — in Hebrew). Jerusalem: Kana.

Black-Michaud, Jacob. 1975. *Cohesive force: Feud in the Mediterranean and the Middle East*. Oxford, England: Basil Blackwell.

Blau, Peter Michael. 1964. *Exchange and power in social life*. New York: J. Wiley.

Boehm, Christopher. 1984. *Blood revenge: The anthropology of feuding in Montenegro and other tribal societies.* Kansas: University of Kansas Press.

Canaan, Taufik. 1927. *Mohammedan saints and sanctuaries in Palestine.* London: Luzac.

———. 1931. Unritten laws affecting the Arab woman of Palestine. *Journal of the Palestine Oriental Society* 11:172–203.

Cohen, Abner. 1965. *Arab border villages in Israel: A study of community and change in a social organization.* Manchester: Manchester University Press.

———. 1974. *Two dimensional man: An essay on the anthropology of power and symbolism in complex society.* London: Routledge and Kegan Paul.

Colson, Elizabeth. 1953. Social control and vengeance in plateau Tonga society. *Africa* 23.

———. 1960. *Social organization in the Gwembe Tonga.* Manchester: Manchester University Press.

———. 1962. *The plateau Tonga of northern Rhodesia: Social and religious studies.* Manchester: Manchester University Press.

Conder, Claude Reignier. 1879. *Tent work in Palestine,* vol. 2, London: R. Bentley and Son.

Coser, Lewis A. 1965. *The function of social conflict.* Reprint. London: Routledge and Kegan Paul.

Dalman, Gustaf Hermann. [1939] 1964. *Zeltleben, Arbeit und Sitte in Palestina,* vol. 6. Reprint. Hildesheim: George Olns.

Deng, Francis Mading, 1972. *The Dinka of the Sudan.* New York: Holt, Rinehart and Winston.

Dodd, Peter C. 1973. Family honor and the forces of change in Arab society. *International Journal of Middle East Studies* 4:40–54.

Durkeim, Émile. 1966. *Suicide: A study in sociology.* New York: Free Press.

Ekeh, Peter. 1974. *Social exchange theory: The two traditions.* London.

Eloul, Rohn. 1984. 'Arab al-Ḥjerat: Adaption of Bedouin to a changing environment. In *The changing Bedouin. See* Marx 1984.

Evans-Pritchard, Edward Evan. 1940. *The Nuer, a description of the modes of livelihood and political institutions of a Nilotic people.* Oxford: Oxford University Press.

———. 1949. *The Sanusi of Cyrenaica.* Oxford: Oxford University Press.

———. 1965. *Nuer religion.* Oxford: Oxford University Press.

Farsoun, Sami K. 1970. Family structure and society in modern Lebanon. In *Peoples and cultures of the Middle East,* vol. 2, *Life in the cities, towns and countryside,* ed. Louise E. Sweet. Garden City, N.Y.: The Natural History Press.

Fyzee, Asaf Ali Asghar. 1953. *Outlines of Muhammadan law.* Oxford.

Gellner, Ernest. 1969. *Saints of the Atlas.* Chicago: University of Chicago Press.

———. 1981. *Muslim Society.* Cambridge: Cambridge University Press.

Ginat, Joseph. 1970. The Bedouin of the Negev in the Ayalon basin. In *The Western Ayalon Basin* (in Hebrew), ed. Shlomo Marton. Tel Aviv: Hakibbutz Hameuchad.

———. 1975. A rural Arab community in Israel: Marriage patterns and woman's status. Ph.D. diss., University of Utah.

———. 1976. *Changes in family structure among rural Arabs* (in Hebrew). Occasional

Papers no. 3. Shiloah Center for Middle Eastern and African Studies, Tel Aviv University.

———. 1978. *Blood revenge in Bedouin societies* (in Hebrew). Occasional papers on the Middle East no. 14. The Institute of Middle Eastern Studies, University of Haifa.

———. 1979. Illicit sexual relationships and family honor in Arab society. In *Israel Studies in Criminology 5,* ed. S.G. Shoham and A. Grahame. Tel Aviv: Turtledove.

———. 1980. Employment as a factor for social change in Arab villages (in Hebrew). Discussion paper, Pinhas Sapir Center for Development, Tel Aviv University.

———. 1982. *Women in Muslim rural society: Status and role in family and community.* New Brunswick, N.J.: Transaction.

———. 1984a. Blood revenge in Bedouin society. In *The changing Bedouin. See* Marx 1984.

———. 1984b. Sedentarization of Negev Bedouin in rural communities. *Nomadic Peoples* 15:13–33.

Glickman, M. 1971. Kinship and credit among the Nuer. *Africa* 12:306–19.

Granqvist, Hilma. 1931. *Marriage conditions in a Palestinian village,* vol. 1. Commentationes Humanarum Litterarum, vol. III, 8, Helsingfors, Finland: Societas Scintiarum, Fennica.

Hardy, M.J.L. 1963. *Blood feuds and the payment of blood money in the Middle East.* Leiden: B.J. Brill.

Harris, Marvin. 1980. *Culture, people, nature,* 3rd ed. New York: Harper and Row.

Hiatt, Joseph M. 1984. State formation and the encapsulation of nomads: Local change and continuity among recently sedentarized Bedouin in Jordan. *Nomadic Peoples* 15:1–11.

Hottinger, Arnold, 1961. Zu'amā and parties in the Lebanese crisis of 1958. *Middle East Journal* 15:127–140.

———. 1966. Zu'amā in historical perspective. In *Politics in Lebanon,* ed. L. Binder. New York: John Wiley and Sons.

Huxley, Frederick Charles. 1978. *Wāsita* in a Lebanese context: Social exchange among villagers and outsiders. Anthropological Papers No. 64. Museum of Anthropology, University of Michigan.

Jaussen, Joseph Antonion. 1908. *Costumes des Arabes au pays de Moab.* Paris: Adrien-Maisonneuven.

Khalaf, Samir. 1968. Primordial ties and politics in Lebanon. *Middle Eastern Studies* 4:243–69.

Kennett, Austin, 1925. *Bedouin justice: Laws and customs among the Egyptian Bedouin.* Cambridge: Cambridge University Press.

Khuri, Fuad. 1968. The etiquette of bargaining in the Middle East. *American Anthropologist* 70:609–706.

Kressel, Gideon M. 1976. *Individuality versus tribality: The dynamics of a Bedouin community in a process of urbanization* (in Hebrew). Tel Aviv: Hakibbutz Hameuchad.

———. 1981. Sororicide/filiacide: Homicide for family honor. *Current Anthropology* 22:141–58.

———. 1982. *Blood feuds among urban Bedouin: An anthropological study* (in Hebrew). Jerusalem: Hebrew University, Magnes Press.

Lancaster, William. 1981. *The Rwala Bedouin today.* Cambridge: Cambridge University Press.

Layish, Aharon. 1984. The Islamization of the Bedouin family in the Judean desert, as reflected in the sijill of the Sharī'a court. *See* Marx 1984.

Layish, Aharon, and Avshalom Shmueli. 1979. Custom and Sharī'a in the Bedouin family according to legal documents from the Judean desert. *Bulletin of the School of Oriental and African Studies* 42:21–45.

Malinowski, Bronislaw. 1959. *Crime and custom in savage society.* New Jersey: Littlefield Adams.

Marwick, Max G. 1965. *Sorcery in its social setting.* Manchester: Manchester University.

Marx, Emanuel. 1967. *Bedouin of the Negev.* Manchester: Manchester University Press.

———. 1973. The organization of nomadic groups in the Middle East. In *Society and political structure in the Arab world,* ed. M. Milson. New York: Humanities Press.

———. 1976. *The social context of violent behavior: A social anthropological study in an Israeli immigrant town.* London: Routledge and Kegan Paul.

———. 1979. Circumcision feasts among the Negev Bedouin. *International Journal of Middle East Studies* 4:411–27.

———. 1980. Wage labor and tribal economy of the Bedouin in south Sinai. In *When nomads settle,* ed. Philip Carl Salzman. New York: Praeger.

———. 1981. The anthropologist as mediator. In *The Future of pastoral people: Proceedings of a conference held in Nairobi, Kenya, 4–*8 August 1980, ed. J.G. Galaty, D. Aronson, and P.C. Salzman. Ottawa: International Development Research Center.

———. 1984. Changing employment patterns of Bedouin. In *The Changing Bedouin,* ed. Emanuel Marx and Avshalom Shmueli. New Brunswick, N.J.: Transaction.

Mason, John P. 1975. Sex and symbol in the treatment of women: The wedding rite in a Libyan oasis community. *American Anthropologist* 2:649–61.

Melzer-Geva, Maya. 1983. Mate selection in the Jewish Georgian ethnic group (in Hebrew). M.A. Thesis, Hebrew University, Jerusalem.

Musil, Alios. 1928. *The manners and customs of the Rwala Bedouins.* Oriental Explorations and Studies, no. 6. American Geographical Society, New York.

Nader, Laura. 1965a. Choices in legal procedure: Shia Moslem and Mexican Zapotec. *American Anthropologist* 67:394–99.

———. 1965b. Communication between village and city in the modern Middle East. *Human Organization* 24:18–24.

Patai, Raphael. 1976. *The Arab Mind.* New York: Scribners.

Peters, Emrys L. 1967. Some structural aspects of the feud among the camel herding Bedouin of Cyrenaica. *Africa* 37:262–82.

Pitt-Rivers, Julian Alfred. 1965. Honor and social status. In *Honor and shame. See* Abou Zeid 1965.

Safilios-Rothschild, C. 1969. "Honour" crimes in contemporary Greece. *The British Journal of Sociology* 20:205–18.

Salzman, Philip Carl. 1980a. Introduction: Processes of sedentarization as adaption and response. In *When nomads settle,* ed. P.C. Salzman. New York: Praeger.

———. 1980b. Processes of sedentarization among the nomads in Baluchistan. In *When nomads settle.* See 1980a.

Silverman, S. 1977. Patronage and myth. In *Patrons and clients in Mediterranean societies,* ed. E. Gellner and J. Waterbury. London: Gerald Duckworth.

Simmel, Georg. 1971. On individuality and social forms. In *Selected writings,* ed. and with introduction by D.N. Levine. Chicago: University of Chicago Press.

Smith, William Robertson. [1907] 1966. *Kinship and marriage in early Arabia.* 2nd ed., ed. S.A. Cook. Reprint. Ooesterhoot, The Netherlands: Offsetbedrifj H. Zopfi.

Spradley, J. 1979. *The ethnographic interview.* San Francisco: Holt, Rinehart and Winston.

Westermack, Edward Alexander. 1926. *Ritual and belief in Morocco.* London.

Index

Only real names have been indexed. Pseudo names of individuals and tribes can be located through the List of Case Histories. Main headings are usually indexed in direct phrase form (e.g., Bedouin of the Negev; Public accusation). The method of alphabetical order is word-by-word; this also applies to subheadings with the provision that beginning prepositions etc. have been ignored in determining the order.

"Mentioned" indicates pertinent case history references. The letter "n" indicates that the referred to endnote amplifies the text in some important way; occasionally, the endnote is directly referenced (e.g., chap. 3, n. 8). *Passim* indicates that the subject matter is referred to in scattered passages throughout the text reference. Index terms are *frequently* alluded to more than once on a page.

Lebanon (continued)
revenge in 28
Leopard-skin chief (Nuer) 63–64, 87
Lineage 18: decline of, corporateness 20–21, 111 (*see also* Individuation). *See also* Descent group; *Ḥamūla*
Lod (mixed Jewish-Arab city) 16

Malam (passive mediator) 68–70. *See also* Mediator/judge
Malinowski, Bronislaw: public knowledge 115
Marabouts *(Marabtin)* 62, 85
Mardawi (neutral man) 68
Marriage(s): between offenders of the sexual norm (*see under* Sexual relations, illicit); first cousin (mentioned 104–5, 123, 125, 143, 144, 149); in-group 108n; to a non-Bedouin peasant male 105, 120; out-group 54n. *See also* Matchmaking
Marwick, Max: public accusation 134n
Marx, Emanuel
anthropologist/mediator role 31–32; Bedouin suicide 135; circumcision ceremonies 37; collective responsibility 46; Jedū'a Abū-Ṣulb 51, 52, 92; insecurity of Bedouin 18; Negev Bedouin relocation mediated by 31, 32
Negev Bedouin sedentarization 16, 18; revenge refrained from 43; Qla'iyya tribe 46, 49; ritual abduction of bride 114
Maṣārwa (peasants of Egyptian origin) 77
Mason, John P: dishonor and shame 114
Matchmaking/marriage negotiations 11, 36–38 *passim,* 89, 146
Mate selection 38, 114, 149, 154 (mentioned 142, 147)
Matrilineal relations. *See under* Descent
Mediation 3
alternatives to 83, 84, 148, 152, 153; a central element of rural Arab and Bedouin way of life/channel by which political relations conducted 32, 37, 67, 153; different types of 89; in elopement case history 143-44, 146
to negotiate seal holder rights/tribal independence 80n; of personal relations 37; Saints of Atlas tribal chiefs elected through 62-63, 85; unsuccessful 72, 81, 83, 85, 86, 89; by women 87-88; mentioned 139
Mediator(s) *(wāsiṭa)* 3, 154
authorities/public use (*see under* Social exchange); authority/prestige/qualities of 3, 60–61, 69, 80, 84-85, 87; disagreement among 85; exiled individuals assisted by 44, 57, 61; heads of tribes/co-liable groups often serve as 64n, 87; interactive comparison between role of mediator-saints-chiefs in selected societies/Bedouin and rural Arab societies/ Simmel's "stranger" 62-64, 85-89
kinship not a prerequisite to become 85; Knesset members/candidates as 75–76, 77; matchmaking/marriage negotiation role of (*see* Matchmaking); payment for services/repayment of indebtedness to 42, 79-80n, 147-58; political/personal motives of 4, 57, 72-79 *passim,* 82, 87
power accumulated by manipulating intergroup relations/dependence of parties 38, 72, 79; power/"power of influence" of 32, 61, 64, 80, 89, 153; status of 64, 68, 80, 84, 86, 89 (mentioned 72, 76-77); shelter/sanctuary arranged by 63, 143. *See also* Anthropologist/mediator; Arbitrator; Go-between; Stranger
Mediator/judge(s) 68–71: fees of 69 (*see also under* Mediator); no legal authority 69, 86; secret (bribing) mediation of 81–82; social exchange relations of (*see under* Social exchange); status of 80, 83–85 *passim*
Meshamas (expelled person) 90–91: co-liable group membership terminated by being declared a 55; individual declared a, as "insurance policy" for rest of family 145–46; reduced stigmatization of 112; shelter not usually given to 92
Melzer-Geva, Maya: abduction 115
Military Government: organization of tribes by 94, 103–4, 107; restrictions on movement of Bedouin by 11, 92n
Ministry of Justice 35, 133
Mu'adi, Sheikh Gaber: and assassination of Sheikh Abū-Rabi'a 30–31, 82; Knesset election of/agreement with Abū-Rabi'a 29, 73, 82
Muhakham (arbitrator) 62
Muḥammad (informant) 10–12